# FORWARD

# FORWARD

*My Life With and Without Boney M.*

Marcia Barrett

with

Lloyd Bradley

Constable • London

CONSTABLE

First published in Great Britain in 2018 by Constable

1 3 5 7 9 10 8 6 4 2

Copyright © Marcia Barrett with Lloyd Bradley, 2018
Foreword © Eddy Grant, 2018

The moral right of the author has been asserted.

A CIP catalogue record for this book
is available from the British Library.

ISBN: 978-1-47212-441-8 (hardback)
ISBN: 978-1-47212-442-5 (trade paperback)

Typeset in Bembo by Hewer Text UK Ltd, Edinburgh
Printed and bound in Great Britain by Clays Ltd

Papers used by Constable are from well-managed
forests and other responsible sources

Constable
An imprint of
Little, Brown Book Group
Carmelite House
50 Victoria Embankment
London EC4Y 0DZ

An Hachette UK Company
www.hachette.co.uk

www.littlebrown.co.uk

# Contents

# Foreword

As I have travelled through the rough and tumble existence of life I haven't met many people who I could honestly say are worthy of being called true 'heroes', neither in the music business nor, dare I say it, even in life in general, whatever the discipline. You see, sometimes one may not even be aware that heroism is being enacted, as life's necessities or wants are pursued. It is most often a question of getting the job done, earning the money, getting the praise – or not – and moving on to the next task, all in the seemingly never-ending process of sustaining what is commonly called a *living*.

But in 1979 I was destined to meet such a hero. The whole world, it seemed, was busy buying the records of two super pop groups: ABBA and Boney M. Each of their individual commercial reach was awesome; they were the Ali and Frazier of the music business and, like The Beatles before them, each single member of both groups had their own individual fans who would almost die for them. It was like that then, a little less so now in 2018.

From my perspective, and bearing in mind that I loved the music of both, it was, and continues to be my opinion, that the most beautiful of them all was the statuesque, Amazonian-looking one in Boney M., Marcia Barrett. There was just something about her that said *otherworldly, spiritual, friendly* beyond all the others.

I did not know at the time quite how much Marcia contributed to the sound of Boney M. That, I would find out much later. But those early days were confusing: with the advent of new recording technology, and more than a little help from session singers of all kinds, what was being heard had very little to do with who was being seen. Nevertheless, like most things in life, it's only a question of time before all is revealed: the love in Marcia's voice, not to detract from Liz's contribution, is the primary reason the world bought and will continue to buy mega-millions of Boney M. records.

It is my firm belief, and I speak it like a mantra, that 'What is for you must come to you'. After tasting major success with my band The Equals, I suffered seven years of anonymity: I was slowly making my way to the top of the international pop charts as a solo artist with my song 'Living on the Frontline' and it was a very uncertain period in my life, as I had not planned to ever have a solo career. At the time, the Caribbean community in the UK was serviced by a newspaper named *The Caribbean Times*, which held an annual award show featuring the successes of each year in the fields of music, film and TV. This is how I came into the orbit of the world superstar that is Marcia Barrett. She was being recognised, along with Boney M. I believe, by our often-denigrated black West Indian community, but only she was there to receive the award. I was impressed and so were all who attended the function. Naturally, more than the usual complement of photographers were present, desperate for a mere smile from Marcia. They would have quite happily turned and gone home without recognising the greatest UK thespian of his time, Norman Beaton (later of the TV sitcom *Desmond's Fame*) and, of course, yours truly.

Marcia, realising what was about to take place, let it be known that there would be no more photographs taken of her that did not feature both Norman and myself. I was extremely grateful and my respect for her rose to a level far outdistancing that of any amount of her records sales, which were already stellar.

Well then, just imagine my elation when a few years later, at a time when I had moved to Barbados and Marcia was not satisfied with her situation in Boney M., I got a call from this beautiful person and artist, asking whether I would consider producing *her* solo recordings!

My studio was some way from being completed, but certainly in a condition for us to make music, so obviously I said, 'Come on down!'. I then proceeded to invite over from the UK my good friend and bassist Marcus James, from my touring band The Frontline Orchestra. We had a great time making music and engaging Marcia in my very normal family life; my entire family loved her easy, non-fussy attitude (even though her wardrobe would leave Imelda Marcos's mouth agape). We were as one family, with Marcia and my wife Anne cooking indoors and outdoors; we would take tortuous bicycle rides along the hilly roads of Barbados, when Marcia would outpace most of the very robust men who thought they were fit, but obviously not in the same league as her.

The shock was immense when, some time after all of this, after she had returned to her then home in Miami, I heard she was battling that non-relenting human adversary, cancer, and that it was serious. I prayed along with my family and we all felt deep sorrow, especially for Marcus, who by now was married to Marcia.

Deep in my soul, I had every expectation that if there was anyone who could beat this affliction, it would be Marcia. But how many times?

Let her, my hero, tell you, and fill you with hope.

*Eddy Grant*

# 'It was hard not to be overwhelmed'

On 9 December 1978 Boney M. flew to the Soviet Union, as it was then called, to play a series of concerts in Moscow, and it was at that point it started to sink in with us exactly how big we were. This might seem strange considering that we'd had huge hits all across Europe and in Australia, New Zealand and Canada practically from the word go. But the simple truth of that period is there hadn't been any time to digest too much of what was going on. We recorded the single 'Daddy Cool', went straight out on the road to promote it, then were right back in the studio to do the next one – and we worked like that until it was time to come back and record the one after . . . All we were focused on was what was going on in our Boney M. world, not the big wide world.

Of course we knew the records were selling well, and during 1978 we had been coming to terms with how much Boney M. had become part of the everyday pop music that was all around us, especially in Germany where we were based. All through that year it had been commonplace for us to walk into a restaurant or a bar and hear 'Daddy Cool' or 'Ma Baker' or 'Rasputin' playing – in fact, by the end of that year we'd just look at each other, nod and smile! Maybe we'd got a bit blasé with that level of fame, or perhaps we just didn't believe we were anything above any of the other acts you'd hear on the radio. After all, there was always a song on before us and another one after us. That trip to the Soviet Union, though, pulled us up and it really sank in that we had gotten so big.

As with everything else we did, from our point of view the trip was arranged quickly, meaning I didn't have any time to think about the finer points of what we might be doing. When the limo came to take me to Heathrow airport it felt like any other trip to any other country, there was the usual mild commotion as we went through to departures, but nothing out of the ordinary. After we'd taken off, however, and I relaxed into my First Class seat sipping a glass of champagne – First Class had been reserved just for us – I could properly consider what we were doing. For me this was the height of Boney M.'s achievements. The album sales, the sell-out tours, the magazine front covers, the new records set and the gold and platinum discs were absolutely fantastic, but this was *special*. No other Western rock or pop group had performed in the Soviet Union. Not The Beatles, not The Rolling Stones, not The Bee Gees . . . Not even Abba who were the biggest group in Europe at that time. It was us, Boney M., who had reached that new pinnacle in the music business. We were making history.

It was hard not be overwhelmed, especially when I thought about how the group had started off three years previously when a virtually unknown German rock hopeful decided he'd be better suited to life in the studio as a producer and had gone looking for three glamorous black women to front the record he'd created. He wanted them to mime to it on a one-off TV show, but had no plans for anything after that. Being on my way to Moscow like that was testament to how a group put together under those kind of fly-by-night circumstances stuck at it, worked hard and became one of the best in the world. I also felt a massive sense of personal achievement as I had come from beginnings in rural Jamaica where we'd slept five in a bed and if we kids didn't go up the mountain to pick vegetables sometimes the family wouldn't eat. On that flight, I savoured the luxury treatment Boney M. had made possible.

I was also well aware how different my life could have been, when I remembered how close I'd come to not joining Boney M. at all. When I was invited to the first interview to join this group being put together with three black girls and one black guy I took no notice! I couldn't have been less interested, it took me a couple of months and the guy I was dating at the time telling me I was too old to join a pop group for me to change my mind and see if they were still looking . . .

*Part One*

# STARLIGHT

## Chapter One

# 'You just have to get on with it'

In 1975, in Hamburg, my friend Dornee told me about a German record producer named Frank Farian who was looking for attractive black girls who could sing, to form a group. It wasn't the first time I'd been approached to be part of a group, but I'd always dismissed any such suggestions as I was very happy with what I was doing. Sure I felt ready to take the next step, but I wanted to do it as a solo artist because I believed that by becoming part of a group after five years on my own, I'd be giving up too much of what I'd earned for myself. The only reason I considered it this time was because it came from Dornee, who was my one good friend on the German music scene. We'd met the previous year, when I was recording for the producer Joe Menke and she was in the studio next door working with somebody else. I was listening to her work and was fascinated by her voice, it was amazing – after I got to know her I used to call her the Black Barbra Streisand. Dornee turned out to be one of the nicest people I've ever met and we became close. When I was in Hamburg I'd visit her in her flat or we'd go out to dinner.

The idea of joining this group didn't appeal to her because she wanted to concentrate on the gospel she sang so spectacularly, but she knew me well and wouldn't have passed the offer along if she didn't think it would be worth my while. So even though I had told her I wasn't interested it stuck in my mind and when I went back to England soon after, it was plaguing me. I got straight into the usual routine with my family, but Dornee must have done quite a number on me because every day I'd wake up thinking, 'What about this group?'

When I returned to Hamburg, I asked the German guy I was dating what he thought I should do, and it may well have been his reply that pushed me into making my decision: he said to me, 'Don't you think you're a bit old to be joining a pop group?' I was twenty-seven! And whatever that might have seemed like to anybody else, or in comparison with other pop singers, it really didn't matter to me because I saw myself just starting out on this journey – standing on the verge of a wonderful career.

So I picked up the phone and made the call to Dornee, hoping the position hadn't already been filled. She said she'd have to track Frank down, then when she did get back to me I was really quite surprised to find he still hadn't found anybody. That was it! If this was still open after what was now a couple of months, I knew the spot was for me – it was destiny. How I justified it to myself after being so adamant I would never join a group was to think, 'This is about making that step up. I might have a record deal on my own, but I've not made much progress in the last few years. Maybe if another producer comes in and he's interested to work with my voice, maybe it will turn to something big – why not give it a go?' It's silly to stick to your principles just to stick to your principles, sometimes you have to make a compromise. Also, I always knew that if it didn't work out then I would have lost nothing because I could always go back to doing my solo thing.

The point of contact was a German woman called Katja Wolfe, who I think was acting as a talent scout for Frank Farian. She came to meet me in a bar in Hamburg, and arrived with Maizie Williams. Maizie was the first to be signed up for this new group, and she was a good mover because had been dancing *oben-ohne* in a bar in Hanover. That means topless, which was very much a fashion in Germany in those days – indeed, it was so commonplace that when I used to go back to London if I told somebody I was a dancer in Germany they'd always raise an eyebrow as if something untoward must be going on! I won't judge anybody who chose to do it, but I never have. When I danced I wore bell-bottom trousers and had my shirt tails tied under my breasts – I can show my photos of those times to anybody!

I had brought my black book of press cuttings and photos to the meeting, and although Katja seemed impressed that I was really a singer – I guess they only expected someone who could dance and look pretty – all she said was, 'Fine, I'll tell Mr Farian. You just have to meet him and do a little audition, if he wishes.' And that was it – I would soon find out that even telling me that was high praise indeed from anybody in that organisation!

I waited a couple of weeks, then I was told Frank wanted me to audition in Saarbrucken, a town near the French border, where he and his musical arranger, Stefan Klinkhammer, lived. At Stefan's flat the arranger played the piano while I sang 'Get Ready' and a couple more tracks. Frank sat there, and when I'd finished said, 'It will do', and my immediate thought was, 'Blimey! Is that all he can say?' He asked me several times if I knew any other black girls for the group, which I thought was a bit weird. Was he really looking for a singer or did he just

13

want a little marionette to stand out in front and mime to his productions?

Frank Farian had produced a record himself, 'Baby Do You Wanna Bump?', on which he had sung all the parts – it didn't have much of a lyric. It didn't get anywhere in Germany but had become a surprise hit in Holland. The name he had given the group was Boney M., after an Australian TV detective called Boney, with the M added just because he felt it gave the name a better ring. Now, through the record company, a Dutch television show had actually booked Boney M. to perform. Never one to pass up an opportunity to sell some records, Frank needed his fictitious group to exist, which is why he put me together with Maizie and this guy Bobby Farrell, who had also already been selected. The original plan was just to mime on that TV show, which was probably the reason he and Katja Wolfe appeared to take our auditions so casually.

Bobby was the DJ at the bar where Maizie had been dancing, so they knew each other already. I met him for the first time on the way to the TV gig in Holland – once again thrown straight into it – and he seemed like an OK guy, a bit of an extrovert, but in our business that's not always a bad thing. He was the only one of us who hadn't come from England: he was born in Aruba, a Dutch colony in the Caribbean, and from there he had been living in Holland before relocating to Hanover. The reason Frank had been so keen to have three girls in the group was because he'd already had a publicity photo done with one guy and three girls in it so he figured he'd better match it up, but I'm sure nobody either noticed or cared there was a different number of people in the group. Or that two of them were different from the people in the photograph – Maizie was in the publicity shot and was the only one of them who became a genuine Boney M.!

The three of us did the gig: Maizie and I mimed the 'Woooh-woooh-wooohs' with Bobby covering the part that repeated the title in a big deep voice – I said that song didn't have too many words! Bobby had quite a reputation as a dancer and brought his own creations with him, Maizie herself was a very good dancer as she could improvise, and I had danced at the Top Ten club for a couple of years, so this was well within our capabilities. We presented the song with some real energy, but from that very day I've never liked it and never liked the dance, the bump, either. When Frank put it on the first Boney M. album, *Take the Heat off Me*, it became part of our set, a part I dreaded, knowing I was going to have my butt bumped on stage for four or five minutes!

Because this was television – the big time! – and because our performance had such a positive reaction, when we were on our way back to Germany Frank seemed to have his light-bulb moment: 'I want to do more of this!' Suddenly he wants to start recording new songs, turning Boney M. into a real group with actual singers, so he started properly auditioning for a second singer. He needed two female singers to give him the sound he wanted. He had me already and although he knew I could sing, for some reason he made me do another audition – thankfully I passed! Maizie and Bobby were already in, he knew they weren't singers and he didn't want them to be: Bobby brought a nice balance to the line-up and his dancing was always exciting; while Maizie looked good and could mime it, she couldn't do the full three-part harmony. This left Frank looking for another girl singer, which is what, unwittingly, caused so much future confusion.

He was looking for another black girl and one of the first he came across was a Jamaican named Millie something. I know she impressed Frank and I think she might have been in, but she had a German husband who was very proper and after the first meeting said he wanted to see the contract. He took one look through it and said, 'Oh no, this won't do, this is not good!' So that was the end of that! She was never asked back and I wonder how much she came to regret that.

Then there was a girl who had come over from England with her to dance go-go at the discotheque in Hanover. She was one of the girls in that first publicity photo, so when Frank started looking for singers after 'Baby Do You Wanna Bump?', she auditioned. She never got through; in fact, the nearest she ever came to being part of our group was when she toured as part of Maizie's Boney M. for a while in the nineties. But that hasn't stopped her using that ancient photo, claiming that she is an 'original member of Boney M.', and forming her own version of the group! Last time I looked that photograph is still on her website showing herself and a couple of others – but she's cropped out the guy who was recruited to complete the quartet at that time (an African guy who I've only ever heard referred to as Mike) and the caption reads: 'Original Boney M. Girls 1975!' For ten years she's been putting herself out there as such, and getting a lot of work because she goes out so cheaply and undercuts those of us who I feel have a genuine claim to that title.

It's not that I want to push her down just because she's competition – I'm all for people being enterprising and doing things for themselves – and I *suppose* because of the way Frank made that and had good-looking black people fronting it, she was there before me, therefore *technically* she is an original. But this ignores the most important aspect of it all – she never sang a note in the studio with Boney M. It is just not her legacy. Anybody who is going to a show today is there because of what we sang and what the four of us performed, not some forty-year-old photo with two relative unknowns in it! That's what makes me mad, and not so long ago I had my lawyer call Fairfield Halls in Croydon, where she was due to perform, to let them know what it was they were getting. They actually tried to argue with us that she was an original member of the group because of that photo – can you believe that? They weren't convinced until they compared the photo she was using with all the others of the real group. This just goes to show how easily people can be taken in.

Claudja Barry was in that 1975 photograph. She was a Jamaican who had grown up in Canada then arrived in Germany via London and had been in the cast of *Hair*. She could sing, too, and I believe she was one of Frank Farian's first choices as a vocalist. She turned it down because she had been having hits in Canada with songs she was recording in Germany and she wanted to concentrate on that. She had a point, too, as that was something that was actually happening and was much more than Frank appeared to be offering in the beginning – I'm sure that if I'd been having hits somewhere I wouldn't have been interested in the 'Baby Do You Wanna Bump?' thing! Even so, she seems quite willing to try to cash in on that same photo. I had never given Claudja Barry any thought until my half-brother in Jamaica told me that she goes over there quite a lot, and describes herself as an 'original member of Boney M.'. Once again, she was never in the studio with us. Sometimes it feels like there's a cast of thousands calling themselves an original Boney M., and I wonder how a group with that many members could even fit on stage!

Meanwhile, the audition process carried on. Frank and Katja Wolfe would regularly ask me if I knew another black singer for the group and eventually I remembered this woman I'd met in Germany a little while before: her name was Liz Mitchell.

I'd met Liz in Hamburg a couple of months previously. She was there with her two sisters Joyce and Jascind who were at university in Germany, and she'd invited me to dinner at her flat. While it made a nice change to eat some good Jamaican food of rice and mackerel – like me Liz emigrated from Jamaica to London as a young girl – the evening wasn't my thing at all. Every five minutes the door would go, people were in and out all the time and it came over as a bit of a hippy scene. It wasn't a very big flat and soon got very full of people and because I was used to living pretty quietly I found it all a bit overwhelming. Also it seemed like everybody was smoking and I've never smoked in my life as it's always affected my eyes and throat, so I spent most of the evening thinking, 'Get me out of here!'

Liz was very pleasant, though, she had invited me after all, and she'd been singing in Germany for a few years. Originally she'd come over to take a role in the stage musical *Hair*, and from there she joined the Les Humphries Singers, who were a multi-racial pop and gospel choir, led by an Englishman but had made their name in Germany. By the time we met she was singing in a group called Malcolm's Locks, which was started by her then-boyfriend Malcolm Magaron who had also been in the Les Humphries Singers. They had made records in Germany but that evening at her flat she told me she didn't think anything was happening with them and she was seriously considering moving back to England where she knew she could work as a studio session singer. Therefore when I was thinking about her for Boney M. I didn't even know if she was still in Germany. I suggested to Katja the best thing she could do was contact Liz's sisters at the flat I had been to. I knew they would still be there as they were continuing their studies.

As it turned out Liz had gone back to London, but Katja got in contact with her through her sisters, and I don't know if she or Frank actually auditioned Liz anywhere, but a couple of weeks later she and I had been booked into a hotel near Frankfurt airport to start recording. She had been flown in from London, I had travelled down from Hamburg, and the next day we were to be driven to the nearby town of Offenbach to Frank Farian's studio where it was straight into doing the vocals on Boney M.'s first proper single 'Daddy Cool'.

Although the record wasn't a hit until quite a way into 1976, this was all happening in the early part of the year, just a few weeks after I'd met the others and gone to Holland with 'Baby Do You Wanna Bump?'. That was the speed with which Frank Farian did things! The backing music was already in place, not completely finished but there was plenty for us to sing to, and while we stood there Frank explained that was how he liked to work – bringing the singers in quite near the end. What it meant was Liz and I had only just met, were in a studio we'd never seen before, with a producer we didn't really know and who spoke no English, and had just been given the lyrics to the song we're going to have to harmonise on in a couple of minutes! Talk about being thrown in at the deep end, but you just have to get on with it. I think we might have been a bit worried if Frank hadn't broken the tension – completely accidentally! When he was running through the song with us, he was going to do the deep-voice bits and he'd start holding his belly and singing 'Crazy like a fool . . .' in this big gruff voice. Liz and I just looked at each other, fighting back laughter, both of us thinking, 'This guy may be a good producer but he's certainly no singer!'

After what seemed like a matter of days, although it was longer than that because I had the time to go back to London, 'Daddy Cool' was mixed and released and Liz and I had met up with Bobby and Maizie to go on the road to promote it. We were told we *had* to do this tour with an organisation called DDU, Deutscher Discotheken-Unternehmer, a business association for German disc jockeys and disco owners, which Frank Farian was plugged into. Most German pop music producers were, because it was a promotional thing and all of the members would showcase new groups, new records and new ideas in their nightclubs. It was taped backing, as the clubs wouldn't pay very much – 400 Marks a show, which even back then was nothing – but it meant people would see you. It wasn't just a few clubs in the big cities, either: DDU took in every little town in Germany, so it meant maximum exposure, and the clubs were always packed. The downside was that we seemed to be constantly travelling and although the club owners were raking in the cash we got paid a pittance. But the bottom line was DDU could be as important as radio play when it came to breaking a new act or a new record.

So there we were with a road manager, a Ford Transit, a little bit of equipment and we're to wear our own stage clothes. However, as we're being rushed into this in true Frank Farian style, we've only got 'Daddy Cool' and 'Baby Do You Wanna Bump?' making up our show and the DDU wanted a bit more than that for their 400 Marks! Frank knew I already had a repertoire I was using for my solo act, which was very well recorded, so we added the two Boney M. songs in with the cover versions and two or three original songs and went on stage with that. It was such a rush job, we had to take my reel-to-reel tape recorder out on the road with us because Frank didn't have one.

This was it! I'm sure I didn't realise it at the time, as I was still unsure about being in a group situation, but as I travelled up and down the German autobahns in that little Ford Transit, staying in run-down motels, I was on a journey that would dominate the next ten years of my life and have a profound effect on practically every aspect of it after that.

When we weren't on the road promoting 'Daddy Cool', Liz and I got down to the serious business of recording the first Boney M. album, *Take the Heat off Me*. We started working on the other tracks quite early in 1976, very soon after we'd done the promotional work for 'Daddy Cool'. We would be recording for up to a month at a time, staying in the Steigenberger Airport Hotel, and being driven to the studio in Offenbach. As we weren't earning any royalties yet, we were counted as part of the production . . . all we had to do was bring ourselves and our voices. This was OK for me – I looked on it as being there to work not on holiday – and so the two of us settled into a routine. We'd come down from our rooms – *rooms*, not suites back in those days! – around mid-morning, perhaps I'd get something to eat, then we'd meet up and have a couple of rounds of saunas and baths to totally relax us, then get ready for the half-hour drive to the studio. We'd start work there early afternoon, then work through until, usually, nine or ten at night – depending on how much Frank wanted to do we could be there until any time between eight and eleven.

Frank's method was the same as it had been for 'Baby Do You Wanna Bump?' – he had already finished the music then we came in to sing on top – and how we worked on that album set the pattern for almost every other Boney M. recording. We would have already had the lyrics to go over and think about, but we would be hearing the backing track for the first time when he called us in, one at a time. After we'd soaked up the music, he'd go through it with us, explaining what he wanted from the vocals in each bit of it, where the harmonies would be, how the voices would carry the melody, what the choruses should sound like . . . I thought this was a fantastic way of doing things as it didn't waste our time and as we came in when it was finished we were hit with the full vibes of the track immediately.

When he got us in there together he would stand behind the mixing desk and tell us 'Do this harmony . . .' or 'Sing this bit like this . . .' and we did it, which might sound like the employ-ees have to take commands from the employer, but it wasn't like that. Of course Liz and I would have ideas to contribute and we would make suggestions, but Frank was the producer, it was his vision. We were professionals and we respected that role just as we expected him to respect ours, which I have to say he did – especially in the beginning – and I really enjoyed record-ing with Frank Farian.

When I first met him it was all friendly enough but essentially it was neutral; at that point I didn't know it was going to be any sort of long-term proposition but I thought he seemed professional enough and everything seemed to be well organised, which really appealed to me. When we began recording with him and Boney M. was taking off, I knew that we would find out just how serious he is. As it was he turned out to be a really good record producer. Not just because he created a sound that became a hit practically all around the world, but because of how he worked in the studio with Liz and me. He had patience, which is most important. He would explain what he wanted us to do, and if we didn't get it straight away he'd never ever lose his cool, he'd just try and tell us or show us in a different way. All this would take place in German, because he spoke no English whatsoever – I'm not even sure he's learned any yet! – but I was more or less fluent by this time and Liz knew enough, and I would translate anything she didn't understand. He was the ultimate producer – doesn't sing, doesn't play, doesn't write, but if he wasn't there none of it would have happened. I've never seen him with an instrument in his hand, but he hired some of the best backing musicians around, and he soon gave up trying to help Liz and I do background vocals after he came around to stand with us and would screw up his face as he tried to hit the high notes that would end up as a squeaking 'Eeeeh, eeeeh, eeeeeeh!' Sometimes it was all we could do to keep from laughing, and he seemed to know when he was beaten as after a couple of songs he left us alone and said, '*Nein, nein, nein* . . . You two do it, I'll just sit here at the mixing board!'

Frank knew I liked a glass of champagne, while Liz preferred cognac so there would be a glass of each waiting for us when we arrived. This isn't to say we needed a drink before we could sing, it was just a little gesture to relax us and always appreciated as that. If we were working late he'd send out for pizza, because that was about the only fast food you could get out there back then, we'd wash it down with water, then it was back downstairs to the studio. He was a happy man, running jokes with us all the time, those sessions were fun, and there was always the hope and anticipation of starting out on a new project.

While Frank Farian was very comfortable to work with, making this album was pretty intense and we worked hard during those sessions. Recording each track took a long time because back in those days studio technology wasn't anything like it is today: there was no looping to repeat something that's only been sung once, and if something needed to be doubled up we had to sing it twice. Also, it meant Liz and I each had to sing everything: we would stand before the microphone and we would sing every melody, every harmony and every octave. I had a track on the board, and she had a track, so eventually Frank could decide what he was going to use and how to mix this together to create harmonies. Or we'd have to sing harmonies with vocals that we'd already recorded. It was full on, but we both understood that this was being aimed at a big audience so we would have to put in a big effort.

It was very different for Maizie and Bobby, who weren't there: they never sang on any of the records so they weren't needed in the studio. I'm not sure what they did during the *Take the Heat off Me* sessions, but later on, because the group couldn't tour when Liz and I were recording, they could go on holiday and didn't seem to take much interest in what was being done back in Germany. This could result in a quite weird situation in which the first time they heard a new song by the group they were a big part of would be when they heard it on the radio! As it went on, they got so relaxed that they didn't seem to do the exact lyrics and timing of the songs – when we did television appearances we were supposed to lip sync but at times it looked like they were just opening and closing their mouths!

As positive an experience as I was having from all of this work, as soon as each session finished Frank needed time to do his mixing and bring the magic out of each track, so we were free! After a few weeks of living in a hotel room, I couldn't wait to get back to London, see my family and fully relax. Mama had stopped work by then, and I was earning enough not to have to work as a stenographer, which was my day job since leaving school, so once I'd taken care of anything that needed attention I could properly chill out.

These breaks gave me the chance to reflect on what I'd done and where I was, and I was satisfied that what I had approached as a gamble – putting my solo career on hold and joining a group – was paying off. I was learning a great deal about the studio and how vocals could be made to work, plus I definitely felt I'd stepped up a level in terms of the music business.

When the whole album was finished I was excited about it. I thought it sounded good, I was happy with my contribution and how Frank had worked Liz and my voices. We had done a lot of cover versions for it – 'Sunny', 'No Woman No Cry', 'Fever' – and I was pleased with the way we had put our own Boney M. stamp on them. Really, I was far more concerned about what the album sounded like than whether it would be a huge hit or not – I knew there were so many factors that would go into making it a hit, yet anybody who listened to it would know if it did me credit or not. I suppose at that point I hadn't fully committed to Boney M. the group as it was still all very new to me – I'd never been in a group before, I'd never had an album out so I wasn't at all sure what to expect, and all I was sure of was I didn't want to jeopardise the solo career that I might have to go back to.

That said, of course I wanted *Take the Heat off Me* to be as successful as it could be, and I won't pretend I wasn't excited as I waited, hoping it was all going to kick off. But I was working hard to keep a lid on things, as was Liz, the other Jamaican in the group. Not long before it was released, she came up to me and said quietly, in patois, 'Yuh t'ink dis go work?' All I could reply was, 'Bwoy, mi no know! Mek we wait an' see.'

## Chapter Two

# 'Suddenly everybody everywhere wanted Boney M.'

'D addy Cool' didn't take off straight away, but we carried on working it around that DDU tour circuit, which was valuable PR for a new act but could be punishing because there was so little money in it. The 400 German Marks a show was much less than I had been earning solo, but it wasn't as if it was costing me anything because I lived frugally on the road, and the bottom line was I was committed to this project for at least that first album. Also, I always kept things in perspective because I remembered what *real* hard work was and it didn't involve any sort of hotel, being driven around or standing on stage singing, it actually meant working hard! So while I might have been tired when I got home to London, I was never going to forget how privileged I was.

We'd go out, do some club dates and whatever TV shows the record company could fix up, then when Frank had a new track ready he would call a halt to the touring and take Liz and me back into the studio. Our part of the album finished in May 1976, it was released in June that year and what we had been doing eventually paid off. We were booked on to *Der Musikladen*, Germany's biggest pop music TV show, and we gave what I thought was our best performance so far. We really went for it, and suddenly 'Daddy Cool' was a hit practically all across Europe – it was as if people saw that and thought, 'Hang on, isn't that the group that's been touring all over? They're pretty good, aren't they?' It was an immediate hit in Germany, then spread to become Number One in France, Austria, Belgium, Spain, Switzerland, Norway and Sweden, it even went Top Ten in the UK, an audience that seemed to come to Boney M. very late. That's when everything seemed to move up a gear and suddenly everybody everywhere wanted Boney M. We were all over the Continent doing TV shows, interviews, photo shoots, appearing on the covers of magazines . . . We could walk into a shop or a restaurant, hear 'Daddy Cool' on the radio, look at each other and just burst out laughing – *that was us*! It was even more special for Liz and me because we knew people could hear our voices and they were loving what we had done. All of us were getting stopped in the street, especially in Germany where we would cause a commotion as soon as we stepped out of the door.

It doesn't matter what anybody says about why they get into the pop music business and what they hope to achieve, this was what it was all about: having a Number One record! It means what you have done is being appreciated by the people it was aimed at. Of course you can't get carried away and start believing you're something you're not – there's a great many factors that contribute to a hit record – but like any other job you want to be told that you're doing it well, and a Number One song means for that week you're doing it better than anybody else. We were as excited as little kids at Christmas, and although Boney M. went on to have countless Number Ones, none of them ever had the same effect on me as 'Daddy Cool'.

The sheer volume of things for us to do and places for us to be increased enormously, and although we were getting a noticeably better standard of comfort on the road, it was still a real workout. 'Sunny', our second single, came out before the end of the year, so as soon as 'Daddy Cool' started to die down we were being taken all over the place to promote that. Meanwhile, the album *Take the Heat off Me* had become a hit in several countries, getting to Number One in a couple of them, so the record company wanted to follow that up while our momentum was still high. Of course, Frank was only too happy to oblige. So before the end of September, while all the promotional whirlwind for 'Sunny' was going on, Liz and I were called back to Offenbach to start recording the *Love for Sale* album. I'm pretty sure the first track we did was 'Ma Baker'.

This put an extra strain on us, because we weren't getting the time off that Bobby and Maizie enjoyed, but how could you complain? 'I'm sorry, Mr Farian, but I'd much rather go on holiday than do the job I've been dreaming about for most of my life, and have finally got the chance to be successful at it!' This wasn't a matter of just getting on with it – I absolutely relished everything that was going on.

Working on a new album while we were still promoting the current one was how we worked all the time Frank was our producer, so there was always a seamless supply of singles and the audience never got a chance to forget about us or discover somebody else. All the groups at the pop end of the market worked like that. Frank rarely came on the road with us, he only made it to the biggest concerts or most influential television shows, so he would stay in the studio working on the next tracks, and as we were still performing to backing tapes at that point, the musicians were available for the studio sessions.

As far as I was concerned, it didn't matter which album the tracks we were singing ended up on as long as the maximum amount of people got to hear them and could appreciate what we had achieved. I believe we always performed to the best of our abilities in the studio – at least I know I did – and we let Frank and the record company take care of the rest.

But recording our music in that way meant that it became difficult to get a grip on how the group was doing in the outside world because Liz and I kept having to focus on what was in the future rather than the present. When a song came out and we had to promote it, it was completely new to Bobby and Maizie, but we would have finished with it ages ago and maybe done a couple more since then. So while we'd be very familiar with it, it wasn't as new and exciting to us as it might have been to them – the song that was freshest in our minds would have been whatever we were working on last. All this was going on with the one-night stands that made up most of the DDU dates, so one morning you'd be here – *somewhere* – by the afternoon you'd be somewhere else, then the next morning you'd be off again. It wasn't much better when we were working in Offenbach: we'd be shuttling between the studio and the hotel, still not fully coming to terms with the impact Boney M. was making as part of everyday life.

So Liz and I existed in a kind of Boney M. Bubble, which I think suited Frank. The group was pretty much what he'd always envisaged it to be: a self-contained thing with him calling all the shots and us reliant on him for a link to how we fitted into the outside world. From the very beginning he was always in between us and the record company, our deal was with him and he delivered Boney M. to them as a finished article – a song to release and people to perform to it on TV, never mind what was actually going on behind the name and who was involved. Not that this was at all unusual in Europe, particularly in Germany, there was a trend for pop/disco with acts that didn't really exist – modern technology made it possible for music to be put together by a producer or anonymous session men, with a jobbing singer brought in to do the vocals. After that, if it was needed, somebody would be engaged to front the performance for television – it might even be different people for different shows, depending on availability.

In fact, I think Frank would have been quite happy with session singers just coming in for each track. It's telling that he didn't credit us as vocalists on the *Take the Heat off Me* album sleeve: he credited the musicians, the writers and the arranger, but not us. But when 'Daddy Cool' and 'Ma Baker' became such huge hits it was with our voices and the public knew Liz and me as the Sound of Boney M. – and they loved it. Quite rightly, Frank wouldn't then take the risk of replacing us in case it changed the sound and the hits dried up.

When we went into the Boney M. thing, none of us had any professional management; I personally hadn't needed it up to that point. When I first went to Germany the agencies I was signed to had looked after everything and I trusted them. Gradually I learned how to understand contracts for doing shows and what to make sure I asked for. I assume the others had been adequately managing their affairs themselves too, but like me most of their work centred on live performances, which involved pretty straightforward work-for-hire agreements.

Now the four of us had nobody who was purely looking after our interests and we were going into a very different situation. Frank was Boney M.'s producer, which is not the same as being a manager because he personally had so much to gain financially from the creative side of the group. However, he had put himself in a position where he decided everything as far as we were concerned, and more often than not this would be to his advantage. That could make things a little awkward sometimes, and if we'd had somebody, a manager, speaking up on our behalf then I'm sure we would have been more comfortable. As it was, during that period everything seemed very spontaneous, evolving as it went along; had it been planned it might have left us more time to look around and properly assess our situation.

Something we couldn't get away from, as regards Boney M.'s status as a group, was how we came together: it wasn't like most groups who started off as friends when they were quite young and then grew together as people and as artists. We were put together by somebody else, and we were all grown people when that happened – I was twenty-seven or twenty-eight when I joined the group. In fact, I was the oldest, one year older than Bobby, three years and three months older than Maizie and four years older than Liz. All four of us had fully formed personalities and opinions; each of us wanted different things out of Boney M. and had different ways of going about getting them. Spending so much time together – often in very close proximity for long spells of time – was never going to be easy.

Sometimes I used to think the four of us had so little in common the only time we really came together was on stage, but it was never true we couldn't get on or used to row all the time. We never had any verbal conflicts, something I was always keen to avoid – I'm not from a street gang! – although sometimes there could be uncomfortable vibes that spoke louder than words. Naturally we had our differences, and just as naturally we quickly learned to put them aside and make the most of the opportunity we had been given. However much we may have got on each other's nerves – I'm sure some of my ways irritated the others as much as things they did irritated me – we knew this was the life we had chosen for ourselves. We were professionals. But it was more than that – we were four black people from the Caribbean, let loose in Germany and then the rest of the world, very quickly making a big name for ourselves. I was happy for all of us because of that and I believe the others felt the same.

Of course we had fun; you'd have to be a very special kind of miserable not to enjoy the situations we found ourselves in. The photo shoots and the video shoots were always a good laugh, because it was a way of relaxing and when we were presented with some of the photography scenarios we could all see a funny side to them. We knew it was serious stuff and part of projecting what Boney M. were about, but when we saw some of those costumes for the first time you had to laugh! In those days when we were working on the first album and there was only us and a tiny crew on the road – before the entourages started – we had so much fun travelling, because nothing makes a long autobahn journey go quicker than a few good jokes. We were always laughing in those vans, and wherever we were going was new so there was always that excitement of wondering, 'What's coming next?'

We were all having a lot of fun, but the bottom line is that if we hadn't all been in Boney M. it's unlikely any of us would have associated with any of the others. This isn't anything horrible, we were all just very different characters.

Liz and I were the two Jamaicans, but that didn't bring about any sense of camaraderie, except perhaps when we used to talk to each other in our Jamaica patois, when we were particularly excited or didn't want something broadcast. True, in the beginning I felt closer to her than to the others, but that was because as the two lead singers we spent so much time working together. We got on well enough, we talked to each other and we could have a laugh, but it was nearly always work-related. I felt that from the beginning she was distant towards me and would confide in Maizie much more than she would in me.

In many ways Liz was as self-contained as I was and we both looked out for ourselves. I was like that because of the childhood I'd had looking after my mother and sister from a very early age, but I sometimes felt that Liz was more about getting on and looking after number one. I used to think maybe she didn't see me as anybody who could advance her career.

Maizie was *jokify* as we would say in Jamaica – she had jokes! Maizie was very good company as she was always funny, she could always lift us up or her wit could prick anybody's bubble of self-importance. Maybe because she didn't have the full vocal workload that Liz and I had and she could relax and enjoy the ride a bit more, but she was smart and bright too. She didn't have a strong voice but was always aware of that; however, after Frank had spoken to her about the lyrics, she made the effort and let me coach her to sing a couple of lines from one of the more simple songs, 'Got a Man on My Mind'. I just thought that since we were all up on stage it would be nice for her to be more involved with the singing. When we were on the road I'd go to her room and we'd try '*Walk around in circles/without peace and little sleep . . . la, la, la, la, la, la, la . . .*' We were getting there too, but it didn't really take off.

Maizie had great taste in clothes too and was usually immaculately turned out. I'd like to think she learned some of that from me but I might just be bigging myself up here! One thing I did advise her on – and she seemed to take notice – was dating. In 1976, the media could be so judgmental, particularly towards young black women and especially in Germany – and I told her she should be ultra cautious and discreet, and she was.

Bobby was Bobby! There's not really any other way to describe him. He was like his dancing – spontaneous, larger than life – and he always worked hard to be entertaining! He had something funny to say about just about anything and could have us roaring with laughter, but that had another side too like when he overslept, which wasn't unusual, if you banged on his door to wake him up you'd be greeted with a stream of cussing! I used to give it right back, which he always seemed to think was funny.

Even though Frank had taken Bobby to Holland for that first TV gig, when he started seriously trying out for Boney M. he had auditioned Bobby before Liz and me and had turned him down. I haven't got a clue why, maybe he was looking for somebody who could sing, or perhaps he wanted the guy Mike from that old photo line-up to come back. Eventually, though, I think he realised how much Bobby contributed and how well he worked with the rest of us, so he fully accepted the fact he was just there to dance.

There was hardly any rehearsed choreography with any of us;

everybody came to the stage each time with their own little thing and we just fitted it in. Sometimes we girls would say, OK, we're going to do *this* to 'Ma Baker' or *that* to 'Brown Girl in the Ring', but usually that would be for a particular TV show and would be something we'd work out just beforehand. With Bobby, there wasn't even any of that, it was all natural! Bobby was on his own with his own creations and any day he wanted to do anything, he did it. It really suited the picture of Boney M., because we girls could look quite sophisticated while this guy was going mad around us! If something he did on stage got particularly big applause from the crowd or if he himself was pleased with a move he'd pulled off he'd do it again the next night. Or not – there really was no telling what he might do!

We girls would often work out individual little routines to do with him, we were all good dancers so Bobby and one of us could end up facing each other on stage and we'd copy the other's moves. Then the next night you'd be preparing yourself and be facing in a certain direction at that part of the song, but Bobby would be over the other side of the stage – he'd got so caught up in something else that had come to him, he'd completely forgotten about it! Then there were the bruised legs and ankles which could happen to any of us when we danced with Bobby because he'd got a bit carried away and his kicks were too enthusiastic – I would just move a little bit more to the left with a smile on my face as if nothing had happened. Or, as my husband and I love looking out for if we catch a rerun of one of our TV specials, sometimes we'd look so surprised at something Bobby did we'd almost miss a beat. That was always brilliant, because I'd think, 'If *we're* that surprised and we work with the guy every day, imagine what effect that had on the crowd!' He did try to sing on stage, and because I was at the end of the line-up he would come next to me and I'd give him his pitch by humming the notes he needed to sing, sometimes he would hit them, sometimes he wouldn't, and at other times he didn't even bother to try! But that was what Bobby brought to the party – a sense of total freedom.

The audiences loved him, they really did. Maybe because he was the only guy he was the most identifiable – I'm sure in the beginning people thought he was Boney M. and we were his backing singers! He was like a tinderbox up there and could explode at any time and nobody knew quite what they were going to get or when they could expect to get it. This was a real asset to the group, because we had a devoted fan base who would go and see show after show, so we always knew they'd be getting something different every time.

Frank found out how popular Bobby was when he fired him in 1981 and tried to replace him: it just wasn't the same and the audience we'd built up was never happy about it. Indeed, the fact that Frank, who could be the most stubborn man I've ever met, called him back after about three years suggests that he too finally understood what Bobby meant to Boney M. Why Frank sacked him in the first place wasn't that hard to understand, as another part of Bobby's spontaneity was he would tell it like it is, to anybody at any time, and he wouldn't hold back! He was always telling Frank where to go, and as he didn't care who he said it in front of, Frank must have absolutely hated it.

To me, Bobby was a lovely guy with a soft side. In spite of his bluster and jokes, I think he was always a bit worried that his position in the group was undervalued. After I'd left the group, I hardly ever saw him and we had a few long phone conversations and he'd end up in tears and that would really upset me. I don't think he fully realised what Boney M. was, at its height, and what he as part of it represented in the music business. Which is a huge shame, but I'll always remember him as a very natural, very big-hearted, very funny guy.

Being in Boney M. at that time was simply a great feeling. As the second album took over from the first and things kept building upwards, we began to see that we were genuinely getting somewhere. Emotionally I felt I had landed in something big and nothing was going to stop me on this path. I knew I was a strong woman before I'd ever joined the group – before I'd ever come to Germany or even got into the music business, for that matter – but now I felt I had the right vehicle to make the most of that strength. Any little obstacles or niggles were exactly that – *little*. I felt like the song I sang on that first album, Sunny: *The dark days are gone and the bright days are here . . .* For the first time in my life I was absolutely certain I was going to fulfil my dreams.

## Chapter Three

# 'We kept bumping into Abba'

When The Bee Gees had that big hit in 1976 with 'You Should Be Dancing', it seemed as if audiences everywhere took that to be some sort of command! Suddenly the pop music world was buzzing as disco was taking over and people not only wanted to dance, but they wanted a bit more excitement and *proper* glitz and glamour from their music. They wanted irresistible songs; they wanted good-looking people in great costumes; and the onstage dancing had to be more exciting than anything they could see in a discotheque. This meant that 1977, the time in which we were progressing from *Take the Heat off Me* to *Love for Sale*, felt exactly the right time for Boney M.

The disco era was loosening people up – it looked to me like everybody was doing the Hustle – then in Europe they bit on to us so fast because we were *theirs*. Back then there was a strong European pop music industry with its own audience that wasn't always looking to America or Great Britain, so while artists like Barry White or Candi Staton could have hits in Germany, they weren't German, so the audience would never embrace them like one of their own. We were *German* – it didn't matter that we were born on three different Caribbean islands, we were based in Germany, we were produced by a German, we were signed to a German record label, therefore Boney M. would always be a German group. This was very important all over Europe, as I'm sure the local radio stations and music press gave preference to 'homegrown' acts over the Americans and the British. It's not the case now as MTV and the Internet means all music is global and everybody has access to everything all the time.

We also had an edge over the American disco acts because we sang pop, while so many of them were singing soul as part of the disco thing, this is because wherever it ended up disco started off as soul music. It sounds like I'm being overly fussy about types of music – anybody who knows me will tell you I am a bit of a music nerd! – and these were relatively small differences between what we were doing in Boney M. and pure disco or soul music, but they were important. They were subtleties that were enough to make the difference when it came to getting on daytime radio or appealing to the broadest spectrum of the public, because it wasn't as intense as so much of the American music. Frank Farian was a pop music producer first and foremost, and he understood the distinctions perfectly; he kept us close enough to disco to make people happy and keep them dancing, but our pop music was always far more accessible because it had so many familiar tones and sounds in it. We were coming in on the back of acts like Donna Summer and Giorgio Moroder, who were both based in Germany, and Chic with songs like 'Freak Out', so everything just sort of melded together with our pop sound, meaning mainstream audiences and radio felt much more comfortable with us. This was exactly the same for Abba: they did pop that worked in the discotheques and got people dancing, but it was always pop, plus they were a European group not American or British, so had that head start on the Continent. Of course it helped they were a fantastic group with brilliant songs, but whoever you are, in the beginning it's always about getting yourself heard!

The fact that we were a black group worked in our favour as well. Firstly, because of how the entertainment industry is, people naturally expected us to be doing something that people would dance to, but when it was discovered these three black women were singing pop it was of immediate interest because it was so unexpected – especially from Germany. There were all those fantastic groups of ladies like The Emotions or The Three Degrees, but they were soul groups, and here were we three good-looking glamorous black women singing pop. Once people in Germany realised we weren't American and weren't a soul group they would look at us like, '*Hmmmmm*, interesting!' And they were curious to hear more. Then there was the fact that we were born in Jamaica, Montserrat and Aruba, so how did we get this grounding in pop? Because three of us were brought up in England and the other had been in Holland from his early teens. Once people in the press and radio got to learn that about us they were fascinated to hear the whole story behind how we became Boney M.

When we did take off with our own music it was like an explosion. Bam! Whereas 'Baby Do You Wanna Bump?' had only been a hit in the Netherlands, 'Daddy Cool' and 'Sunny' were Number One in half a dozen different countries across Europe and Top Ten in most of the others. Then came the album with those songs included, but also the big fabulous presentation of the cover shoot and the big fold-out poster of us that came with the vinyl LP. The idea was to let people have a look at us, put us on their bedroom wall and let their friends who might not know us go, 'Whoa! Is that what Boney M. look like? Let me hear some of their music.' It presented us as a whole package, which I found very exciting, and on the back of all this, the album, *Take the Heat off Me* went Top Ten all over the place and earned us our first gold disc in Germany for sales of over a quarter of a million. By the following year we had grown so much that we were awarded a platinum disc in Germany for the *Love for Sale* marking sales of *half* a million, and it was Number One or Number Two practically everywhere in Europe. The only place we weren't hitting so big was the UK. As I've said, those guys over there were slow to catch on to Boney M. and the first two albums only got to Numbers 40 and 13 respectively. However, good taste prevailed and once they got there, the British were as keen on us as anybody else!

One of the reasons for this Boney M. boom was us being on the road more or less permanently in between those two albums, which in itself created its own escalating cycle: playing so many dates boosted our popularity, which led to us doing even more dates, which boosted our popularity even more and so on! Not so long ago I was looking at some adverts for the tours we did in those days and *every night* there was a show – it was get up, drive here, perform a show, back to the hotel, get up, drive there . . . We'd gone from the DDU set up of nightclub dates to theatres and larger concert halls throughout Germany; we were still using taped backing but we were building up our own repertoire as every time Frank recorded a new song the music track would be added to our playback. During that year our touring expanded to all over Europe – Switzerland, France, Spain, Austria, Scandinavia – then to all over the world: Singapore, Hong Kong, Australia, anywhere where our records were selling and we had an audience to build on.

We were hardly off television in Germany either, as if ever we had a day off the record company would book us in for some show or another, or if were playing in a big city they'd set up something for us to do in the afternoon that could be recorded as soon as we arrived. It was the same when we travelled – no matter which country we were in, if ever it looked like we had two or three hours to ourselves, they'd find a TV appearance for us to do. This started off as performances of whatever single we had out at the time, but it quickly grew into interviews and chat show appearances. This helped us put something of ourselves, as people, out there, which not only increased our popularity but also did a great deal to dispel any lingering impressions that we were just bimbos fronting songs for a producer.

The combination of live work, TV shows and press conferences was exhausting but it was all so important. We knew we were selling records – as long as you had radio play you would sell records – but this was a way of building a bond with the people who were buying them. And we could feel we were doing exactly that. Everybody in Germany seemed very proud of us, for what the group was achieving across Europe and elsewhere. I honestly believed they loved us right from the start, but now, as the size of the crowds grew so did their appreciation.

If we were playing a theatre, they would get up and dance at the slightest urging from us – this was quite unusual for German audiences, even the teens, as if they had a seat for a show they tended to stay sitting in it! They seemed to know all our lyrics – it could be a single that had only come out that week and the crowds would be able to sing the whole thing with us. Those were always really fantastic moments, it would make the hairs on the back of my neck stand up when we kept quiet on stage and the whole audience would take over singing a song like 'Rivers of Babylon'.

The applause could sometimes be overwhelming, and we'd well up when we took a final bow at the end of a particularly brilliant gig. We did one show around that time when were opening for Udo Jürgens, an Austrian singer who has been a massive star in Germany since the 1960s, but we were suddenly the hot thing. We did our set, there was an interval and all through it the crowd didn't stop cheering for us, then when it was his time to go on they just started clapping in time and chanting, 'Bo-ney M . . . Bo-ney M . . .!' We had to get back into our costumes and take the stage once more to do a couple of encores.

For me, having success in Great Britain with Boney M. was the biggest blast of everything that had happened to us. I said earlier that it was a bit of a slow start for us in England, but really that was only in comparison with the Continent and had more to do with the album sales starting off relatively slowly. Some of that might have been down to the British press who are among the hardest in the world to impress – look how they treated Prince or Michael Jackson! Boney M. were never going to get an easy ride! They didn't like disco much, they didn't have much time for European artists in general, and in the beginning they certainly didn't get Boney M.: a German group . . . a *black* German group . . . people from the Caribbean . . . how did that work? In the mid 1970s that was a freaky thing for them to come to terms with and you could almost hear the cogs turning as they tried to work out if Germany had any Caribbean colonies or not! In the early days they weren't as mean to us as they might have been, it was more a case of not bothering to take us seriously because they didn't know what to make of us. For example, they never understood why Bobby was a fully fledged part of the group, and how he would appear to be going crazy while the three of us seemed to be standing off to the side, looking cool, with virtually no choreography at all. It just became easier for them to sneer at us as a 'manufactured' disco act.

But what can you do? They didn't make much attempt to find out about us and I guessed they were going to write what they were going to write regardless, so we just carried on and did our own thing. None of it mattered because the public was all that counted and they started to buy the singles, and once a song gets into the charts they've got to take you on *Top of the Pops*. From there it snowballed and from 'Daddy Cool' for the three years every single we released in the UK went into the Top Ten. We were on *Top of the Pops* so much the staff at the studio used to joke that we must have season tickets! And to give the British press their due, once they saw how popular we were and they were more or less forced to accept us they did become much more supportive − although there was always a few who remained a little hesitant because they wouldn't see us as anything other than *just* a disco group.

Regular people in Britain loved us – partly because we were doing music people could easily get into – pop music – and partly because we were still down to earth and looked like we were having fun. We always got a wonderful welcome anywhere we went in the UK and audiences there were probably the most responsive: practically from the beginning they screamed their heads off and would immediately get out of their seats and start dancing.

Liz, Maizie and I had all grown up in England and so we could identify with the crowds there, make little jokes on the stage and in press conferences talk about stuff that was completely relevant to them. This was particularly significant among the big following of young black girls we picked up in England because they could totally identify with us. We had the same backgrounds as so many of them – with parents from the Caribbean, the kids either born in England or coming over very young. They would see us on *Top of the Pops* or talk about us at school or in the street: 'Have you heard that "Ma Baker"? . . . What do you think of "Daddy Cool"?' So many of the boys loved us too, but the girls would look at us and could see themselves. Girls would copy my braided hairstyle – it didn't cost money to do and their mothers were happy to do something that didn't involve chemicals or a treatment. These days when I go back to London I'm always meeting black women in their forties and fifties who tell me they copied my hairstyles through their teenage years!

More importantly than that, I believe we inspired a great many of these girls to follow their dreams, as they'd look at Boney M. and think, 'She's doing so well, and she went to school in *Brixton*! An ordinary girls' school! That's just like me;

maybe I could go on to do something remarkable too.' I felt the three of us were like pioneers in that respect because when we burst onto the scene I can't think of any other black British woman that was having that effect on the youngsters and teenagers. I still feel proud of the idea that we gave so many of our young sisters a lift.

I loved going back to London as part of Boney M., and doing *Top of the Pops* was a big part of that. It was always the best music show on television and something *everybody* watched every week, not just the kids who might be buying records but their mums and dads, too. It was the one UK show devoted exclusively to the Top 30 – the best acts in the country at the time – so to me, when I was a schoolgirl, it was the most glamorous, most exciting show on television. I will never forget the first time we went on, with 'Daddy Cool', and the guy announced, 'And here they are . . . Boney M.!' We were on a podium with all the kids around us cheering and then they started dancing and I could hardly believe I had made it as far as to get on to this show! It was all I could do to hold it together and sing my parts! Then as I got into it all sorts of thoughts started going through my head: 'I wonder who's watching this . . . I wonder if any of my school friends are seeing this and will remember me? . . . Is Miss Tetley [my old music teacher] watching? . . . Is Elaine [my best friend from school] watching . . .'

From that first time, doing *Top of the Pops* was always a highlight of my time in Boney M., it was never anything other than madly exciting for me, even after we'd been on a dozen or more times. It could be well into our career and I'm there up on one of those stages, surrounded by the audience, and I hear,

'And now Boney M. again!' and I would still be every bit as thrilled. I'd be so chuffed to be up there on that show with the possibility of so many people I knew watching it – I wasn't trying to impress anybody; I was just enjoying what I was born to do.

My one regret when we were over in Britain as a group was I didn't have any time to visit my family or my old friends and show them how I was working and what went on as part of Boney M. We simply didn't have time because our schedule was so regimented, and the routine was: you fly in and do a press conference at the record company offices or the hotel; you do *Top of the Pops*; then there's a record company dinner or a meet-and-greet for the bigwigs; back to the hotel to sleep; and the next day you're in a different country and do the whole thing again. There was a whole team from Hansa Records, our record company in Germany, following us around and they would liaise with their counterparts in London, so we were never unsupervised. You'd be given your flight plans and your itinerary and that was that, they were paying all the bills for this to promote the record so they were going to make sure they got the most out of us. There was no way I could have asked for an hour off let alone a whole day to go and hang out with my family or friends.

One of the funniest things about doing all that travelling around Europe was we kept bumping into Abba, who would be on the same TV shows as us – like *Top of the Pops* – because at that time we were constantly doing battle with them in the charts across the Continent. If we were Number One, Abba was Number Two, if they were Number One, we were Number

Two! The press was always trying to create a rivalry between us and them, saying we hated each other. When they got bored with that, they even tried to say Liz and Benny were having an affair! But it was all nonsense, all propaganda to try to create a narrative or stoke something up to sell a few papers. I'm sure fans used to argue about it, in the same way they used to argue about The Beatles and The Rolling Stones, but we were two completely different groups who just happened to be very successful in the same era. They were much more in control of their stuff because they were two couples, who did all their own writing and seemed to be in control of all their own business, whereas we had been put together and Frank Farian ran it all for us. That said, we were black and more exotic, we could go further and be wilder, and we *definitely* had the more interesting wardrobe!

I always found them to be very nice, very calm people, smiling and friendly, who would always make sure they greeted all of us even if neither of us had time to stop. We only got the chance to actually hang out with them a couple of times, the first time was when we were on the same bill for a show in Switzerland, and we were all pretty wary of each other to start off with. We were in this kind of sitting room in the venue and just looked at each other and smiled for quite a while then one of us from Boney M. broke the ice – it was probably Bobby – we all started talking to each other and got on great. I really enjoyed their company, and I'm sure they were pleased they had met us too, because they never came across as at all cocky. I enjoyed the rivalry we had with them in the charts as well, just as I think they did because it kept things interesting. I loved their music and thought they were very talented people. Nowadays there is almost as much old footage of them on German television as there is of Boney M., and every time I see some of it I'm always reminded of what a privilege it was to have been in competition with them.

*Chapter Four*

# 'It was our job to look amazing'

It was after the UK finally picked us up that I really felt we had made it and I was now what I considered to be a star. I wouldn't say it had a huge effect on me, though, as we were so rushed I really didn't have too much time to think about it. Sure, in the back of my head I was realising what was going on but I never stopped to consider if there was anything I needed to be doing differently. I just said to myself, 'OK, this is good, I could get used to this!' And I carried on. I'm a level-headed person so I was never going to get over-excited about simple things, although I'm not sure being part of group that by then was internationally famous could ever be called 'a simple thing'! I believe that because I was getting to where I wanted to be I simply accepted so much of what was happening and didn't let it send me one way or the other. Ultimately it was all part of my plan, so I think I looked at it in the same way as I had looked at anything else that had happened to me in my life; being famous was just one more thing. My attitude to it was the same as being taken from Jamaica to live in London when I was thirteen years old: 'Mmm *hmmm*! Bring it on! I can manage anything thrown my way!'

This isn't to say Boney M.'s changing circumstances had no effect on me on a day-to-day level. We were squarely in the limelight now and there was no getting away from that, but why would we want to? This was recognition for how well we were doing what we set out to do and I was *so* pleased this was being celebrated. People were getting to know us now as Marcia, Liz, Maizie and Bobby, not just as Boney M.; they were calling our individual names when we walked through places, or journalists were asking each of us different questions. Ironically, I'm not sure how happy Frank was about this as it was never in his original plan: back with 'Baby Do You Wanna Bump?' he was totally the mastermind behind the group and the one identifiable face. Now, quite rightly, we were all becoming stars in our own right and I found that so personally satisfying I wasn't too bothered if anybody else did get a bit miffed! Best of all, our audience were recognising our separate contributions to the group and appreciating our own personalities, meaning the fans all had their favourites and would write to us separately – no, I don't know who was getting the most fan mail!

We could cause a commotion practically anywhere we went, either as the group or individually, but it wasn't like it is today when it's not unusual for celebrities to get mobbed by people wanting selfies with you, or calling for photos from across the street. Back then, especially in Germany, it was much more restrained but our appearance on a street could still block a pavement or stop traffic. In restaurants or shops or airports, you had to accept whatever you were doing was going to take longer than it might. For me, this was never a chore. All people wanted to do was tell you how much they appreciated you, and there are a lot worse things in the world than that, so you'd gladly give them some time which would become a moment they'd remember for ever. I saw it as part of what we did, as important as singing in the studio, and one more thing to be relished.

What this meant, however, was that we were never off duty, and because the whole image of Boney M. was one of fantasy glamour we had to turn heads even when we weren't on stage. None of us girls could be caught slopping down to the shops in an old cardigan or anything like that – any time you stepped outside your house or your hotel room you had to be on point! This was never a problem for me, I've always been an elegant woman on and off stage; I didn't create that as a character because I was in Boney M. – I brought it *to* Boney M. with me! When I was solo I used to dress in a lot of Ossie Clark gear, he was a London designer who was really big in the late sixties and the seventies. I loved his designs, most of all the blouses and trousers in fabrics like chiffon and crêpe, which used to cost me a small fortune because this was before designers would give clothes to acts to wear just for the exposure. Back then the UK fashion industry was just getting going – Swinging London, and all that – thus many of what became big names were just establishing themselves and were as hard up as the groups and singers!

Ossie Clark was my favourite, but I didn't wear it exclusively, I knew what suited me and tended to stick with those shops or designers, which I would check out on the rare occasions I was back in London. I kept it simple because I've never been a Shopping Queen, and the idea of trailing round shops in whatever city while we were on tour never really appealed to me. I was well aware of what it took to look good, and I didn't deny myself anything, but I've never believed in spending money for spending's sake. Maybe this is because things had been so tight for my family when I was a child, but I just couldn't bring myself to squander money once I had it. Later, Maizie and I would sometimes look at jewellery together – usually in airports – but if you know how expensive that stuff is you'll know I probably didn't buy too much!

As for window shopping, a few people in our touring party loved to browse the stores if we were in Paris or Milan somewhere. I hadn't done that since I was much younger and it was a lot of fun to wander the upmarket shopping streets eyeing up gear I couldn't possibly afford and putting together fantasy wardrobes. Once I was in Boney M. I could have gone inside those shops and bought more or less anything I wanted, but that would have taken all the fun out of it! I was always happy to keep up with the latest styles and so on in magazines, but time was so precious to me I couldn't have even imagined spending it just looking at shop windows. When I did spend the money, I was always sure it was worth the expense, because I believe good clothes will always pay you back as they tend to fit better and look good for longer – it's better to buy a few classy pieces than to fill your wardrobe with a load of cheap stuff.

I've always felt good about displaying my attire to the fullest: when I was a child in Jamaica I loved my school uniform and would be careful how I sat so I didn't crush the pleats in the skirt I would have painstakingly ironed the night before. As soon as I started earning good money I was flamboyant and proud of it, nobody wore gear like Ossie Clark on a day-to-day basis, but I would walk down Oxford Street in one of his chiffon blouses. Even now, as my husband Marcus will tell you, I won't leave the apartment unless I am absolutely satisfied I look the part – hat and gloves have to be matching, then they've got to complement the main colours, and I've got so much to choose from. If I can't be bothered to do all of that properly then I'm not going out!

What was expected of me as part of Boney M. appealed to the extrovert in me, and if I spent a small fortune when I was solo I was spending a *large* fortune as part of the group. I would buy clothes for myself from Dagmar Englebrecht, the seamstress in Hanover who made our stage wear, because I knew I could get exactly what I wanted. Also it saved me the trouble of shopping, something I was never keen on and by that point literally didn't have the time for. Dagmar is still a friend of mine, and back then she quickly understood me well enough to know what I wanted, that it had to look special but shouldn't look like I was about to take the stage as I'd still have to wear it out to dinner or somewhere. She was able to modify some of the ideas I might have and she usually improved them! If she had got her hands on a particular fabric or had an idea she thought would suit me she would get in touch, then as she had all my measurements − which didn't change as long as I was in Boney M.! − I could leave her to get on with it, and if I knew I needed something for a certain event she would always come up with exactly the right garment, and have it ready on time! Hence I had all these wonderful one-offs that fitted me perfectly, so I really didn't need an excuse to dress up and put on full make-up just to walk through an airport! It meant being a bit more careful about getting dressed, thus spending a bit more time, but so what? This was our job, and as it was turning out it was the greatest job in the world.

The schedule was busy, we could be on the road for anything between one and two months taking in twenty different countries, but it was so enjoyable. We were making money for the record company and for the concert promoters so the budgets had got much bigger, which meant life on the road got far more comfortable. The hotels were smarter and when we were being driven around to dates within Germany, or met at airports, they would send a Pullman for us, which was like the Mercedes version of the stretch limousine, which was so luxurious inside.

The big difference after that first year, though, was that when we went abroad I demanded they fly us First Class, which became so important to me I would *have* to have it. Sometimes I would have to pay for it for myself because the promoter or the record company would have promised it, but when we got to the airport we'd only been booked on economy, or First Class had been booked but it hadn't been paid for – so many people were full of tricks like that. This wasn't me being a diva and thinking I was above other people, it was just that flying was one of the few chances I got to relax and unwind, even if it was only for a couple of hours. I needed my space when I got on the plane because flying is stressful enough, and I knew that to be able to perform properly and to look good I had to be rested. In First Class I was at least going to be able to put my feet up, sip some champagne and gather my thoughts. After we were thrown into all this air travel I quickly worked out this was the best way for me to get some 'me time' while we were on the road. Too often when we were touring we were sleeping at strange times and snatching bits of food on the go, flying First Class represented a little patch of calm so it became my method to cope in those unusual circumstances.

There would always be journalists waiting at the airport, or there would be a press conference immediately at the hotel, so I had to know what I was doing and be alert enough to answer questions. We had to look good, too, because photographers seemed to follow us wherever we went. In First Class I could put on my make-up in comfort or adjust my hat ready for getting off, without somebody banging on the bathroom door! Then the chances are there would be no time to eat when we arrived at the hotel, we'd have to go straight out to the venue where there would just be some cold cuts or something in the dressing room, or we'd get to the hotel so late I wouldn't want to wait up to get dinner. Flying First Class allowed me to get a decent meal and eat it in comfort. Then there was the baggage allowance, which was a real downside of having to look glamorous all the time! The bigger we got and the longer we were on tour, the more of our own gear we seemed to be taking with us – by the time I left Boney M. I had seven suitcases on the road with me. In First Class that wasn't a problem, but otherwise we were constantly being charged extra because our luggage was overweight.

Anybody who has been pitched into any sort of unusual, demanding situation like we were *has* to find their own way of handling it, otherwise they'll wear themselves out. I'm sure Liz, Maizie and Bobby had their own methods, but this First Class travel was so worth it to me, at one stage I went to war with the record company to make sure we had it all the time – not just me but the whole group because I knew how much we'd all benefit from it. I put my foot down on behalf of the others, telling the record company and Frank how much it would be worth their while to have us happy and well rested when it came to promoting the records or doing shows.

I put my foot down over the hotel accommodation too. OK, so we had moved up from single rooms in cheap motels to double rooms each in better class hotels after *Take the Heat off Me*, but we still only had rooms. I wanted a suite, with a separate living room. This was to give us some privacy so when anybody comes in, even the other group members, you're not receiving them in your bedroom, especially if the bed has not been made. I'm from Jamaica and your bed must always be made and fresh if anybody is going to enter your room! Also, it made it so much easier for us to relax if we didn't want to go to bed or lie down, so I told them, 'Look, I'm working hard, so you'd better give me a suite not just any little one room t'ing!'

It was around the time the *Love for Sale* album was released, I really took stock of my first eighteen months as part of Boney M. All I could think of was how much it had been worth it. Pure and simple. And this was in spite of the fact that before I'd joined the group I was determined to stay a solo artist, then even after I'd first got together with the others I remained unsure about it. When I looked back I saw that nothing had happened to justify my apprehension, indeed everything seemed to be working out very well. What I was most fearful of was not being in control of my own career like I believed I always had been, and then worrying that we weren't getting the best treatment possible. However, the record company was putting a great deal of effort and resources into us – especially as we started having hits. We were able to come across very well, and we were *definitely* getting maximum exposure – we couldn't possibly have done any more promotional work or television appearances! So I was very happy with all of that, because I felt as if I was arriving at the level I had imagined myself getting to as an artist, somewhere where I could show what I do best to as many people as possible.

Naturally there were a few arguments to be had and demands to be made along the way, which I tended to handle because I had the experience of a solo career. Sometimes these were financial, which mostly concerned what they should be paying for when we were on the road, but generally I had to speak with the record company people about our comfort or well-being. Although there were times when it would seem like a constant battle, usually we got what we wanted, like the First Class travel, because that part of it was a bit of a game – the record company knew what they had to do, but sometimes weren't going to do it without some prompting. Also, they were pretty wary of the four of us in the beginning because Frank had always put himself in between them and us, so they didn't really know who the Boney M. people were – in fact they weren't even certain they were getting real singers! Frank hardly ever came on the road with us, so we were more or less thrown together with the record company people and during the promotions of those first releases they had to kind of feel us out.

Whatever my negotiating skills were, the bottom line was they gave us what we wanted because it was us who paid for it in the end – whatever they pay out to you or for you in the early days they will take back when they subtract it from any royalties you are owed. Once they're certain an act is going to be successful enough to earn it back they don't mind laying out for anything. However, everywhere within the recording business there is the very real consideration that artists' royalties get *misplaced* and that accounting always favours the record companies. You have to look after yourself when it comes to dealing with whoever put up the money for you in the first place as they are only ever going to worry about getting their investment back as quickly as possible, so I figured I might as well take as much as I could from them up front. Then as this is business they'll want to capitalise on what you do to the absolute maximum, so what you need as a person or where you want to go in your career will always be secondary, unless, of course, it helps them in pursuit of their goals.

I'm sure that if anybody was to do all the sums from those early days in Boney M. it would add up that, financially, we didn't get our dues, but it was never as simple as that. Sure I worried about getting paid, but I was getting the chance to achieve my goal – my name was being known and to this day I have a global following.

Most importantly, as I took stock after the *Love for Sale* release, I didn't think I was losing any sense of myself as an individual now I was part of Boney M. Much of this was to do with us all being fully formed characters by the time we joined so had enough confidence not to get submerged in the group identity. Personally I felt self-assured and therefore secure in myself as Marcia Barrett because I was getting the respect I deserved for my contribution to the group's success. Maybe not from everybody, but I was getting enough, especially as the fans got to know us better they knew how to appreciate us.

## Chapter Five

# 'The Boney M. Bubble'

The main thing I had come to terms with during that first period was that Boney M.'s success was all about teamwork: the only reason the group had got so big was because we all played our roles within it. Although the press would often try to make a big thing about who sang and who didn't, ultimately it didn't matter because the public didn't need to analyse that. Liz and I sang, Maizie didn't, Bobby danced – that was Boney M. as was presented to them and they loved it. To our fans it was purely about the group, which was always going to be bigger than the sum of its parts, even though it couldn't have worked without all those parts. Although I was really enjoying it by then, this group mentality had taken a bit of getting used to because I had always been so self-contained, right from when I was a child through to working as a solo artist. Indeed, I'll swear that in the beginning I saw myself as a bit like a solo performer existing within a group setting, but I soon got used to it and came to terms with the sacrifices involved, even if some of them meant just keeping quiet, which was sometimes the hardest one to make!

This way of thinking meant early Boney M. was even further insulated against the outside world, as thinking about the group first it made us mentally as well as physically self-contained

– the Boney M. Bubble I mentioned earlier was a very real state of affairs! This was probably for the best in the beginning, for me, because I found Boney M. a unique state of affairs: I was thrown in with three complete strangers, we were spending twenty-four hours practically on top of each other, then almost every evening we had to perform as a unit. If we hadn't formed that sort of bond we could have been pulling against each other on stage, which wouldn't have done anybody any good – us or the fans. Most importantly, though, it meant we had a good laugh.

Once we'd finished feeling each other out, we had some beautiful days when we were on the road. Quite quickly, as the hits started to rack up, we could see that what Liz and I had initially called 'dis Boney M. t'ing' was actually going somewhere so there was no point in being overly cynical about it. The happier we felt in committing to it fully, the more relaxed we became around each other. I think we'd all worked out none of us were going anywhere, so we might as well have some fun.

There would be jokes flying around in the limo or on the plane, we'd all be laughing about the little things you'd observe on the road that could be spun into a story. There's always so much sitting around waiting when you're touring that all groups have these kinds of jokes going on: you'd go mad without them! We'd eat together in restaurants and just enjoy ourselves noticing that as the band progressed so the service got more attentive and more and more people started to recognise us. We weren't being swell-headed – at least, I wasn't! – we were simply thinking how it was absolutely great, how we'd worked hard together for that recognition. We thought, 'We've earned it so now let's enjoy it together.' It was the same in the hotels: we'd hang out in each other's rooms, often after shows the four of us sitting in the same one, we'd have a couple of drinks, tell stories, compare notes . . . and we'd all be laughing hard. Then it was getting late and OK, see you all tomorrow, when it would all start again.

Everything was new and exciting for us so those sessions could be beautiful, but as what we had to do increased so did the pressure it was putting us under and those times seemed to become fewer and fewer. We'd have more and more functions to go to and people to meet before and after gigs, so we'd have less time to socialise amongst ourselves. If we had to do an after-show dinner, with the record company or something, by the time we got back to the hotel I was not going to be able to stay up and still look good the next day. I'd just say goodnight and head off to bed. Also, as the workload increased, there was a sense of everybody needing more of their own space. I know I used to look forward to time on my own. In the beginning, though, it was just great to have that sort of camaraderie and to be making real progress in the business.

Where the bond between us was strongest was when we were actually on stage together, in front of a packed house of Boney M. fans. It would begin when we arrived at a venue and usually went straight into the dressing rooms – Bobby had his own, but we girls shared – and got into our pre-show routines. Each of us had our way of doing things before a concert – a time for focus and concentration – and although we were definitely in the Boney M. Bubble, we would each be in our own zone, so it wasn't like sisters, sharing the mirror or borrowing each other's make-up! In fact, these were more like rituals than merely routines but what that did would make each new dressing room seem as familiar as possible, helping us settle down. I never used to get nerves before a show, I still don't, I never ever experienced butterflies – why would I? Right from the beginning I couldn't wait to get out there on stage and start performing; that was what it was all about so as we were getting ready to go on I never experienced anything other than anticipation.

Our costumes would be laid out for us or hung on rails, everything each of us had to wear grouped together – we stopped doing costume changes very early on because we didn't want to break the bond we'd made with the audience: we'd go on, nail it and then stay there! In the dressing room I'd try to time my getting dressed and fixing my make-up so there was as little time as possible between that and show time. Each of us would be minding our own business, putting on what we had to put on, not discussing anything, so it would be best to get out there as soon as possible. Then somebody would come to get us to lead us to the stage, which was probably the most important job of the night. Some of the older theatres were like rabbit warrens with little corridors branching off all over the place, then the arenas were so big it seemed as if you had to walk miles to the stage! In many cases it would be so easy to get lost in between the dressing room and the stage, maybe end up in the car park!

As we got closer to it we'd hear the band or the playback and the MC announce us and that was it! Every time we actually hit the stage there was a one-ness . . . we were all together . . . this was us . . . this was Boney M.! From those very first gigs, that never changed. We did have our differences as time went on, but when we burst on to that stage, our band, Black Beauty Circus, would be playing behind us, the horns were going, the rhythm was pumping and we are already killing it. I'd look round at the others and any disagreements were forgotten.

Then there was the audience, who I believe were as big a part of the show as everyone on the stage: once they saw us they let loose a barrage of noise that went with a rush of energy that could almost blow you off your feet. It didn't matter what country we were in, or what size the gig was, each audience went mad at that moment. It was a wave of love coming for us that lifted us even higher than we already were and we in turn gave back to them by putting everything we had into the show. It was better than being called back for an encore, because by then the crowd is practically as drained as we are so there wasn't that initial energy. Again, I would look at the others and just think, 'Oh my God! This is brilliant! *We are Boney M.!*' That really was the peak of it for me. Even towards the end of my time in the group, when I came to believe that we were being exploited it was, and still is, an almost indescribably brilliant feeling.

Of all the gigs we ever did, I think my favourite was at the Royal Albert Hall in London. It definitely wasn't the biggest we played – we did arenas and stadiums sometimes with audiences of over a hundred thousand – nor was it our most spectacular, but in terms of what the venue meant to me as somebody who had spent their formative years in London, performing at the Albert Hall was about more than tickets sold or special effects. Going out on stage before the audience came in and looking out at those lovely red velvet chairs and the boxes around the sides, then up at that fantastic domed ceiling, it was all so grand and so classy I'm literally going, 'Wow!' It was astonishing, it's a venue and a half, because all you can think about is how some of the greatest acts in the world have stood on this very same stage – I know it affects other performers that way because they've told me. When Boney M. got out there for me it was like, 'Wooooh! *This is it!*' As we'd say in Jamaica, 'Yes, mi reach, and mi reach good!'

One of the strangest things about the Boney M. Bubble was very little other music found its way in to us, I suppose we heard the other stuff in the charts in shops or while we were dashing through airports, but there was never any time to digest it. In what little leisure time we did get I needed to relax so I would listen to music I was already familiar with. I had this little red radio cassette player I bought in Curry's in Croydon, and for years I took that on the road with me and would enjoy my own tapes – B.B. King, Barry White, and so forth. When I had time to myself I was in my own little world within the Boney M. world!

It wasn't that I couldn't be bothered with other music, as I'm sure that if I had been contributing to the writing of Boney M. material, I would have made it my business to know what was going on out there. But the songs were just given to us, so we trusted that Frank knew the current trends. And for those years *we* must have been the trend because we were doing so well. I didn't even know what was in the charts unless it was Boney M., as people around us would tell us that we'd gone in this country's charts at this number, or moved up to that number. Other than that I only knew about Abba – people would tell us where they were in the charts because of the so-called rivalry.

We knew most of the other artists, though, because this was before videos became such a big thing and acts had to do television shows in person so we met just about everybody once or twice in the corridors at TV studios. I still had no idea what their music was because usually these meetings weren't anything more than, 'Hi. Bye.' In fact, there was seldom even time to catch their performances. I tried to be pleasant to all of them even though a few blanked us or made disparaging remarks, which could be a bit awkward if we then had to appear on the show at the same time. Forty years later it wouldn't be fair to name them, they were probably just a bit threatened by our success and aren't at all like that these days!

Completely by chance we spent a bit of time with Michael Jackson, when we shared First Class with him and his brother Jermaine on a flight from London to Bremen in Germany. He had left the Jackson 5 then, but this was before he hit mega big as a solo artist and although he must have been a proper teenager by then he seemed really young – he was still Little Michael! He had his teacher with him, and I thought it was interesting he was taking advantage of those couple of hours in First Class for undisturbed personal time, in the same way as I did. Because of that, I didn't speak to him much, but he was very polite and very quietly spoken, exactly the same demeanour he had as a man.

With our schedule being as tightly planned as it was, the other aspect of the Boney M. Bubble was that it seemed as if everything was done for you. On the road everything had been booked in advance: cars were waiting, hotel suites were ready; if we were taken to a restaurant we were expected and somebody else took care of the bill . . . I just locked my suitcases, a hotel bellman knocked on the door to pick them up and the next time I saw them they were in the next hotel room. There were always people around, usually from the record company in whatever country we happened to be in, whose job it was to make sure our lives ran smoothly, that everything was done right and to answer any questions we might have. After shows or TV appearances they'd take us out to a restaurant or a nightclub and be really disappointed if it didn't look like we were having a good time, because it was their job to make sure we were!

It wasn't quite clicking your fingers and whatever you wanted would arrive, but it was pretty pampered and meant you didn't really have to think too hard about anything or what it might be costing. We didn't even have to think about what food and drink and comforts were laid out in the dressing room for us, that was all decided between Frank and the promoter! It must seem like many people's idea of heaven, but what it really did was serve to isolate us even more because when we were touring as Boney M. we didn't interact with too many people who weren't on Team Boney. As we got bigger so did the touring party – at one point there were about seventy-five people on the road with the four of us – which meant there were even more layers between the group at the centre and the world outside.

I'm not saying I didn't enjoy having this sort of attention and service: I did, I took advantage of it as much as the others and I loved every minute of it! But I always knew the Boney M. Bubble wasn't really *real*, therefore it probably wasn't going to last for ever. I personally rather resented losing so much control, as I had been looking after my mother and my younger sister since I was a little girl, and by this time I had a son at home – which we'll get to later – so taking responsibility came like second nature. However, after living in that world for a while, and as every big touring act must have these sort of walls around them, I understood why so many artists who get into that sort of life when they are young end up going off the rails.

It would have been easy to start believing our own hype too, especially by staying in Germany or France or any of the northern European countries when we weren't actually touring or recording. Anywhere there if you were on the street or went out socialising it would be 'Oh my God! She's from Boney M.!' or 'He's the guy from Boney M.!', even before they knew our names. I should imagine if you were in a nightclub you wouldn't have to buy a drink all night! Because I had family I used to go back to England at every chance I got, and there was nothing like that to bring you down to earth! We did much less in England than on the Continent – we weren't on television all the time – so I wasn't recognised as often, and even if I was there was never that sort of excitement like I'd get in Europe. I don't know why, it's not as if we weren't selling records in the UK, and at the concerts the British fans were every bit as enthusiastic as anywhere else, but it was actually quite a relief to get a bit of respect!

I loved the Boney M. Bubble, it protected us and allowed us to get on with what we did best, but it was nice to be out of it and to be my own woman for a while. I was secure enough in who I was, plus I had a full life outside of the group, and I knew if I needed to get my ego stroked I would only have to wait a couple of weeks until I went back on the road.

## Chapter Six

# 'Frank Farian came in with a bag of chains'

Boney M. was teamwork away from the four of us as well, because although it was often assumed that it was all Frank Farian's doing – not that he was going to correct anybody in that respect! – the reality was that he had surrounded himself with a team of very brilliant people who all contributed their great ideas, which is actually a real skill in itself. The themes of our songs were so wild and so wildly different – 'Ma Baker', which is about a Bonnie and Clyde-style gangster lady; or a Jamaican nursery rhyme like 'Brown Girl in the Ring'; or 'Rasputin', the story of a mad monk in Tsarist Russia; or 'Rivers of Babylon', which was psalms from the Bible reworked into a song. They could never all be the product of one imagination, however vivid. The reality was there were several people bringing their own ideas, so of course they were going to be different. One thing about Frank was that he was open to absolutely anything when it came to song themes – maybe because he spoke no English the subject matter of a song had no resonance with him, but it made for a fabulously mixed bag. 'Brown Girl in the Ring', Liz and I knew just how infectious it was from our childhoods in Jamaica. It became one of our biggest hits. It was the same with my song 'Belfast': he saw it was going down very well in the discos so he had Boney M. do it, and I don't think he even noticed it was a politically aware song. Or the title of our fifth album, *Boonoonoonoos*, which was a word invented by the Jamaican folk poet and comedienne Louise Bennett – Miss Lou – meaning anything or anybody beautiful or special. Frank couldn't possibly have known that word; somebody must have said it to him or he heard it in Jamaica when we were filming there, and decided he liked the sound of it so it became a theme for the album.

After the first album had so many cover versions on it he organised a crack writing team. Hans-Jörg Mayer was the brainchild behind so many of the songs, he was really smart, a university guy who really *knew* music. Hans-Jörg was there working with Frank from the beginning as he wrote 'Daddy Cool', and would take his writing credit under the name of George Reyam – Mayer backwards. The other main writer was Fred Jay, an American who had German parents and was bilingual – I think he was born in Germany, he and his wife were such lovely people. Fred had written 'What Am I Living For?', a huge hit in the US in the late 1950s that had been covered by dozens of artists, then he moved to Germany where he had written all sorts of pop hits. The first time I met him was in Frank's studio in Offenbach, when we were recording 'Ma Baker', a collaboration between Hans-Jörg and Fred. The first idea was a song called 'Ma Barker' after the real-life gangster mother, but we couldn't sing that very easily, so Fred said, 'OK, what about Baker? Baker? That's better for you to sing, you can call it "Ma Baker".' That's the kind of teamwork that went on around the group.

Then there was Stefan Klinkhammer, who was a genius musical arranger. He was with Frank from the beginning too – I met him when I first auditioned for Boney M. So many people don't realise the importance of the arranger, especially in the kind of big productions Frank wanted to do as Boney M. progressed. Stefan was vital in taking the basic song and fleshing it out into those sounds that were pure pop music but with the little touches of disco or reggae or rock or whatever to make them stand out from the crowd.

Later on there were other writers involved with Boney M., but in the beginning it was these collaborators and Stefan who were responsible for what Frank got to work with in the studio, and, in my opinion, they were as important as Frank in shaping the sound of Boney M. I'm not trying to take anything away from what Frank actually did; I've said before he was a damned good producer, and he was the ringmaster who brought all of this together. It was proper teamwork, different mentalities and different people from Germany, America and the Caribbean all working together – I fully believe that the true creatives behind Boney M.'s music should get the credit due to them.

Although Frank was shaping the sound rather than composing he still had a writing credit. This meant he got a share of the writers' earnings. This has long been a grey area in the music business. The songwriters often have to put up with giving away a percentage of their earnings or their songs wouldn't be accepted in the future, and seventy per cent of the money from a massive hit is better that one hundred per cent of nothing.

How we looked as Boney M. was also down to collaboration, although letting someone else decide on our look could be a bit scary at times, as we found out quite early on. From the beginning the esteemed German rock photographer Didi Zill had been shooting us. He was one of the best in the world and has shot fantastic studio sessions with just about everybody from Little Richard to Tina Turner to Culture Club to Alice Cooper. He did some great live stuff with us, too, and I loved working with him, so was very happy to find out he was shooting the *Take the Heat off Me* sleeve. We met up with him in a photography studio in Berlin, and were sitting around waiting while they set up the lights when I thought something was missing. I asked Frank where our costumes were, and he told me not to worry, he was just going out to pick them up. Fair enough. Then when he came back all he had with him was this one little carrier bag! I didn't think much of it immediately, and asked him again where our costumes were, to which he just kind of smirked and held up the bag!

Even before he opened it up our jaws had dropped. Then when we three girls got our first look at the flimsy little bits of lingerie inside we were shocked. My first reaction was, 'Oh no! What is he going to expect us to do for this photo shoot?' Although we could sometimes come across as raunchy on stage, away from those performances we were just four regular people who had regular inhibitions and no way did we want to stand about half naked in front of the three or four men in the studio. It was Didi who came to our rescue, because it is a big part of a photographer's job to make his subjects feel at ease, and he was very good at his job. He didn't make a fuss, he simply told us to go in the dressing room, get changed into the, ahem, *costumes*, but to leave our own underwear on and to put on the dressing gowns that were there. When we came out he arranged us on the studio floor for the shot as he saw it, with us still in the dressing gowns. One by one he got the three of us posed properly – Liz and my faces are so close we're looking at each other like we are lesbians; Maizie is angled so her slip appears to be coming off; and Bobby is standing behind us so macho. Then when he was finally satisfied he said, '*Ja*, now you can take off!' One of his female assistants came out to help us off with the dressing gowns, and to remove our brassieres, without moving us or showing anything we weren't supposed to. He was looking through his camera going, 'Ah! Fantastic . . . Marcia, can you move a little left? Hmmm, fantastic . . . stay like that, everybody . . .' Then he began clicking away, and we felt like we were in a fashion shoot.

That is what I thought was the genius of Didi Zill, because in a very short space of time he had taken us from being quite nervous about looking like strippers to feeling like fashion models! We really started to enjoy it because of the care he was taking to make sure we didn't feel uncomfortable and to let us know there was no way this would look cheap. Even though I was exposing more than I expected to I didn't feel *exposed* in any kind of dodgy sense.

Following that session I worked out very quickly that this was going to be part of what we as Boney M. were, and there was no complaining after that. It was what we had to do, and we felt secure in the fact it wasn't anything we would ever go on stage wearing, but in the privacy of Didi's studio it was fun. We really began to enjoy it among ourselves. Personally, in the beginning I didn't understand why the record company, Frank and just about anybody we dealt with in the industry was so obsessed with us showing that much flesh – I honestly thought some of it was porno and kept asking myself, 'What does this have to do with our singing?' Then I understood how the music business needed something a bit outrageous at that point because it needed shaking up again.

Posters of the album sleeve would go up everywhere, so they were on view to everybody and not just our fans, which was a bit of a worry but it turned out people were ready for them. They weren't that sort of quickie cheapness that was so often associated with the disco of the time; they made us look like we were here to stay because they were classy. That had so much to do with Didi and how he saw Boney M., he took trouble with the lighting and would keep making subtle alterations to get our poses just right – the *Take the Heat off Me* sleeve that gave me so much concern turned out really elegant, all done in white. Regular people loved our artwork because it was exciting and intriguing; the gay crowd loved it because some of those pictures were so camp; and the kinky people loved the sleeves like *Love for Sale* because it took them wherever their minds wanted to go!

*Love for Sale* was the next album sleeve shoot we had to do and our approach to it, just a year later, showed how much our attitudes had changed, given that it was so much more porno-looking than *Take the Heat off Me*! We were at Didi's once more, only this time Frank has come in with a bag of chains, handed them out and we literally couldn't believe it! We three girls don't even know how we're supposed to wear them – if you can call it *wearing* them – then we see Bobby staring at that little piece of silver jock strap, that looked like aluminium foil. He's turning it over in his hands and says in his Aruban accent, 'So this is what I've got to put on?' And we all cracked up. After that he started fooling about with it and we were in stitches laughing. That was what was so great about our photo sessions – we had a laugh. Didi was a really funny guy himself and he would encourage it because it relaxed us and he knew we were professional enough to calm down and stop when we had to pose. He was also very persuasive and would always get rid of any misgivings we had, as in the case of *Love for Sale*, when both Liz and I, being well-brought-up Jamaican girls, worried about what our mothers would say when they saw it!

So back in Didi's studio, we put the chains on, then came out in our underwear and dressing gowns, and Didi arranged the three of us so we could keep our knickers on but it gave the impression we were naked. Then the lady came and took our dressing gowns and bras, while we were told to hold our breasts in a certain way to preserve our modesty. Then Didi is all, 'Marcia, do this . . . Maizie, do this . . .' And it's done.

When I saw the finished work, I didn't think it was dirty or pornographic at all, I thought it was certainly odd but it was rather elegant and made us look a bit mystical. The American and Canadian record companies didn't seem to think so, however. When they put the album out they wouldn't use that picture and those editions feature as their front cover what was the back cover for the European releases – us fully clothed. Although we had fun doing that one and it worked out well for us, I was very relieved to do the next one, *Nightflight to Venus*, because in spite of us having to look like we were hanging off a rope, at least we got to keep our clothes on!

There weren't any more risqué sleeves, which is a good thing considering the amount of photo shoots we were doing for sleeve artwork: so many of the singles had picture sleeves and soon there were different compilations being released all over the place. Some of the concepts – *Nightflight, Oceans of Fantasy* and *Ten Thousand Lightyears*, in particular – were a bit nuts, but they continued to keep us in the forefront because people had never seen anything like them before. After those first two sleeves our images became more of a collaboration between Didi and Dagmar Englebrecht, who made all of our costumes. Of course Frank contributed, but once Dagmar started to make the clothes we didn't have to rely on whatever Frank could fit into a carrier bag!

Once that was the case I loved doing those photo sessions even more. It didn't matter who had the original concept, Dagmar would conceive how we'd be dressed for it then make the clothes, adapting them or making last-minute alterations in the studio. I trusted her completely because our stage wear always looked elegant and by this time she was making my own personal clothes too. I wasn't too happy about wearing a swimsuit for *Oceans of Fantasy*, but Dagmar was making them and reassured me everything would be all right. And it was. Didi was always full of ideas for how to get the shot he wanted, on the *Nightflight* shoot he was balancing on a ladder while we clustered round beneath him. He could talk us into anything too, when we went to Jamaica to shoot the *Boonoonoonoos* photos, we did the cover shot at Negril in sunset, then he wanted to do another session of us climbing the famous Dunn's River Falls. I thought, 'Great!' Until he gave me this chiffon top to put on and I knew as soon as the water touches it it'll be completely see-through! He was just so charming: 'Oh Marcia, Marcia . . . *Komm, komm . . . Das is gut* . . . It's only a cover!'

Like that's supposed to make me feel better! But it worked, and when I saw the finished pictures, I just had to smile because, of course, there was nothing for me to have worried about. We all loved shooting with Didi, but me especially because I am such a poseur.

When I look back, I have realised those sessions were always more than just getting our picture taken, they were events. They were glamorous and they were exciting, but what was so great about them was it was away from the pressure of performance or even being in public. We were all together, working, so there was all the Boney M. fantasy world in there, but we were behind closed doors, so we could behave how we liked. Because it was only us we would run jokes like nobody's business, with Didi joining in. That trip to Jamaica was pure laughter, and the one with the silver suits, *Ten Thousand Lightyears*, stands out as just being joke after joke.

Sometimes I think those visuals summed up our life in the group, even the ridiculous ones – or perhaps I should say *especially* the ridiculous ones! There were so many photos taken of us that our apartment is full of them, they make up for the lack of any pictures at all of me when I was a young girl in Jamaica. When I look at the Boney M. photographs it can take me right back to a particular session and really good memories of the four of us, having a laugh and getting the job done. This was so much of what I expected from life in Boney M. – to do a good job and enjoy myself. In many ways Didi's pictures can mean as much to me as the individual songs.

## Chapter Seven

# 'Two drinks and that's definitely it'

While it was good to be part of the group, it was important to maintain my own methods and routines, because it was essential for me to feel like I remained in charge of as much of my day-to-day life as I could be. I didn't want to just leave it all up to other people, because you never know what's happening next and when it comes down to it *you* are the only person you can truly rely on.

When we were going on the road, the limo would come to pick me up at my house in Davis Road, Croydon, which I shared with my mother and my son Wayne, and the moment I got in the car and settled back in the seat I was in Boney M. mode – it was as if the big *clunk* of the car door flicked a switch and now I'm the artist, not the family woman. When I went away I was always secure in the knowledge that I had done everything I could for those at home, as I would have been cooking like a maniac to prepare meat and chicken and all the gravies that they liked, labelled them and left them in the freezer, so Mama didn't have to do any serious cooking. I knew I would have taken care of anything else that needed to be done around the house and paid all the bills, so I could get completely into what was expected of me on tour.

Sometimes I'd meet other members of our touring party in the VIP lounge at the airport, depending on who was getting on the flight. Liz and I would often be in London on our down time, sometimes Maizie too, but Bobby lived in Holland. If we had a very early flight, we would usually spend the night before in a hotel near the airport. Most flights were pretty much the same, especially in First Class, they only varied in length, but as soon as we got off the plane, it would be press everywhere, escorts, record company people . . . That's why when we got to our hotel I would find out what our schedule was then head up to my suite to have some alone time. After the stresses of travel and the whirlwind at the airport, this was important, so even if it was just half an hour I'd grab it. If this was after I had met my husband Marcus, it was even more important, because I could use that time to call him or just sit and think about him!

After we were married Marcus never came on the road with me; he might come to a gig if we were performing in London, but that was as far as it went. He knew that Boney M. was my thing, he had his own life in music – he was Eddy Grant's bass player – and was writing songs for my solo project, but in the Boney M. situation he would have had nothing to do. He took that decision himself, saying the last thing he wanted to do was hang around me in hotels looking like a groupie! I completely agreed – that wasn't for Marcus, so although we sacrificed that time together it was definitely for the best.

I was quite happy in my own company, taking care of things for myself. Of course later on I missed Marcus, but I didn't feel lonely without a bunch of hangers-on. I would keep diaries, and I found writing them was as good as practically any conversation. I've got piles and piles of Cartier desk diaries from those days, and I could be totally occupied with writing my story down, diving into my diaries whenever I got the chance on planes, in hotel lobbies, or if we were waiting around somewhere. The others were always nagging me about it: 'What are you writing, Marcia? What's so interesting you have to write it down?' I'd just say, 'Never you mind.' That was my substitute for an entourage, and I'm sure it helped me keep my feet on the ground, not having a group of people around me telling me how great I was all the time, just so they could carry on living the so-called pop star life at my expense.

I looked at what I did as my job. In spite of having to put so much of my personality into it, it was always what I *did* more than what I *was*, and although it was all very exciting and I loved being recognised in so many different countries, after all that was finished for the day I would rather be by myself. Also, I needed time in my own suite because I am a very organised person. I'd always sort out what I was going to wear the next day and then I'd have to iron it – I always did my own ironing because I didn't trust hotel laundries with some of the fabrics my clothes were made out of. That was about the only thing I insisted on in my hotel suite – an iron and an ironing board! Not very rock 'n' roll, is it? Once that was all laid out ready, I'd put on my cassettes, maybe drink a glass or two of wine, and take a leisurely soak in the tub. After that, I never had any problem getting to sleep, so I would always be prepared for whatever the next day would bring.

As I've already said, after a show we would often be taken out to dinner, which was always fun – lovely restaurants, good food, excellent wine and I met some really interesting people at them. When we were doing full-blown tours there were after-show parties too, so the opportunity to over-indulge was ever present, but I was always careful. I'd think, 'Two drinks, maybe three, then that's definitely it!' I'm not a teetotaller, far from it, as every so often Marcus and I might go over the top a bit at home, but I think we're allowed to – it's just the two of us, nobody is driving and we can just roll into bed!

But on tour there was a responsibility, as part of Boney M., that we represented something to millions of people, therefore nobody was going to see me drunk in public. I didn't want to put the group in a situation where people were pointing at us in restaurants for all the wrong reasons! Also I still had vivid memories of getting *very* drunk at an office Christmas party when I was eighteen years old and worked as a stenographer. I didn't understand about mixing drinks – that you can't do it! It was all, 'Oh Marcia, have another drink . . .' And it was vodka, it was gin, it was vermouth . . . it was everything! And there I was, silly little teenager who doubtlessly thought she was sophisticated and carried on knocking them back! I was *poisoned*! I had to go home because I thought I was going to die, and then I vomited for about a week! Who wants to experience that again – especially when you're getting older and, supposedly, wiser? That evening has been in the back of my head for fifty-odd years, and these days nobody knows how to do sensible drinking like Marcia Barrett!

Something that gave me no trouble at all in Boney M. was living out of a suitcase – I had to be comfortable with it, because for most of the year that became my daily routine and if I hadn't learned to live with it I would have been miserable. It was another big reason why I couldn't do shopping as a leisure activity while we were on tour, because if you start accumulating more clothes you end up accumulating more luggage, because you just have more and more stuff to carry around with you. I'd got used to it when I was a solo act, and the only difference was now I had seven pieces of luggage instead of one or two. That was everything except for my cabin baggage, but as it included the case for my shoes and my hatbox and considering they were all suitcases not great big trunks, it actually wasn't very much. Especially when you take into account the expectations placed on us girls in Boney M.

*Maybe* we three could get away with looking a bit casual at sound check — and that's still a pretty big maybe — but the rest of the time we had to look the part. We couldn't be seen in the same thing twice in the same city, and if we'd been photographed then probably not even in the same country! If we arrived somewhere in one thing, then went out to the press conference and finally out to dinner after the gig each time we'd have to be seen in something different. Then of course there'd be one more outfit to wear to leave the hotel the next morning! And everything had to match: handbags, shoes, hats . . . We had to take so much more stuff than Bobby because, essentially, as long as what he was wearing was ironed and halfway decent he'd be OK, then as long as it was clean he could wear the same thing the next day — nobody was looking out to see what he was wearing and then writing about it!

It was all down to how I packed, I'd learned how to make the most of the space in a suitcase when I was solo, and now it was even more critical. I was very organised and could fold the garments properly then look down over the suitcase and plot where the space was and what was best to put in it. There wouldn't be a gap anywhere, and that's why I needed an iron and ironing board waiting for me in my suite! I could pack so much into a small space, when I went to Barbados to record solo material at Eddy Grant's studio, Eddy said to me, 'But Marse, where are you getting all these clothes from? You're getting changed twice during the day and you arrived with only two little suitcases!'

The downside of packing like this was having to lift it afterwards, as they could be so-o-o heavy! In the Boney M. days there were always bellmen and porters to do that for me, and these days I have my husband! When we're going out doing gigs I've put so much in a case he can hardly lift it and is always telling me, 'You might be able to pack like that, but you'd do it differently if you had to carry it too!'

Another aspect of having to constantly look glamorous was being able to get the right cosmetics for my skin tones – make-up artists didn't exist back then, or at least not for us, so we each did our own make-up. We had to work hard to make sure we stayed moisturised, because it's so easy to get dehydrated travelling all day then on stage at night, and black skin is particularly susceptible to drying out. But after that it was a matter of getting our make-up right and I felt very lucky because around the middle of the 1970s the American cosmetics range Fashion Fair became available in London. It was a relatively new company that had been started a few years earlier by the Johnsons, a husband-and-wife operation who owned *Ebony* and *Jet* magazines, America's premier black publications. Those cosmetics were a huge range of top quality products designed specifically for women of colour; it was really the first time, in England, we'd been able to easily buy make-up that good and that reliable. All three of us used Fashion Fair, and it was so reassuring to know that we could look our best all the time, with ease, unlike when I started as a performer and finding the right make-up to look good under the stage lights was much more difficult. I used to have to hunt down somewhere that was importing a limited range, usually from West Africa, or you had to mix your own foundation, because the cosmetics firms in Britain hadn't yet woken up to the lucrative black market. Now, with Fashion Fair, there was this fantastic range of American products acknowledging the fact that not all black women were the same black, and I was able to exactly match my shade every time.

Of course it hadn't reached Europe yet, but it was easy to buy what I wanted when I was in London and travel with it. Although if I had time to look for the right shops, I probably could have found the right make-up in cities like Paris or Amsterdam, but it definitely hadn't reached Germany at that time!

Hair care on the road turned out to be relatively straightforward. Before Boney M., when I was doing my solo project, I had a big Angela Davis-style afro as, so it seemed, did everybody else! Taking care of it wasn't so different to what I'd been doing for most of my life: keeping it clean, combing it out, greasing my scalp and hair with coconut oil or jojoba oil, and plaiting it when I could. Of course it took regular maintenance with the trusty afro pick to make sure it remained perfectly round as the day went on, but that was about it – much less effort than looking after my hair if it had been straightened or permed. Because the style was so popular and if you had a decent 'fro you *had* to keep it looking immaculate – there was nothing worse than a raggedy-looking afro – by that time the American products Afro Sheen and Ultra Sheen were easy to get hold of in London, especially in Brixton. They made hair and scalp grease, although I always preferred the natural stuff, but most popular were their sprays of a very light oil that could give the hair a real shine. They reckoned it would hold it in place too, but really Afro Sheen was about finishing your afro off with that healthy sparkle every time.

I got into the braids around 1977 when they were becoming very fashionable, and my life became even easier as regards hair care – I could be on the road for what seemed like ages before they grew out, and the only maintenance I had to do was to keep my scalp clean and greased. When I was doing a cover shoot for this British black hair and beauty magazine called *Root*, I met a young lady they had working for them called Sylvia Edwards and I was so impressed with the way she looked after me that day and made sure everything was looking just right, that I asked her to take care of my braids on a regular basis. Each time I got back to England, I would call up Sylvia and ask if she could refresh them, and that was me finished with the hairdresser until after the next tour. I don't wear braids like that any more, but I'm still in touch with Sylvia and would use her again if I needed.

The fantastic thing about the braids was they were very easy for our young fans to copy, and because they were so little trouble to maintain the girls' mums were always approving! There might have been a few tears or just eye-watering when they were being put in, but after that their daughters would have a hairstyle that was natural, it didn't cost anything and would be trouble-free. I loved my braids, because following on the afro that style became another expression of who we are. I was so proud when the fans started identifying them with me as my trademark and as I've mentioned I'm still overwhelmed today when I meet women who tell me how they copied that style when they were teenagers.

It was only when I started having those conversations with women years later that it came home to me how much of an effect Boney M. had had on youngsters, especially black women or girls in Britain. In the 1970s, you never really heard the phrase 'role model' and for so many of us we simply weren't aware of what sort of influence we had beyond entertaining people. Personally, I think my own modesty would have made me shy away from that sort of thing, because back then I would have found it difficult to believe anybody would have listened to me beyond Boney M. I am certainly pleased that we made such an impact, but at the time it was more a case of thinking that what was happening to us was great and I was glad we were making people happy. Naturally I wanted to set a good example in how people saw me behaving when I wasn't on stage, but that would have been exactly the same if I hadn't been in Boney M.

As long as I've been an artist I've cared about what was going on – 'Belfast' was my song before it ever became part of the Boney M. catalogue, and I was so pleased when 'We Kill the World' became a hit around Europe and Number One in a couple of countries. As a solo artist I recorded a song that was written for me called 'You Can't Fight While You're Dancing', which was another appeal for peace. I've always tried to bring a message to my music. I believe had I realised I was a role model, and we had been allowed the time, I would have got into charity work as an individual, and given speeches, the kind of inspirational and motivational speaking I've been doing for quite a while now.

So I would have done more things like that, indeed it remains my goal to do everything I can as a missionary for peace and for encouragement to people who might be suffering from a disease or just afraid of being attacked by one. I try to inspire my sisters, wherever that might be, not to write themselves off even if they think that other people may have written them off. That God won't have written them off, so there is always the possibility they can conquer whatever has been put in front of them. Like I did, twice, first of all getting to where I got to with Boney M., then beating cancer, five times.

I didn't have too much time for boyfriends while I was in Boney M., the combination of the hectic life I was leading and the fact I had a mother and son in London who relied on me didn't help matters. I was never going to have a string of affairs or casual relationships or even one-night stands when I was on the road because that's not at all how I am; also I always had a phobia of any disease passing on to me. I don't think women can behave like that on tour, and although men can get away with the sex and drugs and rock 'n' roll – in fact sometimes it even seems expected of them – it's very different for us. Anyway, if we three girls had the male equivalent of groupies trying to get near us, I can honestly say I never noticed!

There was a German man I was dating for quite a while who was a stockbroker from Hamburg, and I kept some clothes and things at his flat. Although the relationship lasted quite a while

– from before Boney M. through to the first few years of the group – I don't think it was ever really very serious. This was because my family responsibilities in London meant if I wasn't on the road I wanted to get back to them, also I didn't like the attitude of his family who made it clear that black and white didn't suit each other as a couple. I don't think I ever thought he was or ever would be The One for me and when I called it a day I left quite a few of my gold records at his flat – I wonder if he's still got them!

I met a Jamaican guy, named Peter, when were over there filming the 'Boonoonoonoos' video, and we dated very briefly. Although he was a lovely guy, what kind of relationship would that be? He lived in Jamaica, I had my family in London and was in a group based in Germany. And Jamaican men aren't exactly known for waiting patiently for their wives or girlfriends to return. So that was that.

I never felt I was missing out on anything, even when Liz and Maizie had their partners on the road with them: I used to think it wasn't such a big deal being without a man at that point, in fact I felt my life was a bit like a fairy tale as it was. I wanted to get everything I could out of that experience, and as I already had my son it was a real concern that I could get pregnant while at the peak of my career. Then what's going to happen? I can't take a year off from Boney M. and expect to slot back in again afterwards. That is a real worry for so many female artists but at least the solo acts have a better chance of planning for it, because of the way our group had come together and operated we couldn't plan our career around such eventualities. So I got to thinking it was for the best that I was on my own, I spent my time well, both in the group and when I was at home with my mother and son. I wasn't looking for anybody when I met Marcus and just as I am a lucky woman in meeting him, he is a very lucky man that I took him into my life – I tell him this frequently, but I think up until this day he doesn't believe me!

## Chapter Eight

# '200,000 people started to chant "Rivers Of Babylon"'

It was in 1978 and 1979 that Boney M. reached heights that still amaze me. In my home in Berlin both walls of the entrance hall and corridor leading into the apartment are lined from floor to ceiling with gold and platinum discs – and that's just some of them. All in all I had picked up about eight hundred but have misplaced quite a few along the way. Even though I walk past a record of our achievements practically every day, it's still very possible for me to feel a bit overwhelmed by my Boney M. adventures. This is mostly due to the speed with which it all happened and how steep the curve had been. Three years previously we'd been slogging around Germany, Holland and Belgium in a Ford Transit, performing to my backing tape in front of tiny audiences on even tinier nightclub stages. During 1978 and 1979 we'd played to six-figure crowds; become the first Western group to perform in the Soviet Union; been presented to Her Majesty Queen Elizabeth; appeared on the legendary American TV show *Soul Train*; sold over 60 million records in 1978 alone; had a Christmas Number One; got two singles into the UK all-time best-sellers Top Ten; and even had a Number One in Jamaica – 'Rivers of Babylon' – which made me very proud. Crucially, though, Liz and I were finally credited as the vocalists on 1979's *Oceans of Fantasy* album, which meant as much to me as any platinum disc or concert attendance record.

Boney M. had been building steadily from day one, but it was during 1978 and 1979 we took the jump from being just a successful group to a *mega*-successful group. The signs had been there from the year previously when our concerts had started making enough money for us to take a live band on tour, and we did away with the backing tapes when we toured to promote *Love for Sale*. It was an obvious step, because as our audiences had gotten bigger so had the venues and it would look a bit silly to have just the four of us on a great big stage in a sports arena! It was a big deal at that time, though, because in the disco era so many of the studio-created groups and singers didn't get as far as live backing, they remained like Boney M. were in the very beginning and nobody was going to invest in them for the long term. Getting a band was an acknowledgement that we were a genuine group, never mind what the critics might have said.

For me personally it was fantastic, because that was what I had been used to: even in my first show business job dancing in Greece I had been with a seven-piece live band, and as a solo artist I'd done a great deal of touring with bands. I'd always loved the power and energy of a live band, so I was really keen to be back in front of one. Indeed, one of the few things that would improve my life today would be if I could do gigs with a full live band again instead of a half playback, but I'm in no doubt that will happen.

The band we got couldn't have been better; they were a thirteen-piece group called Black Beauty Circus with horns and backing singers, who hailed mostly from the Caribbean, West Africa and London, although there was one Brazilian and a guy from Sicily. Real multicultural! Black Beauty Circus evolved out of a band called The Eruptions who Frank had been working with in the studio. Precious Wilson was their singer, and Frank seemed to have a lot of faith in Precious and wanted to produce her as a solo act, which of course led to rumours that he was going to bring her into Boney M. and kick me out! I couldn't have cared less because I knew he couldn't change the sound of Boney M., especially as we were going stellar at that time. The best thing is Precious and I are still very good friends and we've had many a good laugh about that.

Frank wanted to get The Eruptions as much exposure as possible and he put them on tour with us as our opening act, then when we needed a band they would continue after the break, supplemented with a few more musicians. As things grew so did the size of the band backing us – horn players like Eddie 'Tan Tan' Thornton and Mick Eve who used to be in Georgie Fame's Blue Flames. Gradually The Eruptions evolved into the new bigger group, Black Beauty Circus, with a five-piece brass section, four backing singers, a rhythm section, guitarists and keyboard players. When we were touring the really big venues it was with a party of up to seventy-five people, including technicians and roadies. Black Beauty Circus would do their own set to open the show, then they'd return to line up behind us. They were brilliant, bringing a real injection of energy into our stage show. Many of them had been regulars on the soul and R&B scenes so they knew how to just keep the groove going and when to really kick up a storm, plus they could play some amazing solos.

The band gave Boney M. a much wilder and more exciting stage presence and they looked utterly fabulous in their costumes, which was a real bonus for the whole show. Another big difference they made was we could always hear them! This may sound obvious, but one of the things so many people don't realise about backing tapes is that it is very common for the artists on stage to have difficulty hearing them, meaning they have to concentrate so hard on listening for the music it doesn't allow them to put one hundred per cent into their singing and presentation. Then, of course, there was the whole spontaneity thing that went with having live musicians, which was something that meant so much to me. Because of my previous experience I knew how to be a showwoman on stage and knew how to interact with musicians and what to expect back from them.

We used to rehearse with the band and I understood how to talk to the musicians on their terms; I knew how to engage with them and we would work out things to do and certain flourishes to put in certain places. It was such a nice atmosphere working with them because they were having great fun, telling me they could do *this* or put *that* there, allowing them to free up their creativity. They were always good enough to go with it if I just said, 'Hit me, gentlemen . . .' or something like that, and I felt safe enough with them that they would never let anybody down or miss a cue. I always thought that if they knew it was one of my lead songs coming up they would perk up a bit: 'Aha! Here comes Marcia, we'd better be ready for some action.'

The others weren't invigorated by Black Beauty Circus to the degree I was, because Maizie didn't sing so she wouldn't understand it in the same way. Bobby, too, didn't know anything about music, he didn't know how to count the bars or anything like that, and he was all about doing his own thing anyway. Liz would act like she understood, but sometimes I wasn't sure she knew what was going on. This didn't matter, though, the other three all gained from the upsurge of energy the band brought to the stage, so that boosted everybody's performances.

A big live band is very useful in another respect, too. We once did a massive show in a football stadium in Poland to an audience of 200,000, and when we came on the people surged forward, only held back by a line of policemen with their arms linked. The crowd was pushing and these policeman were really straining against them. As soon as we stepped up to the mics and said 'Hello!', Liz beckoned to the crowd and the whole place erupted – the audience tore away from the police and came charging at the stage. It was like a stampede, they were coming to grab us and even though we knew they loved us it was very frightening. The band were picking up their instruments, we were trying to run, people and equipment were tumbling over, but the guys in the band were so good at helping us girls get off that stage it was as if they physically carried us off. I dread to think what would have become of us if all we'd had were backing tapes.

As the shows got bigger so did the hits. This had been happening through all of the *Love for Sale* releases, and we knew from the reports of our record sales we were doing really well, but nothing prepared us for *Nightflight to Venus*. The first single was 'Rivers of Babylon', with lyrics adapted from Psalm137, which had been a huge hit for the Jamaican rocksteady group The

Melodians. They had put in lyrics about Rastafari and it made sense as a spiritual song coming out of Jamaica, but when we covered it I really didn't expect anything out of the ordinary would come from it. I wasn't doubting it would be a hit, but there we were, a pop group, singing a Psalm . . . Why would people take to it like that? I treated it the same way as I treated all our other recordings, so when it was done didn't really pay much attention to what's going to happen to it – just do it and get on with the rest of the work.

It came out in April 1978, with 'Brown Girl in the Ring' on the other side – another song I wasn't paying a massive amount of attention to – and I was off on holiday to Jamaica with my mother and my son as it climbed the charts. As usual when I did get time off I did my best to stay away from Boney M. business, but after a while out there I heard 'Brown Girl in the Ring' was Number One in England. I was baffled – that was the B-side. Then it was explained to me that Babylon had been in the charts for so long, then when it started slipping and there was no new Boney M. record out there radio DJs started playing the other side, 'Brown Girl'. It was lively and fun and different enough from 'Babylon' for a new crowd to start buying it and it went back up the charts. This had never been planned but when it happened the record company started calling it a Double A-side, as if it had been their intention all along.

All of this worked wonders for the sales figures, 'Babylon' went to Number One all across Europe, Australia and South Africa and gave us our biggest American hit – Number 30 in their charts – and was massive in both Canada and Japan. It's still the best-selling single ever in Germany, while in the UK it became the seventh best-seller ever and is still in the Top Ten all-time best-sellers forty years later. It was on the British charts for nearly a year, forty weeks, and is one of only half a dozen records that have sold more than two million copies in that country. At one point in Britain the record sold 147,000 copies in a single day, and there were all sorts of reports of pressing plants not being able to keep up and copies having to be shipped in from abroad.

So Boney M. got into the *Guinness Book of Records*, then that same single got us into a far more controversial book when it got us a mention in Salman Rushdie's *The Satanic Verses*! That book came out at least ten years after the song, I'd left the group and we were living in Florida, where my neighbour said she had a present for me. She handed me a copy of *The Satanic Verses* and told me how she'd been reading about me in it! I was shocked! I knew this was the man everybody was looking for because of that book, and I said, 'What has this got to do with me? They might come and kill me if they can't find him!' I felt a bit foolish when she said to me, 'Didn't you know?' Then she opened the book up to page 175 where it reads:

She says, 'Right!' And she slapped his knee. 'That's really right, Mr Reeljck, it's well and truly like that, actually.' Another drink they took, then she leaned over to the tape deck and pushed a button. 'Jesus Jump.' he thought, 'Boney M.? Give me a break!' All the tough-raised professional attitudes, the lady still had a lot to learn about music.

Here it came, Boom shaka boom, then, without warning, he was crying, provoked into real tears by counterfeit emotion by a disco beat imitation of pain, it was the one hundred and thirty-seventh psalm, Superflomina, King David calling across the centuries – 'How shall

*we sing the Lord's song in a strange land?' 'I had to learn the psalm
at school,' Pamela Charmsha said, sitting on the floor, her head
leaning against the sofa bed. Her eyes shut tight. "By the rivers of
Babylon where we sat down, Oh, oh, oh we wept." '*

The record's other A-side, 'Brown Girl in the Ring', gained
its own place in cultural history, too, with the English moun-
taineers in Peru, Joe Simpson and Simon Yates, who were
climbing in the Andes when Simpson slipped and fell onto a
ledge. They were roped together so Yates eventually had to cut
the rope to save at least one of them, himself. Simpson had slid
into a crevasse, but eventually freed himself and, going several
days without food or water, managed to get back down the
mountain – literally, he hopped. When the two of them spoke
about their ordeal he said that after he had been left alone all
that was going through his head was *Brown girl in the ring / Tra-la-
la-la-la-la! / Brown girl in the ring / Tra-la-la-la-la-la'* And he was
asking himself, 'Why am I hearing Boney M.? I don't even like
Boney M.! Bloody hell, please don't let me die to Boney M.!'

But he didn't, his life was saved to Boney M. as he lived to
tell the story. He told it on Oprah Winfrey's show and so many
other big American talk shows, meaning our name stayed out
there because then you had people asking, 'Who is Boney M.?'
The director Kevin Macdonald made a film about their adventure, *Touching the Void*, which was really successful and called
the best British documentary film ever made, and of course
'Brown Girl in the Ring' is part of it.

It could be said that in both of these instances people are
making fun of the songs and of Boney M., but so what? Those
two songs went on to break all those records and score Number

One hits in all those countries, so why should we care if somebody wants to tease us? Especially if it keeps our name alive. And it certainly wasn't everybody who thought 'Rivers of Babylon' was a bit naff: when Pope John Paul II went to Poland he held a mass for over 200,000 people who spontaneously started to chant the 'Babylon' lyrics, then ended up singing the whole song. That must have sounded absolutely awesome, and provided the answer to the question I'd asked myself when we finished recording it – why would people take to a pop group singing a version of that song? Obviously, it was a very special song that touched people in a very special way.

'Rasputin' came next, which was probably the maddest song we ever did! It told the story of a monk who, around a hundred years ago, supposedly manipulated Tsar Nicholas II and had an affair with his wife Alexandra, but turning him into some kind of disco-era nightclub playboy – *Russia's greatest love machine*! What was all that about? That song was so much fun to do. Putting the Cossack twist on a funky beat was really lively, and of course Bobby came up with some Russian-style dancing and even wore a big Rasputin-style beard for some of the performances! I know people had a great time dancing to it in discotheques, because they could get a little crazy. It went to Number One in Germany, Austria and Australia, Number Two in Great Britain and Top Ten practically everywhere else it was released. It was even really popular in nightclubs in Russia, apparently reviving an interest in Rasputin who had pretty much been written out of history. This was in spite of it not being released there, as talk of the affair with Tsarina Alexandra was deemed too disrespectful towards Russian rulers. Another country that wasn't too happy with the song was Poland, which was part of the Soviet Bloc back then: we played a big show there in 1979 and apparently the promoter had been asked by the authorities not to let us perform 'Rasputin'. This didn't filter down to us or the band, though; in fact, we only heard about it after the event. We did the song in the set as usual – it went down very well, as I remember – and in spite of the show being broadcast live on the radio, when the film of it was shown on TV the next day the song had been edited out.

As successful as 'Rasputin' was, it was nowhere near 'Babylon' levels, which I believe was because the *Nightflight to Venus* album had been released about a month previously and gone straight to Number One in so many countries that many of our fans already had the song. So I'm not complaining at all! In fact, it showed exactly how internationally popular we were going into 1978 because the anticipation for a new Boney M. record had contributed to the reception for 'Babylon' and 'Brown Girl', then the album sold out as soon as it hit the shops. A state of affairs underlined when our next single, 'Mary's Boy Child'/'Oh My Lord' was released: it wasn't on any album, and it immediately became our second-biggest seller.

Like so much of what happened to Boney M., that single hadn't been part of any long-term planning. Liz and I were called into Frank's studio in early November to record a Christmas song, a cover of the lovely Harry Belafonte hit from twenty years previously. It was finished quickly, then put into our live set for the concerts we would be doing over the festive season as a Christmas gift for the fans, then the single was to come out at the very end of November. It was perfect timing because by a couple of weeks into December we could accompany it with the magical video we'd shot in the snow in Moscow's Red Square, of us wearing these beautiful white feather coats. That was another first for Boney M., as, at that time, we were the only pop group to be granted permission by the Soviet authorities to film a video in Red Square. By Christmas it was Number One in so many charts. In Britain it was at the top for four weeks and ended up selling 1.8 million, which put us in the UK all-time best-sellers list *again*! We are the only act there is to have two entries in that Top Ten: not The Beatles, not Michael Jackson, not Abba – Boney M.

Even disregarding those sales figures, back then getting the Christmas Number One was fantastic, a really big deal – I think it still might be, but back then competition for it was intense as so many of the big groups would put out a special Christmas single. To get that top spot in Germany, the UK and so many other countries was the perfect end to an absolutely extraordinary year: we were even on the BBC's Christmas *Top of the Pops* three times, with 'Rasputin' and 'Babylon' as well, because they had been such huge hits. 'Mary's Boy Child' really became a special song to me because it became part of the whole Christmas tradition, one of those songs I'll hear every year on the radio or in shops or airports, no matter what country I might be in. Likewise, the video of us all in white fur performing it is always cropping up on television in Germany when they show anything to do with Christmas music. It even gets played a great deal on the radio in America, which I find very interesting because it wasn't a hit over there at the time. It's something I am really proud of, and feel so privileged to be so regularly reminded of my contribution.

## Chapter Nine

# 'All these black people enjoying themselves in Red Square'

After the excitement of 1978 and that Christmas Number One, 1979 was always going to have a great deal to live up to. Our first single of the year, 'Painter Man', came out early in the year and was only released in Great Britain, the Republic of Ireland and the Netherlands. It was another track from *Nightflight*, and had been the B-side of 'Rasputin' everywhere else on continental Europe. I think the only reason for its release was to cash in on the success we'd had during the previous year, and it got to Number Ten in the UK charts. Immediately there was an outcry in the media about 'Only Number Ten . . . Is it all over for Boney M.?' It didn't bother me because I am a very positive person and instead of thinking '*Only* Top Ten', I was thinking '*Wow!* Top Ten!' and savouring the moment we were still being talked about.

I never really looked at the charts as being the measure of how well we were doing anyway, inside the Boney M. Bubble I always felt we were detached from them. Of course, it was nice to be told that your records had reached Number One in whatever country we were in at the time – especially if it meant we were above Abba! – but it didn't mean nearly as much as being on stage in front of a packed house of Boney M. fans going mad. We were on tour all the time, so keeping up with what was happening in various charts wasn't a priority and the only way I judged how well we were doing was how the concert audiences reacted and that couldn't have been better. During those mega years, we played some of the biggest concerts we'd ever done, which were fabulous, but we also played some very interesting ones, opening up experiences I never would have believed possible when we set out on the Boney M. journey.

The first totally amazing event for us was that trip to Moscow in December 1978. It made a very deep impression on me, although not all of it for the right reasons. As I've said, we really were pushing back the boundaries of Western pop music – the first group to be invited to play what was then the Soviet Union. Up until that point the government hadn't wanted to be seen approving of Western culture, but as we'd sold 100,000 of the *Nightflight to Venus* album over in Moscow, clearly the Russian people were quite keen on it so they were willing to make an exception! It is said that we were there at the personal invitation of the president of the Soviet Union, Leonid Brezhnev, and although he never came to meet us while we were in Russia, the way things were over there concerts like ours couldn't have happened without his say-so, so it was a big honour for us.

Many people assume we'd been invited there because of 'Rasputin', which had been such a big international hit, but that couldn't have been further from the truth – the single had been banned in Russia and the album was pressed without 'Rasputin' on it. We had actually been given strict orders not to perform the song at any of the shows, although after our visit I was told plenty of local Russian bands had the song in their repertoire – I guess for them playing a banned song was quite an act of rebellion!

It seemed to us that, as per usual, the trip was arranged quickly, meaning we didn't have a lot of opportunity to think about the finer points beforehand, so at first it was just like flying to any other country. It was only when I arrived at Heathrow that I realised something special was happening, although the full magnitude didn't hit me at that point. Heathrow was much smaller in those days, with far fewer planes flying in and out, and there were certainly not many flights to Russia. But there was this great big Aeroflot jet, the Soviets national airline, sitting on the tarmac. It was the biggest plane anybody could see, so I could hear people asking, 'What is *that* doing here?' And the replies were, 'Oh, that's for Boney M.!' And *then* I remember thinking, 'Wow! Somebody's pulled out all the stops for us!' As it turned out the plane wasn't *just* for us, but we had the First Class section to ourselves, and the stewards and stewardesses looked after us so well it might as well have been a private flight! And so, after we'd taken off, I finally had the time and space to properly consider where we were going and what we were about to do and that's when I got excited – *nobody* had been there from the West to play pop music before, so Boney M. were true pioneers.

When we touched down in Moscow there was a reception committee to greet us – Communist party bigwigs and politicians and government officials. Because we'd been invited by the government, naturally they wanted to schmooze with these exotic creatures from the other side of the Iron Curtain. There was a massive press turn out, too, because bringing in a Western group – a *black* Western group, no less – and one as lavish and as glamorous as Boney M., was a big coup for the ruling politicians so they wanted to show us off and make sure the people knew we were there. When we got into the terminal building there was a battery of cameras clicking away, film crews, the whole works, and we did lots of interviews. To my surprise nearly everybody spoke English, which is how we could do all those interviews. I hadn't expected that at all as it was the language of the competition – America! – also, in Germany if people could speak English it wasn't unusual for them not to let on!

For me, that felt like a very warm welcome; I felt everybody who was out at the airport was genuinely happy to meet us. More telling than that, though, was the 'Welcome to Moscow' we got in Red Square, as that was from ordinary Russian people.

Our hotel was actually on the square and physically seeing Red Square was an experience and a half . . . a really fantastic sight. Pictures can't really prepare you for the real thing; it is so vast, and the colours of those domes are so vivid it simply looks like nothing anybody has ever seen in the West. When we were there it was covered in snow, so it really did look like something out of a fairy tale, and that totally entranced us. And I'd never seen so much snow! As soon as we'd checked into the hotel we rushed out there, and were playing in it, throwing snowballs at each other, falling over in it, laughing, shouting . . . just acting like four big kids. Then our backing band arrived and jumped right into the action with us. They were easily having as much fun as us and probably making even more noise. The passers-by, regular Moscow people, were *amazed*! They'd certainly never seen anything like this, all these black people in their Red Square, laughing and enjoying themselves in this way. They had to stop and look. It was like they were glued to the spot, so pretty soon there was a huge crowd there, which really was as exciting for us as it was for them. They were speaking their own language, so we didn't know what they were saying, but their tones were so enthusiastic and they were smiling all the time, those with cameras were taking pictures, and they seemed so friendly and welcoming. The same thing happened when we did the 'Mary's Boy Child' shoot out there, but that was an organised affair so the shoot was roped off and people couldn't get so close to us.

The hotel we were staying in Moscow was the Hotel Rossiya, which was owned by the state and was huge – I mean *enormous*! I found out later that, at the time, it was the largest hotel anywhere in the world, it could accommodate 4,000 guests. It had its own full-size concert hall downstairs, which is where we were going to do ten shows in six days, one at four in the afternoon, one at eight o'clock in the evening. Each floor had its own reception, and each of us had a suite that was bigger than most apartments I'd seen in England or Germany. Mine had seven rooms and the living room was big enough to have a full-size Steinway grand piano in it – my first thought was that I'd get lost in there and miss the first show! In spite of all this luxury, it was still Russia and when I looked up to the ceiling I saw some wires poking through next to the light fitting. I'd heard about their spying, especially on Westerners, so all I could think was, 'They're not going to watch me when I'm naked!' So when I was using the shower I would turn off all the electricity and feel my way around the walls into the bathroom in the dark!

Something else that happened on the first morning that really spooked me: Maizie came knocking on my door looking for her clothes, the dresses she was going to wear on stage – all brand-new dresses – meanwhile, I'd woken up to find half of the piano that was in my room was missing. We went to one of the reception desks and tried to make ourselves understood, mostly using our hands to make signs, which got us nowhere, so we went to look for ourselves. We walked and we walked and we walked along those endless corridors, eventually coming across this room with an open door that must have been house-keeping. In there we saw this woman polishing the piece of piano and Maizie's dresses hanging up soaking wet after they'd been washed! That was spooky. We just looked at each other and I said, 'Oh my God! They came into my suite when I was sleeping and I didn't hear one thing?' In a way I was relieved because I had thought I was going crazy – I knew the piano was in one piece when I went to sleep – and, presumably, they thought this was the sort of service we should get. On the other hand, though, they'd just walked in and out of our suites. But that was the experience in Russia – it didn't matter who you were, you still didn't really have any privacy.

We didn't see much of Russia at all, or even of Moscow beyond Red Square, which was a shame but there wasn't really any time even to reflect on that, let alone do anything about it. The simple truth was that we had no reason to leave the hotel for anything, and that's probably how the authorities had planned it so they could keep an eye on us. Our stage wear was all left in the theatre dressing rooms, but because they weren't too comfortable we would come down in just our underwear with our mink coats over the top to get dressed for the show.

One evening they did a banquet in our honour that was attended by many delegates and party officials, it was really something else but also it brought home to me what life was really like in Russia. This banquet, again in the hotel, was a genuine feast, it was magnificent, the *best food you could ever imagine* . . . caviar . . . champagne – not domestic sparkling wine, genuine champagne – all the Western labels like Moet & Chandon or Bollinger, which I had assumed wouldn't be available in Moscow. It was served with beautiful-looking silverware and the finest china, and the thing I remember most is how the silver was polished so so shiny – I've never seen silver shine like that before or since – fantastic! I never expected anything like this, because when we used the restaurant upstairs in the hotel it told a completely different story. In there, where the ordinary people ate, the plates and the mugs were chipped, the cutlery was tarnished, we even saw some people eating out of newspaper, and once we watched this couple who brought their own food into the restaurant, sat down, unwrapped it and ate it – if we hadn't seen that, we wouldn't have believed it!

That whole situation of the wealthy class having only the best while the everyday people had virtually nothing immediately reminded me of my own little island of Jamaica – beautiful as it is, there is such a difference between the elite – the politicians – and everybody else. As I travelled more, with Boney M. and later as a solo singer, I came to realise that while I don't want to term it as *normal*, this sort of thing happens all over the world. To this day it still exists: the politicians live like kings and queens and don't do anything for the average person on the outside of that exclusive set. That really hit home with our shows in Moscow – Russian people were the fans who had bought the album and knew the songs, but none of them could go to the concerts; there's no way they could have afforded to buy tickets, yet each one of the ten shows were chock-a-block, packed with the delegates who were just there because it was a privilege, I doubt if too many of them were genuine Boney M. fans.

Going to the other political extreme, quite early on in 1979 we found ourselves on *Soul Train*, the iconic American black music TV show. In many ways that was as unexpected as performing in Russia!

We'd had a tiny amount of success in America, as a couple of singles had ridden on the disco wave to get into the very lower reaches of the Billboard Top 100, while 'Rivers of Babylon' made it into the Top Thirty. This wasn't bad, considering the amount of competition from American groups and the fact our record company had never really given us a push out there. Things changed when Frank decided to take us out there to do the rounds of television promotion around the single 'Hooray! Hooray! It's a Holi-Holiday!' In one week we did four US TV shows. Hectic as that was, it wasn't nearly enough, so America didn't get to see what Boney M. could really do and I believe a few of the people who did see us didn't quite get it – 'Holi-Holiday' wasn't perhaps the best song there could be to represent us. When we did *The Merv Griffin Show*, one of the biggest chat shows of the time, he introduced us in this big booming voice: 'And now . . . here's reggae!' I'm sure that confused a few people, especially if they'd expected us to look and sound like Bob Marley. We did *Dinah!*, with Dinah Shore, and an entertainment talk show called *Soap* – not, I stress, the comedy soap opera of the same name! We did a lot of interviews, too, and then they booked us on *Soul Train*!

When I look back at that now it was so funny, but at the time I actually felt a bit embarrassed: *Soul Train* was a groundbreaking black music show, which had launched in 1971, then become the first black produced show to be nationally syndicated on American television. By the time we got on there every soul music legend you can think of had performed on the show – James Brown, The Temptations, The Jackson 5, Stevie Wonder . . . then we come out with, '*Di-di-di-di-di-di-di/It's a holi-holiday*!' On *Soul Train*! It was ironic because after the fantastic year we'd just had some critics, especially in the UK, wanted to find something to snipe at us about and decided we were selling out as a soul group! They hadn't taken on board the fact we'd never said we were anything other than a pop group, so I wonder what they would have made of us getting a gig on *Soul Train*! With 'Holi-Holiday' no less! Everybody on the show was really nice to us, and the kids in the audience danced as enthusiastically as they would have done to a genuine soul group, but I really don't think we should have been there, or at least not with that song.

After a week in the States Frank suddenly took us back to Germany and we never returned to America. To this day I still don't know why he did that, he obviously wanted to break us there or he wouldn't have taken us over in the first place, but then to take us back when we were just starting to get noticed is a mystery. Obviously I would have liked to have had a chance to make an impact there – we all wanted to – and I think with disco hitting so big we could have done it too, although I'm not sure where we would have found the time to work in the States given our commitments in Europe, our core audience.

Those two years finished off on a real high for us, from a live point of view – we were privileged to be invited onto the bill of that year's Royal Variety Performance in November. That was a real honour. I remember that Yul Brynner, Elaine Stritch and dancers from the Bolshoi Ballet were on the bill, but what I got most out of that was being presented to Her Majesty the Queen. At the time Jamaica was still a British colony – England was the Mother Country – and we were brought up at home and at school to respect the Crown. Practically every Jamaican of a certain age will have a picture of the Queen on the living-room wall next to the picture of Jesus, so you can imagine what it was like to have come from one of those very houses in a yard in the hills above Kingston, to actually shaking hands with Queen Elizabeth. I couldn't have hoped for a better end to those two brilliant years.

## Chapter Ten

# 'We were all looking for different things out of Boney M.'

In 1979 we flew to Hong Kong to do a show. It was just one show but as we had such a big fan base out there it was in an open-air arena where over 100,000 tickets had been sold and the promoter had gone completely over the top with the presentation – we made our entrance into the arena on chariots! Genuine Ben-Hur-type chariots, pulled by horses, on which we were paraded round the stadium before being taken to the stage. The band was giving it their all with our introduction music but we could hardly hear that as the audience was going totally nuts! It was absolutely amazing, and from an opening like that we could do no wrong. It was a fantastic show on a fabulous scale and something I'll always treasure, although it was one that nearly didn't happen at all and my first reactions weren't quite as enthusiastic.

Bobby and Maizie had travelled out with Black Beauty Circus a few days earlier, but Liz and I were in the studio working on the *Oceans of Fantasy* album until the very last minute and only arrived in Hong Kong the day before the show. When we arrived there it was raining quite hard and I got up to my hotel suite, and lay down actually hoping it would still be raining the next day so the gig would be postponed.

When I woke up the next day it was still pouring down, the same the day after. In fact it rained solidly for three days before it was dry enough for the show to go ahead – each day I would hear on the radio: 'The Boney M. show has been postponed until tomorrow evening . . .' I was so relieved, because it meant I had those days with nothing on the schedule and I could catch up with my sleep. It turned into a lovely relaxed trip: we got out a bit and met loads of our fans, we did some press – Maizie and I went to a gym and photos of us lifting weights made newspaper front pages – I bought some shoes and a traditional oriental dress that were made to measure for me in a day. We had time to do all these things and such moments are so touching, it was like no other concert trip I can remember.

Which in itself presented a dilemma: on the one hand I thought postponement of a show was a terrible thing to wish for, because our audience had waited a long time to see us, spent good money and would have made all their arrangements to go out on that particular night. On the other hand, I was exhausted, I arrived in Hong Kong thinking, 'Sleep . . . sleep . . . sleep!' and I knew that if I could get just a little bit of rest I could deliver a much better performance. I honestly believe it wasn't too bad for me to be glad of the rain because I knew the show was only being postponed not cancelled. I did feel so much better for the days off, and the crowd was in a state of even higher anticipation because they'd been waiting those three extra days. They went *mad* for us and we responded with a real extra energy.

I still get tears in my eyes thinking about that show. It was as if God had looked down and thought, 'Child, you need your rest', and put the show off for three days, as right after the ninety-minute show the skies opened up again.

The Hong Kong show neatly summed up where we found ourselves during that period of such astonishing success: everybody wanted us all the time; we were doing massive shows and so many of them, which was keeping us under such increased pressure we needed time off more than ever. Yet the stakes were so much higher now because there was a much bigger audience that would be let down if we didn't come through. A good example is the recording of the *Ten Thousand Lightyears* album in 1979. I so desperately needed a holiday, and the only time we had off from the road was when Frank had scheduled the sessions for Liz and me. So he moved the recording to a studio in the South of France, where we could go on holiday and still get the work done! It wasn't too bad, but it shows what the demands were on Liz and me as the vocalists. I went down there with my mother and my son, we stayed in a lovely villa, but every night around ten o'clock when they'd gone to bed, a car would come to pick me up for the studio where I'd be recording sometimes until three or four o'clock the next morning. It wasn't a real holiday, but at least I could get some rest and spend a bit of quality time with my family.

The cracks were also beginning to show within the group. By the time we hit it really big we had been Boney M. for three full years, and when we got into those super-hectic years we each seemed to need our own space more than ever. It was a mutual thing, but it meant we hung out less and went to fewer dinners or receptions together, so any closeness that was there in the beginning was definitely fading. Sometimes, when we were on a long tour, I used to think the only time we were all in the same place was on stage.

Also, very importantly, we were no longer the people we had been when we went into it, all hopeful and looking to see what might happen. After this length of time in Boney M. and because of where the group had gotten to, our personalities and expectations had changed and we were all looking for different things out of the group and out of life as we settled into fame in our own particular ways. As I said earlier, we were all fully formed personalities when the group came together and had become familiar enough with the situation now, not to relax and worry about creating a good impression.

Where this used to affect Maizie and me most of all was with punctuality. She was always on time, as was I, and so often we would be sitting in a hotel lobby or the Pullman car waiting for Liz or Bobby or, as was usually the case, both of them. We'd be sitting, sitting, sitting, waiting for anything up to an hour after the time we were told to meet, and I used to think ten or fifteen minutes is excusable – just! – but *an hour*, when you are only coming from upstairs? Maizie was pretty tolerant of it, but I was brought up to believe that if you are late you are telling whoever it is you are meeting that your time is more important than theirs, so it used to drive me mad! *These people are adults same as us, we got up in time to spend the necessary hour or two making ourselves look good. Why couldn't they?* In the end I couldn't take it any more and made sure that when we were travelling by road there would be two Pullmans, one for Maizie and me that would depart on time and another that would leave whenever Liz and Bobby were ready.

This wasn't ideal in terms of the group's togetherness, but it was definitely for the best in terms of my sanity, as there had been trouble with us all travelling in the same Pullmans. These stretch Mercedes had two rows of seats facing each other in the back, we used them for travel in Germany or northern Europe when it was easier to go by road. How we usually arranged ourselves was Liz and I shared the forward facing one and Maizie took the backwards one by herself, Bobby would always sit up front with the driver and close the glass partition separating him from us. It seemed to suit everybody because we all had plenty of room and could stretch out or sleep if it was a long journey.

I was starting to question the amount of money we were getting for live work, although I must stress this was just me, nothing to do with the other group members – I don't know what they were being paid.

The concerts helped to sell the records, I was well aware of that, and yes, I was getting some cheques from the record sales, but then the touring really started to get intense. If we weren't on the road in Europe there would be dates fixed up in places like Bahrain, Abu Dhabi, Dubai, Hong Kong or Singapore, which involved so much travelling to maybe do one or two dates it became really gruelling. These were lucrative gigs, we all knew that, but because we were still tied to the same agreement we'd had when we were promoting 'Daddy Cool' all we were seeing from them was 400 marks per show – which wasn't even such a huge amount back in the beginning. We were the first group from the West to go to Russia yet we were getting paid the same as if we were a band starting out in the discotheques! Where was the rest of it going? Once I went to war with a promoter who handled all our work in Africa and was clearly making a fortune out of us, and my getting involved with that side of the business didn't go down well with Frank at all.

People often ask me if I got rich from Boney M. – because we were so famous and sold so many records they assume I must be. I always reply to them: 'It depends what your definition of rich is!' I moved my family from a flat in Peckham to a lovely house in Croydon, I had a fabulous little Mini Cooper, I had a fantastic holiday home designed and built in Florida, I wore lovely clothes, I ate well . . . So I couldn't complain at all financially – well, not as the 1970s rolled into the 1980s. But after that, when Boney M. became more about touring than selling records, I began to question that side of things, and it coloured the way I felt about something I'd previously been very happy doing.

One other aspect of my life that very definitely contributed to the shift in how I thought about Boney M., however, was that I met the man I would marry, Marcus James.

## Chapter Eleven

# 'Blimey! He's handy!'

When I met Marcus I definitely wasn't looking for a man. This wasn't because of Boney M., or having my mother and son to look after in London, I just always figured I was too much of a loner. I had never been too interested in finding a partner, even when I was at school in Clapham and the other girls would be talking about who they were going to marry I didn't join in, and I definitely wasn't the kind of girl who thinks, 'Well, as soon as I finish school I have to be married and have kids.' At school I was the only girl without a boyfriend, and even though I had my son at sixteen, that was never planned.

I wouldn't ever say it worried me, but I will confess at a later stage in my life playing that game with myself thinking, 'If I was going to get married what type of man would my future husband have to be?' I decided he would have to be Jamaican, first and foremost, and a natural man – or *ital*, as we'd say in Jamaica, which means healthy, loving life for what it is and not ruled by material things. Also he would have to be a musician so he understood my career and my ambitions; but more than just a musician he would have to be a bass player. That might sound like I'm being overly picky, but to me the bass is the foundation of a piece of music, it's the first thing I hear when I listen to a track – especially if it's sweet and melodic. It's carrying the whole song, so why not look for that sort of solidity in a man? Apart from when I was very young and I cried when I couldn't go to organ lessons, the only instrument I've ever wanted to play is the bass guitar, so I guess I thought if I'm not going to learn to play the instrument myself then the next best thing would be to marry somebody who could! Finally, of course, he would have to be a gentleman.

Imagine how I felt when I found all of that rolled into one man? And the thing was, I almost didn't notice all these boxes were being ticked because we became very good friends before we got intimate. Which is why I believe we've been so happy together for over thirty years.

I'd like to say it was love at first sight for us, but although, like the old cliché, our eyes did meet across a crowded room, there were no sparks – at least not from me, I just thought, 'Oh, he seems friendly.' And that was that. It was at a black beauty contest in London's West End at the very beginning of the 1980s. I had been asked to go on the judging panel – of the three of us it was usually me who was asked to do stuff like that because I always enjoyed it and I was the most flamboyant, therefore the best representative of Boney M. Marcus was there with Eddy Grant's brother, the reggae artist Mexicano, who I knew through Eddy; and I was there with my mother and my son. The five of us ended up in the lift together where we all exchanged perfectly cordial greetings. Later when we were all seated for the dinner, my party was about six tables away from his, and I caught him looking at me more than once, even though he still denies he was!

The next time I saw Marcus was over a year later, in January 1983, when I was still in Boney M. but about to do some solo tracks with CBS Records. They had suggested Eddy Grant as the producer and were sending me to his studio in Barbados to record, so as soon as I was able to take a couple of weeks' holiday from the group I flew down from my house in Florida. When Eddy met me he told me although he could play all the instruments himself on our sessions – he frequently works like that on his own recordings – he had brought his regular bass player down from New York because he thought that would benefit my material. Naturally, as a lover of the bass, I was very pleased with that. It was in the evening when Eddy's wife Anne cooked a big dinner for all of us to sit down together at, I was introduced to that bass player, Marcus, and I genuinely didn't recognise him from that event in London! In fact, when Marcus told me, 'Oh, I've met you before,' I thought he was just trying an ancient chat-up line! I wasn't overly impressed, and replied, rather coolly, 'Oh *really*?'

In spite of Marcus sounding like he was giving me an old line, this wasn't some guy trying to pick me up in a nightclub, I would be working with him for the next couple of weeks. We chatted during dinner, when he refreshed my memory about our first meeting, and was so funny and interesting. We found out we had similar backgrounds in Jamaica: we both left the island to come to Britain at age thirteen. I am just a year older than him so we both had memories of the country as it prepared for Independence; and we were breaking into a little patois too as we cracked jokes. I would say we became friends immediately – just normal friends, nothing romantic.

The recording sessions at Eddy's went very well. They were very relaxed – Eddy is that sort of producer, very patient and encouraging but still a perfectionist. In typical recording studio fashion, the sessions would start in the evening and go on into the night so the whole crew down there would have nothing to do during the day, which was exactly the sort of break I needed. At first we all started going to the beach together – seven guys and me the only woman, which suited me fine because I've always gotten on better with men than I have with women and I love having men friends. We'd go jogging or swimming or we'd just hang out on the beach; but after two or three days the others started disappearing. I don't know if they saw something happening that even I hadn't noticed yet and they were being discreet, but I'd be asking, 'Where's so and so?'

Pretty soon it was just the two of us, having the whole days to ourselves, when we would borrow Eddy's kids' bicycles and ride all over the place having real fun. One day we cycled into town, went down to the market and bought flying fish and a bottle of Mount Gay rum; when we brought it all back Marcus made a really good wood fire outside. I saw that and thought, 'Blimey! He's handy!' But it also showed me he was very natural, with no airs and graces, which really impressed me. We borrowed a couple of pans from the kitchen, fried up the fish, took it indoors and told the rest of the crew to help themselves. Although they tucked into the fish, they were shocked that I was outside cooking fish over an open fire in Eddy Grant's yard, because they knew me as the star who was at the peak of Boney M. who was down there to record. I was all of those things, but I was also the girl from Old Harbour in Jamaica, and I loved to cook if I had the time because it was something that took my mind off all that show-business palaver. Marcus understood this straight away.

*(above)* My guardian's little shop in Jamaica, thirty years after I used to help out there as a child.

*(right)* Receipt for the £127 Mama paid for my sister and I to fly over and join her in England.

### 2
### DESCRIPTION *SIGNALEMENT*

| | Bearer *Titulaire* | Wife *Femme* |
|---|---|---|
| Profession) Profession) | Olof Harbour | |
| Place and date of birth) Lieu et date de naissance) | St. Catherine JAMAICA 14th October 1948 | |
| Country of Residence) Pays de Résidence) | JAMAICA | |
| Height) Taille) | 5 ft. 5 in.5 | ft. in. |
| Colour of eyes) Couleur des yeux) | Dark Brown | |
| Colour of hair) Couleur des cheveux) | Black | |
| Special peculiarities) Signes particuliers) | | |

### CHILDREN *ENFANTS*

| Name *Nom* | Date of birth *Date de naissance* | Sex *Sexe* |
|---|---|---|
| | | |

Bearer
*Titulaire*

Wife
*Femme*

(PHOTO)

Usual signature of bearer
*Signature du titulaire*    Marcia Barrett

Usual signature of wife
*Signature de sa femme*

My first passport, aged thirteen. I do my best to look grown up as I get ready to leave Jamaica.

'And on, Macduff!' I played that character in my school play, and of course I'm centre stage.

The Parkside Secondary School girls – my best friend Elaine is far right, I'm next to her.

*(left)* As a very self-assured fifteen-year-old, posing in a studio in Brixton.

*(below)* Sweet sixteen at home in Kepler Road, Brixton, London.

*(left)* Aged nineteen, on my first trip to Germany – I haven't changed a bit!

*(below)* My first driving licence was German.

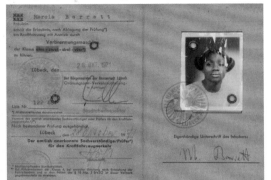

The wildest dancer in the Top Ten Diskotek, Harburg, Germany, early 1970s.

On tour in Europe in the very early 1970s.

In the early 1970s, in Germany. I had to be prepared to present a variety of moods and looks, as these publicity photos prove!

Early publicity picture from my first recording deal, Hamburg, 1971.

metronome
MARCIA BARRETT

A couple of years before Boney M., but obviously a star in the making.

Boney M. in concert at Tivolis Koncertsal, Copenhagen, 24th March 1977. *(left to right)* Liz Mitchell, Maizie Williams, Bobby Farrell, me. *(Torben Christensen)*

Boney M. receiving their gold disc for *Take The Heat Off Me* in Copenhagen, March 1977. *(Tass/PA Images)*

Boney M. in Moscow, December 1978. One of ten concerts at the Rossiya Hotel. *(Ritzau/PA Images)*

Patrons
Her Majesty The Queen
Her Majesty Queen Elizabeth The Queen Mother

we the undersigned tender our sincere congratulations to

*Marcia Barrett*

on being one of the representative artistes selected to appear before

**Her Majesty The Queen**

on the occasion of the

*Royal Variety Performance*

held at the

**Theatre Royal, Drury Lane, on Monday, November 26th 1979**

the performance being in aid of the Entertainment Artistes' Benevolent Fund

Vice-President                                    General Secretary

To be invited to perform in front of royalty is one of my greatest honours.

One of the very rare moments for quiet contemplation during the Boney M. days.

I'm sure people down there thought we were having an affair, I think even Eddy imagined there was something going on, but that wasn't the case; we had just become very good friends. As I said, I wasn't looking for man, I had my career, I had my family, if I date then so be it – my life wasn't finished – but at that point I just felt I'd made a really good friend in Marcus. At least until the night before he had to return to New York.

There was a three-storey residential building as part of the recording complex. I was on the first floor and Marcus was on the next one up; sometimes I would see him looking out of his window but I never went up there because the way I was brought up I was taught not to go into a man's room. On his last night there was no recording, and he came to my room and just wouldn't leave, he was lying on my bed and we were talking, cracking jokes, laughing . . . but he wouldn't go. I resorted to hiding in the bathtub! I told him I had to have my bath, went in the bathroom and locked the door. After about two hours I thought he had to have gone by then, although I was sure I hadn't heard the door close and when I finally peeped out he was still there and had got under the sheets! Then he was bare-faced enough to smile at me and pat the other side of the bed! I must admit I was a little shocked, but really, that was it – for me from that moment on it would be Marcia and Marcus.

After Marcus had gone I had another week down there finishing off my recording and it was one of the worst times of my life! As soon as Marcus left I realised there was a different sort of feeling there, I felt a bit lost and got very sad: 'Oh my God, he's gone . . . What am I going to do . . .?'

We had exchanged details and he had told me after he had finished the gig in New York he had to rush back for he would be staying at his sister's in Atlanta, so I knew I could call him there. This became pretty much all I could think about. We were recording the tracks that would effectively kick-start me as a solo artist, so career-wise this was a pretty big deal, but all I wanted was to get it done and get back to America. Things kept breaking down, because Eddy had literally just finished building the studios – I think I was the first act to work in there – so there were quite a few teething problems. So all I saw were these delays! I was actually quite bad tempered, I started huffing and puffing and saying to him, 'Eddy, man! Jus' fix de ting so we can finish an' I can go home!' Because by that time I knew that I was falling in love.

Of course Eddy was very calm and was saying, 'Don't worry, Marse, everything's fine, we'll be finished soon.' Which did nothing to make me feel better. In fact, I think his being so cool and collected just made me feel worse, and I'll admit I did get vexed with him. I've never done that before in my life – got impatient with a producer, especially not a good friend like Eddy Grant – but I'd never felt like this before, it was like I was in heat! All I could see was this man, Marcus, is gone and I can't imagine what is going to happen next.

We got finished pretty quickly because Eddy was scheduled to go to Jamaica to shoot the video for 'I Don't Wanna Dance', and we were both very pleased with the work we'd done. The main thing, though, was it was time for Miss Barrett to travel. Maybe it was a bit prophetic, but when Eddy took me to the airport I was all dressed up for First Class: in a white dress with flounces and a leather band made for my 24-inch waist, and a cap to match my bag, also in white. One of the stewardesses on the flight asked me if I was going to a wedding or was it my usual attire. When I replied 'The latter' little did I know that my wedding would be only months away.

I flew into Miami, got my car for the two-hour drive up to my house in Hobe Sound, and all that time the only thing on my mind was this man – I'm thinking, 'You wait! I'm going to show you exactly who you interfered with!' I got home, opened the door, threw my suitcases down in the hall, turned off the alarm and with my gloves still on, got on the phone! His sister Lucia answered, and I introduced myself and asked to speak to Scissors. Imagine what went through my head when she replied, '*Who*? There's nobody of that name here. You must have the wrong number!' Every Jamaican has a nickname, and Marcus had told me to ask for Size or Scissors, his nicknames; he told me that was what everybody knew him as. Everybody except his sister! So I said, 'No, sorry, Marcus!', which made sense to her, and she told me he'd gone jogging and she didn't know what time he would be back, did I want to call back? By this point I was starting to feel a bit deflated, then she said, 'Hang on, hang on, I can see him coming over the hill. Do you want to hold on?' Silly question!

So I was waiting on the line for what seemed like ages, a good five minutes, before Marcus took up the phone, out of breath and panting. I asked him how he was, and my second question was: 'When are you coming to West Palm Beach?' His response spoke of having to check the Greyhound bus schedule. I said, '*Greyhound bus?* How long is that going to take?' The Greyhound bus is so-o-o slow and uncomfortable, Americans call it 'riding the dog'! This trip could've taken a couple of days and I didn't have that much time to wait before I had to join up with the group again. I told him I'd book him a flight, let him know what time, then he could pick his ticket up at the airport and I'd meet him at West Palm. He sounded a bit hesitant and asked when would this be? 'Tomorrow!' I said. 'What would I be waiting around for?' And we both had a good laugh at that.

The next day came, I got dressed, bought Moet & Chandon and set it in the ice bucket to cool, and drove to the airport – I don't like to think I was rushing but I actually got pulled over by the police on the I-95 highway going down to the airport! When Marcus came out he was looking well rock star in green leather trousers – my favourite colour is green – carrying this duffel bag over his back, but he had this John Shaft era hat on, real pimp styling! I thought, '*That* is going to have to change', and 'advised' him that it was far too hot down here to wear hats like that.

By the time I'd driven home the champagne was nicely chilled, everything was set, we sat and we drank and we talked and we laughed and then we went to bed.

After that Marcus had to go back to New York for some gigs and I was off with Boney M., so we arranged to meet in London because he would go there a great deal and stay at his brother Sam's house. Although Marcus is Jamaican he had spent a long time in London – like me, he had practically grown up there – and he had known Eddy Grant since he was a teenager. Convenient as us being together in London was, it brought with it a huge consideration for me – what would Mama say on meeting Marcus?

It seems ridiculous, I was a grown woman of thirty-something, but up until then I hadn't brought any boyfriends home and because she and Wayne lived with me in London I didn't want to scare her by announcing, 'I am bringing a man into this situation.' I wanted to ease Marcus into it! To make matters worse, when we first arranged to meet in London Mama had been taken ill and was in hospital – she'd had a mini-stroke – so I definitely didn't want to shock her in any way. Marcus knew all about my situation, that I lived with my mother and son, but was still a bit shy about meeting them – that was very funny, because he was so self-assured in every other way. However, this may have been partly my fault because I believe I was so concerned about this going well I tried too hard to prepare him, telling him how Mama could be a bit funny with some people, and not to worry too much about any first meeting. I think I scared myself as well, which shows how seriously I was taking things – this wasn't just some man I happened to be dating!

He came to my house to meet Wayne, which was fine, but when I went to the hospital we decided he wouldn't come with me because we didn't want to make it look too blatant! I was very nervous when we stepped into the room together and I introduced him as my dear friend, but I needn't have worried at all – even I was surprised at how nicely she greeted him and I immediately felt more at ease. On the second evening I went by myself because I didn't want to overdo it with her, and instantly she asked me, 'Where's your friend?' All my tension vanished as I registered that Mama liked Marcus and after that they got on like a house on fire. So I told him, 'You don't have to stay at your brother's; my family love you too, you can stay here with me, we've got plenty of space and the bed is big enough!'

That's when our relationship started properly. Sometimes it could be a bit long distance because I was away so often with Boney M. and he was still touring with Eddy, plus he had his own gigs, usually in America. I missed him very much indeed when I was on the road, because Marcus, Mama, Wayne and I had quickly become such a good little family it was as if it had always been that way. He had just eased into our lives and it made me feel much more relaxed when I went away because I knew he was there to look after them; they were in the best possible hands. Mama really loved him, she trusted him completely, you just had to look at her around him and you could see that, while he and Wayne became so close they were like brothers. We would get away to Florida together as often as possible – once Marcus had to join up with Eddy somewhere in the US and left Hobe Sound so late he was late for the gig! Marcus said he had never been so embarrassed in his life, but Eddy took it well, he understood that we were young lovers therefore time will always slip by faster than you want it to.

Although we did spend a lot of time apart, we soon became sure enough of each other that we got married in August 1984, about a year and a half after meeting at those sessions in Barbados.

Until I got together with Marcus I was always a loner. I honestly enjoyed my own company and often preferred not to have anybody around me, especially with the madness that could go on when we were on the road. I was never lonely, I was a *loner* – I just did everything on my own! After I became half of Marcia and Marcus I still understood what it meant to be self-contained in particular circumstances, but I was finding out how much more fun it was to be part of a couple. Especially when I was away. Marcus had made me cassettes of all my favourite tracks, plus a few surprises he knew I would like, so I would set a bath, drink a glass or two of wine and play that music and think of him. If my schedule allowed it we would talk on the phone for at least an hour in the evening; sometimes he would phone in the morning to wake me up, just to say, 'Good morning.' This was high romance!

It gave what I was doing in Boney M. a bigger sense of purpose, too – of course I enjoyed being part of the group, but it was no longer an end in itself. Now I had a whole new life outside the group that I was really enjoying, and enjoying discovering. This was a new experience for me as I'd spent nearly all of my life looking after other people, and although I loved Mama and Wayne it was so great to have somebody who was going to look after me. I was like a little kid and I used to rush home every time a tour or recording sessions ended, looking forward to having some fun.

As my life outside Boney M. grew easier I found my approach to life within the band was changing. Although I never gave it anything other than my best, the group was no longer my only focus. I'd had solo ambitions from before I'd met Marcus – that's why I was at Eddy's in the first place – and he's a brilliant musician so of course the two of us were working on new material together. This was to be so exciting, side by side with this wonderful man, making the sort of music I had always dreamed about, and the only downside of it was, I believe, Frank was caught out by it a bit and he felt it was loosening his control of the group. This was a shame because in the beginning he was a nice man, always cracking jokes and it would have been good if he had been more supportive.

We had wanted to get married during the year we met, but the Boney M. schedule meant we couldn't book a date or if we did we'd have to cancel it so we ended up putting it off for about a year. We did have a lovely low key wedding at the Half Moon Hotel in Montego Bay, Jamaica. Marcus's brother Sam was best man, my father and brother who had never left Jamaica were there, Wayne and my niece Samantha who lived with us in London came over, a school friend of mine who had moved back to Jamaica was there – I hadn't seen her for almost a decade, what a reunion! – and Liz and her husband attended. Dagmar made my wedding dress, everybody stayed in the hotel's cottages and two guys from Boy George's band Culture Club came to the reception because they were on holiday at the hotel so we invited them along. It was a beautiful event and I was savouring every minute of it, then I got a telegram from Frank. Not the traditional wedding day congratulations but a summons to come back to Germany, *urgently*, for a TV show in Belgium. I had to start packing and leave immediately.

When I got there I realised it wasn't a big TV show at all, and our record company Hansa had never taken Belgium as seriously as the bigger European markets, so why bring me back from my wedding? Especially after we'd put the wedding off several times for the sake of Boney M. business. To this day we've never had a honeymoon – I know there are people who will say my whole life has been a honeymoon, but I didn't get a single day to lie down on a Jamaican beach with my new husband, and that simply wasn't right.

I suspect this was Frank sending a signal, to me especially, about who was in charge. You know what they say, that if you're not paranoid you're not paying attention but I used to feel this sort of thing had been happening on a smaller, petty level all the time. I suspect he manipulated the levels of our individual voices in the mix to keep us competitive about who was singing lead, which didn't worry me – it was all Boney M. – but having to think about this sort of thing all the time could get very wearing.

The difference now, though, was I had a collaborator, and not just somebody I could talk about it with, but somebody who had been around the music business and understood most of the personalities in it. Marcus would get quite upset about the stuff I told him – he's a bit more sensitive than me – and just having him to sound off to made it much easier to put up with so much of the stupid stuff that came my way. I just focused on the future and what I had planned for myself. The dynamic within the Boney M. Bubble had definitely shifted as a result of Marcia 'n' Marcus instead of just Marcia Barrett.

However that affected the group as a whole, personally I couldn't have been happier – I still am and I must say a big thank you to Eddy Grant for that. I'm sure the reason Marcus and I have been together for over thirty years is because we began as friends before we got intimate, and it was those sessions at Eddy's that allowed that to happen. The environment for those sessions in Barbados was so relaxed, but most importantly everybody there was a musician or part of the process. We were all the same, nobody was trying to show off or star-tripping, so we could all relate to each other like everyday people. Marcus approached me as a woman, not The Star From Boney M., so we could be very natural with each other and become friends, properly. That was something that hadn't happened that much since Boney M. became huge. It was so refreshing.

Nowadays we are still natural, we have been very good for each other as he is something of an introvert and I am a complete extrovert; I think I have brought him out of his shell a little bit and he has probably calmed me down! Most importantly, though, we are good, good friends. We hardly go out if it's not work related or somebody is visiting us, but we don't need to. We're happy enough in our apartment, we can talk about anything and we enjoy ourselves so much laughing so loudly at some of the jokes that are going on I'm sure the neighbours think there's twelve people in there! What makes us both laugh is when we're watching television and running a joke about something on the screen and we're deep into our Jamaican patois and I'm shrieking at Marcus, '*Look 'pon 'im! Look 'pon 'im, nuh man!*' Then the phone rings and as I pick it up I make up my face and say, very properly, 'Hello, Marcia Barrett . . .' Then if I look over at Marcus he'll crack up.

We're planning to go down to Jamaica some time soon to renew out wedding vows, all we need to do now is to sort out the honeymoon.

## Chapter Twelve

# 'We'd become our own tribute band'

It was sometime in 1990 I got back to Florida after time spent on the road in Europe, had my seven pieces of luggage brought into the hall and said to Marcus, 'This is it! *This is it! I've had it!* This is the end of Boney M. for me! Let's get into our stuff. Now begins my solo career.'

It was always my plan to return to the solo career I'd been enjoying before joining Boney M., indeed I had never expected to stay in the group as long as I did; I'd just got really lucky in how things turned out. I always knew at some time I'd be ready to call it a day and I had arrived at that moment. There was no single incident or blinding flash of light that pushed me into making that move, it was more like a set of circumstances that had been building up for quite a while, and although I had to think hard about it, it was a pretty easy decision to make.

The biggest factor in my deciding to move on was that Boney M. wasn't – moving on, that is. We were still out there performing live all over the world as a very popular touring act, but we had so little new material I felt as if time was standing still. In the three years between *Boonoonoonoos* and the *Christmas Album* in 1981 and *Ten Thousand Lightyears* in 1984 we didn't do any recording; then we didn't go into the studio from the *Eyedance* album in 1985 until the single 'Everybody Wants to Dance Like Josephine Baker' in 1989, a record that wasn't even produced by Frank – and Liz was long gone by that time. While I loved performing on stage, without the fresh recordings there were so few new songs being added to the repertoire. This got worse after *Eyedance*, as it didn't produce the big hits of previous albums so there wasn't a huge demand to feature anything from it in the live act so we were just running over the same stuff. It was going stale for us and I wasn't enjoying it as much as earlier because I couldn't see any progression for us – there were times when it seemed as if we had become our own tribute band!

It was also after *Eyedance* that Frank decided he wasn't going to produce any new Boney M. material, but it was a while before he actually announced that he had *left* Boney M. On the surface this makes no sense as he wasn't actually in the group, but it meant it now became all about the back catalogue, which we carried on selling because we kept it alive by continuing to tour. During the 1980s alone Frank put out seven different compilation albums – *The Best of Ten Years . . . The Fantastic Boney M. . . . The Greatest Hits of All Time . . . The Beautiful Ballads of . . .* and so on – all remixes or repackages of the old stuff. With the exception of the first one he released, *The Magic of Boney M.*, which went Top Twenty everywhere, they sold negligibly. That didn't matter, though, because as the producer of all the recordings and the co-writer of so many of them, whatever they sold he stood to earn a relatively large amount.

This is why Frank has never objected to the different manifestations of Boney M. that have been doing the rounds since the four of us split up – in fact, he granted permission for Liz,

Maizie, Bobby and myself to each use the name, and nobody has had any problems using the original songs in their stage sets. People have often assumed that if a group of three black women and one black guy was using the Boney M. name they must be official or they would have been slapped with a lawsuit.

I always knew that we were making money for Frank, and as long as it was benefiting me and my long-term goals then fair enough. I understood the deal, but as time went on it became less and less appealing. What I really wanted to do was go home to carry on with my solo project with my husband, writing the songs that I know will take me forward.

It was the lack of new material that, for me, was the biggest issue with my continuing in Boney M., as times had changed massively since we first burst on to the scene with 'Daddy Cool'. There had been such a movement away from the kind of pop we had started out doing that our live show was appearing very dated. Everybody knows the public's tastes change, and the early 1980s would have been the perfect time to update our sound, but it seemed Frank wasn't interested – maybe he saw us as a moment in time and moving on would mean another group.

I believe this left him distracted, which is why *Eyedance* doesn't seem to have the energy our other albums had. The cover versions like 'Dreadlock Holiday' and 'Ma Cherie Amour' were a pleasure to sing, but there were no hits from that album, so I look back on it as being the real beginning of the end – Boney M. aren't even getting into the German Top Twenty!

One of the worst things about that whole situation was when Frank took his decision not to produce Boney M. any longer he didn't tell me – there was no discussion or group meeting or anything like that. If he'd come to me as a lead singer and the voice of Boney M. to say, 'Well, Marcia, I'm going to pack it in, I've had enough and I want to do my own thing,' then I could have made plans accordingly. Instead, he just stopped doing it. We were busy with the live work and didn't even start thinking about anything like that for a while, then I'm pretty sure I either read about it or was told by somebody else. In a way, it wasn't such a surprise, as Frank's interest had definitely been on the wane since *Ten Thousand Lightyears*, but it would have been nice to have been told properly after all we'd been through together, and, ultimately, all Boney M. had done for him.

Looking back, I can see that there were two distinct sides to the group – the recording Boney M. and the touring Boney M. With Frank gone we had to take charge of the studio side of things for the live side to have any chance. Even five years after our biggest hits we were playing stadiums and huge arenas, so we had an audience we knew could sustain us, and I could see a future if we put out some new material that would make us relevant again without compromising who we were. I am certain we could have built our own empire after Frank Farian, with room for solo projects as well – I always figured I could have a solo career parallel to Boney M. Although I didn't see myself being in Boney M. for ever, at that point I don't think I was ready to quit because I felt there was still a potential for us to move into the next phase. I thought the others did too, but it didn't turn out quite like that.

Marcus and I had written five tracks that would be just right for Boney M., they were damn near finished productions and, we believed, ticked all the boxes for what the group needed. I told the others I had some songs I believed were suitable for us and called a meeting at a hotel in London for us to listen to them and discuss what we should do with them or where we needed to be going next. *Everybody* was late for the meeting, and when they did finally get there they were all so non-committal it was as if they'd been forced against their wills to listen, then couldn't be bothered to give anything any thought. It was all, 'Hmmmm . . . Oh . . . OK . . .' Nobody made any constructive comment or talked about us going into the studio or making any alterations. I was very disappointed, especially with Liz, because we were the lead singers and I thought she would want to carry on the sound and update the music without Frank Farian. None of them were writing, so I figured it was down to Marcus and me to at least get the ball rolling. But nothing. I saw no interest in anything.

I know I would say this, because we wrote them, but they were very good songs, and even if there had been a couple of duds in there we presented five and they couldn't all have been of no interest. Why I was so shocked at the reaction – or *lack* of reaction – was because I knew they wanted to find some new material, so I now believe they couldn't really find that new material from anybody within the group. I'm sure they would have been happy to accept songs from a stranger, but maybe they were fearful of giving a colleague too much power and altering the dynamics. Writing credits of M. Barrett & M. James would definitely have caused a stir!

Whatever their reasons, it was such a shame because not even having a discussion about what sort of direction Boney

M. ought to be taking held the group back at a time when we should have been striking out for ourselves. Liz left Boney M. soon after this, and like Frank she didn't tell me. The first I knew about it was when she didn't appear for a gig. We were doing a show, ironically, in a group of islands near the Seychelles called the Reunion Islands, and she never arrived, so the guys we had managing us arranged for a last-minute replacement – Madeleine Davis, an American soul singer – and she completed the tour and stayed with us as part of the group.

One thing we had learned post-Frank was to get representation, and we did a management deal with Simon Napier-Bell, the guy who was managing Wham! at the time. Simon was very good, he knew we needed to start recording again and put us together with the writer/producer Barry Blue to do the single 'Everybody Wants to Dance Like Josephine Baker'. Barry was perfect for us; he'd had a hit with 'Dancing on a Saturday Night' in the 1970s, he had written for Lynsey De Paul and produced Heatwave's 'Mind Blowing Decisions' and 'Boogie Nights', so he perfectly understood pop music, pop soul and the area we needed to be in. Recording that single was a complete joy – I had practically forgotten what it was like to make a record without either Frank or Liz and I loved it. Madeleine came down in time to do some ad-libbing in French for the song's outro, and we both sang the B-side, 'Custer Jammin'' from top to bottom, all the melody and all the harmonies.

When the song was mixed we were all really keen on it and advanced copies were being well received by the radio and the press. Because it was recorded in England and Simon had so many connections in the UK industry it was sent out there first and everybody started to like it. We were suddenly doing a lot of interviews on the radio shows, in which presenters were telling us things like, 'Wow! Boney M., long time no hear . . .' and 'At last you're back, with a hit on your hands . . .' All this was really lovely, then it came time for the record to go on sale.

There we are, Bobby, Maizie and myself, all pumped up for our first hit in years, and Madeleine looking forward to her first hit with Boney M., and we're told it's been pulled from the shelves. We were told that Frank has stopped the single going on sale, as legally he is the only person allowed to produce Boney M. He was quite happy to have us tour to sell his greatest hits packages, which he continued to use our voices and images on, but he wasn't going to let anybody else produce and make any money. Maybe he expected us to just carry on touring or sit there and rot, and while Simon Napier-Bell was undoubtedly a very good manager, he wasn't able to get the deal we needed. Up until that point I don't think he realised what he would be up against.

Coming after the group's reaction to the songs Marcus and I had written, this really was the end for me – there could be no moving forward with Boney M. Life on the road wasn't too much fun by then either: Bobby's behaviour was wilder than ever, he was very unpredictable and was always getting in heated rows, sometimes even fights. Madeleine had been really great when she first joined, she had been a pleasure to go on the road with as she could be so charming and so funny, but even she got caught up with Bobby's loud scenes in hotel lobbies and airports when the mood turned.

The Boney M. I found myself a member of in 1990 was very different to the Boney M. I joined in 1975. For me it had totally run its course and I couldn't see why I should stay as part of it when I had a husband waiting in our little demo studio in our lovely house in Florida and a pile of songs ready to prove what we could do.

I have never looked back or felt sorry that I left Boney M. when I did, or felt that I stayed too long, the only real regret I feel is that the legacy of what was for a while one of the biggest groups in the world has been handled so badly. After I left, the others went their separate ways and Maizie, Bobby and Liz all started their own different Boney M.s. These usually had Frank's blessing, although sometimes he'd change his mind on who was authorised. I didn't get involved in any of that because I wanted to be a solo performer: the whole point of quitting Boney M. had been for exactly that – to quit Boney M.! The last thing I wanted to do was to carry on in some sort of embarrassing, cut-price version of the group. However, I was damn sure that I was going to use being in Boney M. to my advantage as a solo singer. And why not? I'd contributed as much as any of us to the group's success. I took the best from both worlds and have always billed myself as 'Marcia Barrett of Boney M.', obviously a solo performer, but equally obviously once a part of Boney M.

I would never have begrudged Maizie, Bobby or Liz making a living off the Boney M. name, but I will stand by what I've said about some of the manifestations with the more, er, *tenuous* links to 'the Original Boney M.'. However, I can't say I was entirely happy about three or four Boney M.s criss-crossing the world and competing for the same audiences. I still get annoyed about it these days, when I also see the totally bogus Boney M.s are taking gigs just because they go out so cheap, and this is more than just an objection on financial grounds.

Naturally, if there are several groups on the circuit all claiming to be the genuine article it is plain confusing for anybody looking to buy a ticket, but more than that I think it has been destroying the Boney M. legacy. Most obviously if fans go to see one of the so-called genuine Boney M.s and the show is put on cheaply or the performances aren't up to scratch they'll have a bad view of Boney M. as a whole, not the individuals who were putting on that show. It associates the name with nothing more than trying to make a quick buck at the expense of the fans. Also, while there are so many different line-ups at the same time, the critics who have claimed we're a made-up group are saying, 'I told you so!' It means people might not take the genuine Boney M. seriously, which I think is a situation that has detracted from the work Liz and I had put in at the studio and what we had all achieved on stage. Nobody being sure who is in these groups, and the fact there are so many of them, means they appear to be interchangeable, which, more than ever, gives substance to the myth that it was all about Frank and the rest of us were his anonymous puppets.

I also believe the ridiculous amount of compilations and reissues and remixes and Christmas albums Frank has put out harms our legacy: during the last thirty years he has released sixteen hits packages and six Boney M. Christmas albums. Usually, there's a couple of tracks different here or a remix or two there or an extended version of a particularly big hit – just enough to attract a bit of attention and maybe sell to the diehard fans. I think this is over-releasing and again it is the group that gets talked about in terms of being money-grubbing.

Back then, though, I think I was just so grateful to leave it all behind and get stuck into the next phase of my life, because when you consider my beginnings all of it was a truly fantastic journey.

*Part Two*

# ROOTS

## Chapter Thirteen

# 'Ours was a rural existence'

The first time I can remember hearing music and actually being affected by it, was when I was four or five and lived in a tiny village called Mount Charles, high up in the Jamaican Blue Mountains. We lived on a hill and quite often in the early evening, from a house up above us, there would be this rich, deep music ringing out across the whole village. I had no idea what it was at first; I would be asking, 'What's that? What's that?', and the older children would look at me like I didn't know anything and tell me, 'It's *music*!' Which of course meant nothing to me, so I probably just assumed the word 'music' must mean 'something magical that just appears'.

Many of the bigger kids used to walk up the hill to be closer to those sounds. When I joined them and grew bold enough to peek in through the window, I began to grasp what was going on. There was a guy playing the organ, a small upright organ about the size of a piano, with bellows that had to be pumped with a foot pedal giving it such a lovely bass sound, reminding me of church. Watching him, as he rocked backwards and forwards working the pedal as he played, we kids were transfixed.

Even when I knew it wasn't magic, I was still captivated by that playing, because this was pure music – not singing like in church or in school, just the melodies floating through the open window. I'm sure that's where I got my love of melodies, because all through the Boney M. days and right up until today, the first thing I hear in a song, whether I'm listening to it or writing it, is the melody; I'll worry about the lyrics or the hooks later. The man who played that organ gave lessons, and later my auntie arranged for her children, my cousins, to learn to play, but as my mother couldn't afford it I would be left behind. That was probably the most upsetting experience I had to bear as a child, as I loved that music so much! When the others went off to their music lessons, I would go down into the gully in the backyard, where I cried and I cried and I cried. It didn't do me any good, though, except maybe to teach me that if there's no way you can shine instantly then keep it in your mind and hope to shine one fine day – something that has remained with me my entire life.

I knew about singing much earlier than that, but the funny thing was I didn't consciously connect it with the music I heard coming down the hill. Maybe that was because singing was just something I did, so it didn't seem that special. Together with all the other kids, I used to sing in church and sing in school, so it was everyday. At that young age I loved singing in church, I didn't understand the prayers and the sermons, so I would really look forward to the hymns because that was my one chance to sing with a congregation of grown-ups, and I could join in as loudly as I liked. All of us kids felt the same way and we'd be waiting for the moment that the big pipe organ would start up, we'd take deep breaths, glance around at each other grinning and, '*Rock of ages, cleft for me* . . .' That was always such a thrill.

Beyond the singing I always enjoyed the whole church thing,

because as a young girl growing up in the country in Jamaica, church was a big part of life. It was a ritual to so many Jamaicans, so on Sunday absolutely everybody would put on their best gear and come out to church, where they would look so nice and act so polite. It seemed like that day was their release from the trials and tribulations of the rest of the week. This filtered down to us kids, so provided we didn't mess up our good clothes it was as if the adults were more relaxed with us, and church was at the centre of all that, and therefore one of the highlights of our week.

We kids used to sing in school too, and as far back as infants we all used to sing and dance to nursery rhymes, some of which were English and some of which were traditional Caribbean. That was where I got to know 'Brown Girl in the Ring' – it's a hundred-year-old Jamaican children's song and we would dance round in a circle, holding hands and singing, with one of us in the middle. *Show me your motion* meant the child in the middle had to do their best dance moves; the next verse of the nursery rhyme was *Skip across the ocean*, and the child in the middle picked a partner from the ring to dance with; then that child stayed on to become the next brown girl in the ring.

That was such a popular singing game at infants' school, but it wasn't something you'd do as an older child and I never came across it as a child in England, so I hadn't heard it for years, and then I was presented with it to sing as a Boney M. number! At first, as an adult, I felt silly singing this childish song, but once I got past that I got to love it all over again. Right up to today it's still in my set and it takes me right back to Jamaica when I was five or six, so I always feel really happy singing and clapping and acting like a little kid again.

We sang in elementary school, too, and we'd make music as a kind of percussion orchestra with triangles, tambourines and little drums, which for me was great as I had missed out on those organ lessons. We'd do performances at school for the other children, then at Christmas we'd go carol singing, the whole group from school setting off early in the morning to go round to different places. It was then, when I was seven or eight, I got my first taste of showbiz proper, and I loved it!

The choir from my school had been invited to go to the Ward Theatre in Kingston to do a little performance – or as we called it in Jamaica, a *pantomime*. This was a really big deal, because the Ward is a great big theatre, dating back from colonial days, very grand and very plush inside. We were all so excited, but when my teacher, Mrs Cohen, was choosing the kids who would be part of it and giving out the instruments, I had a huge gumboil. My mouth was badly swollen up on one side, the other kids were sniggering at me and I was so vain, even back then, I tried to hide at the back of the group of children. She went through the whole class, got to me last of all and said, 'Marcia Barrett, you are going to conduct.' My first thought was, 'I can't go on stage at the Ward Theatre looking like this! What will happen?'

I went out in front of the class for the rehearsal at school, they started to sing, and to my mind – my seven-year-old mind! – it sounded dead, with no feeling. So I thought, 'Right, let's get into this properly!' and I led the singing, 'Oh we can play on the big bass drum . . .', urging them on by waving my hands, just as Mrs Cohen had shown me. And it worked! Any of them that were still laughing at how my face looked stopped and they really got into the performance.

148

The day of the show at the Ward was a day of the highest excitement among us kids, an open-back truck picked us up and drove us down the hillside to the capital. I was still very nervous and had to tell myself, 'Go out there and do what is expected of you. It doesn't matter how you look or how you feel, that will only last for a little time, but you can't let your fellow performers down, or the people who have come to see you.' I don't know how I knew that, I just did, and years later it would become something I would never forget. At the Ward Theatre, though, I knew what my teacher expected of me and up there on that big stage, at seven years old, with this big gumboil, I gave it everything.

When we finished and I turned round to face the audience and curtsey, I'd forgotten all about my swollen mouth, and the people stood up to give us a standing ovation. That was it for me – an experience I would never forget, and even though I'm sure I didn't realise it, my future path was being plotted.

Of course I had no idea that anybody could do music as a job and make money from it, singing was something people did for enjoyment or spiritual uplift – in Jamaica people are always singing as they go about their daily tasks. I had no concept of what music was beyond singing and the organ playing up the hill or in the church. This might sound strange, considering I was in Jamaica, coming up to the end of the 1950s, when to the outside world the whole island was going music mad, but I lived in the country. Although my village was only about ten miles up from Kingston, the capital might as well have been on the other side of the world – the truck ride to the Ward Theatre took over an hour, most of us kids had never been to the city and wouldn't go again for many years.

Back then, as indeed now, rural Jamaica was nothing like Kingston where there was hustle and bustle and music all around, with the radios, the jukeboxes and the sound systems. It was as if Kingston was pure music on every corner, all the time, but up in the mountains life was much quieter. When I was young, there was hardly any mains electricity up in the hills, some people had it, but it didn't come up as far as Mount Charles. We had oil lamps and bottle torches, which were bottles half filled with water and kerosene oil with a twist of newspaper for a wick, then we might use candles to go to bed and people cooked on wood fires or wood-burning stoves. Batteries were so expensive, and the way the people were up there, if anybody had a transistor radio they would just keep it to hear the news or to listen to a boxing match. There were no jukeboxes or Rediffusion cable boxes up there, so music for pleasure was very rare. That's why the organ playing sounded so sweet.

I was born in Old Harbour, in the Church Pen district, which is about twenty miles west of Kingston in the parish of St Catherine, and we – my mother and younger sister Dorrett – moved up to Mount Charles when I was very young. Mount Charles is part of a district called Mavis Bank, that was also the name of our nearest town, which was quite a way down the hill – that was where the police station and the post office were, where I as the oldest child had to go and pick up the letters once a week. It was a real countrified situation, not too far from Blue Mountain Peak, the highest point in Jamaica, from where, on a clear day and with really sharp eyes, we could see Cuba, which is only ninety miles away.

My family went up there to live with my Aunt Sodahl because money was so tight. Mama could barely afford to keep us: she and our father, Mr Barrett, were never married and she was bringing us up by herself. He was a police officer stationed in Old Harbour and was already married. Mama knew this yet still had this on-off affair with him, resulting in us girls, and although she gave us his name, I had no relationship with him and never knew him as anything other than a visitor. I was about eight the first time I properly remember seeing him; he was looking very dashing in his full uniform, all crisply pressed. I think Mama was very excited to see him, and she had built up the visit so much that when he appeared in the yard we went running out of the house to greet him, shouting, 'Daddy! Daddy!' – I even fell down and chipped my tooth. There was no doubt he could be charming and it wasn't difficult to see why Mama had fallen for him, but the other side of that was, as a police officer, he had business all over the district so he had sweethearts and other children everywhere. He didn't take any responsibility for us and he never paid my mother anything to support us.

In Mount Charles we went to live in my aunt's yard, which was the country equivalent of the tenement yard in Kingston that Bob Marley used to sing about – three or four little houses, with their front doors facing on to a shared open space. It was communal living in its fullest sense, as everybody would talk to each other out there, making for an atmosphere that seemed as if people had all the time in the world. My cousins, my auntie or other relatives were always popping round, just as we'd be in their houses – the situation at home was always very open.

The kids were usually in that shared space too, they would play there, they would be put in the tin bath out there, and there was always somebody to keep an eye on them, or to discipline them if they got out of order. Nobody cared whose kids were whose and all the adults would take responsibility for all the children. For us kids it meant there was always a grown-up around if you needed one, but on the other hand you could never get away with any sort of mischief! Any adult who saw you would tell you off there and then, and your parents would know about it long before you got home, and the worst crime any child could commit was to pass an adult on the street and not greet them properly. If Mr Williams didn't get a 'Good morning, Mr Williams, how are you?' you might as well not bother to go home!

Back then, in a yard like that there was hardly any crime, not simply because nobody had anything worth stealing, but because nobody really had anything more than anybody else. At that time nearly everybody in Jamaica was poor, but *country* poor was far worse than Kingston poor, and it meant people used to share. There would usually be a fire for cooking burning in the communal space, everybody would contribute what they had, and they could all eat out of it. It was the same if somebody was cooking in their house, they didn't need to be related to you to give you a hot meal and you would do the same for them.

There were a lot of our cousins in my aunt's yard and she used to feed us all with what she could get, which was mostly good Jamaican food: ackee and saltfish, dumplings, fried dumplings, cornmeal dumplings, fritters, green banana, yam . . . Sometimes there might be some meat or chicken, so each of us would get a little twig of that and we would always save it until the last bite. Or if not you would save your dumpling until last

– we kids used to love dumplings, making them as well as eating them, mixing the water into the white flour or cornmeal then kneading the dough with our fists! We would eat everything around the dumpling, everything on the plate that wasn't so interesting – the vegetables like chow chow or pumpkin or corn – but then you couldn't sit back and savour your dump-ling, you had to watch out! Another kid, or sometimes even a big person, could look at it, ask you, 'Why is this still on your plate?' and take it up before you could get to it! Once you'd saved it, you had to eat it quick!

Meals were the only time I noticed a bit of discrimination, as sometimes I'd look round at other children's plates and see they had a whole dumpling when I only had half – *half a dumpling*! I'd be outraged! It was as I got older I realised that those were times when there wasn't enough flour so my aunt was making sure her own kids got enough to eat before she worried about me. I won't say I was ever completely happy about it, but as I got older I understood.

From a tender age all of us kids had chores to do; that's just how it is in Jamaica: every child will be given their household duties, although sometimes I did think that Auntie was working me and my cousins too hard. From when I was about six or seven, when I came home from school I'd hang up my school uniform, then the first thing I would do is sweep the floor. That was important because most of the places we lived had a clay floor and even if it had hardened like wood or there were stones set in it, there was always loose dirt to be swept up. Next came scouring the cooking pots and pans with handfuls of ashes from the previous day's fire – these ashes were like our Ajax out there, and we would use that before the pots were washed with soap. After that, if there was a fire to be made, I'd go outside and bring in the firewood and kindling to spark it up. Finally, if any of the animals that would be round the yard needed food, like the pig or the chickens, I would have to see to that. Also, my mother was a seamstress so I'd have to help her and it was my job to do the bobbin for her sewing machine, winding whatever thread she would be using around the spindle by hand. This was so boring, and all the while I was doing it I would be thinking how, when I grew up, I didn't want *anything* to do with this . . . I didn't want to learn to sew anything . . . I didn't want to crochet . . . nothing! To this day you will not get me with a needle in my hand!

Sure, these duties were demanding, but most days I would get to play a little in the yard, then be called in if I had to have a bath – an open-air bath, in the big washing pan. First I would have to catch the water from the standpipe in a bucket, cold water, then we kids would stand in the washing pan and get washed down. All of us together – we didn't know any different. After that it would be time for bed, and at one place I lived there were five of us kids sleeping in one bed when we would have to be arranged: this one sleeps here, that one sleeps there, this one sleeps this way!

On other days my aunt would send my cousin and I to wash the clothes up at the Yallahs River, which ran through the mountains, we'd walk up there carrying pans of clothes to wash and then spread out on the rocks to dry. That wasn't too bad, but Auntie had a boyfriend who wore these khaki trousers to work every day and they had to be starched and ironed, which was my responsibility. I wouldn't simply have starch from a packet, we'd have to make it ourselves extracting it from the cassava root by grating and crushing it and soaking it in water – it was the same starch we used to make bammy flatbread and tapioca pudding. It was serious stuff, though – once I'd washed those trousers in that I could iron them as stiff as a plank of wood. Although ironing was an adventure in itself, as with no electricity the irons were either hollow and filled with coal or solid iron, each of which would have to be heated up until it was nearly red hot, then I was ready to go. The ironing had to be done by the open fire, so not only was the iron really heavy but everything was dangerously hot and I was only seven or eight years old! I used to do it, though; I'd take pride in the fact those trousers would come out with creases like knives, and I honestly believe it was because I could cope with that that I was able to deal with what would be thrown at me later in life.

Because ours was a rural existence, we kids would also have farm-type chores to do. We'd have to tie out the goats if they were up in the fields above the village, and go up to the farm-land way up in the mountains to where some cultivation had been done. This was known as going to 'wood bush', where we'd pick peas – green peas, gungo peas and red peas – and the other produce that grew up there. What we'd bring home would be our provisions, for the people in the yard to live on for a week or two, then we'd go up for more. Sometimes there would be a surplus that would be taken to Coronation Market in Kingston, when a truck would come by picking up people and their produce in the surrounding area. Mostly, though, this was the definition of subsistence farming, and it was how people survived in the country communities all over the island.

Some of the children would pick coffee too, because up there we were actually in the clouds or above them, which is where Jamaican Blue Mountain coffee grows – it's one of the best coffees in the world, and that is supposedly because it grows at such an altitude. Although on a very small scale, the coffee-picking was much more of a commercial thing, because it was such a valuable crop most of it was sold on by whoever the kids were picking it for, which would be their parents or maybe a small farmer.

The hardest part of going to wood bush was collecting the firewood we'd use for cooking or heating water at home, as the only way we could get up the mountains was by foot – there were no roads that high up, and no vehicles even if there had been. When we gathered the wood we would have to walk all day with it on top of our heads, which could be a real pain – *literally* – because the wood was so heavy and we only had these things called *kattas* protecting the tops of our heads. The original *kattas* were pieces of protective cloth, but we used makeshift ones, constructed on the spot from big leaves or the wispy branches of the trees and they were even more uncomfortable than the cloth version.

By the time we'd get back, it would be twilight, just in time to have an outdoor bath. We really needed it because the worst thing about being in the field all day is that the grass used to get all over you, so your skin used to itch like hell. After that, we'd only have time for something to eat before bedtime; then it was up just after dawn the next morning to do it all again.

## Chapter Fourteen

# 'Kids are more adaptable than people realise'

I moved around a great deal as a child, sometimes being sent to live in situations without my mother, because in Jamaica at that time it wasn't unusual for children to be brought up, temporarily, by relatives or family friends who were in a better situation financially. People seemed more inclined to help each other back then: everybody was striving to make a living and as the island knew Independence was just around the corner, there was a real optimism about being a *Jamaican*. People wanted the whole island to be doing well. As for the kids themselves – I think most of us looked on it as a bit of an adventure. I honestly believe children are far more down-to-earth about such matters than they are given credit for; mostly they're not stupid and although they may not know the whole story, they know what's going on. I knew things were harder for Mama because I didn't have a father at home and she had to play both roles for her daughters. I trusted my mother, and while I may have been too young to be fully aware of the circumstances, at no point did I feel as if I was being abandoned or sent away – I knew I had to exist and if this is what it took then so be it.

We were taken from Mount Charles back to Church Pen, where we lived in another yard with another auntie. This was a big yard, full of kids – with my sister and I and our cousins there were ten of us and we used to sleep five in one bed, five in the other, which could get pretty interesting! But ends still couldn't meet and Mama thought it would be best for us girls if I went to Kingston and Daddy took Dorrett to live with a relative of his in Savanna La Mar in Westmoreland at the other end of the island. Mama simply said to me, 'All right, your godmother is going to bring you up for a while, so you can go to school in Kingston.' I could have looked at that and said, 'What choice did I have?' and simply resigned myself to it, but I chose to be positive. I was determined to make the most of going to school in Jamaica's capital and of staying with my godmother, Miss Sylvia Sinclare, who was a very refined black woman.

Staying there was a very nice experience and I didn't think she was so upscale just because I'd come from the country! Really, Miss Sinclare was kind of hoity-toity, but in a good way as it was class all the way and everything had to be perfect: she had a very nice house and I had to help her keep it that way; I had to go to school; I had to have my afternoon sleep; I had to have good table manners when we sat at the table to eat; and so forth . . . It was from Miss Sinclare I learned how it was worth taking that extra effort to make sure things are classy. This stayed with me for ever – it's still there – and it made a real difference with Boney M., because we stayed above so many of the other bands of the day by keeping things classy all the time. I know some of those album sleeves might seem a bit much now, but back in the seventies that was pure class – I promise you!

We lived just across the road from the school that I would be going to, Central Branch School, so it was a much easier jour-ney to school than I had been used to, and I fitted in with the

Kingston girls just as effortlessly. This last point was far from given as – especially among girls – children from the country could get a hard time in the capital, but then I never considered myself any sort of bumpkin so I wasn't going to be intimidated by anybody! What I particularly liked about Central Branch School was that everybody had to wear full uniform. I loved wearing that uniform and always made sure I sat properly on those pleats in the skirt so they wouldn't get crushed. Even today I still love to see little kids in school uniform; I have to stop and look because it brings back all these memories of my childhood. I think it was important, too, so there was no competition with our appearance, meaning we could be focused on our school work. I still think children attending school should wear uniform so they can concentrate on their education and not on fashion or style, which will come later as they get older and ready for the world. It must have worked for me, as I did well there, and my school report was good all round, but really I had no choice in the matter – with my godmother Sylvia Sinclare, doing well was the *only* option!

I stayed with Miss Sinclare for between eighteen months and two years, Mama would come and visit when she could, which wasn't all that often but when she came she'd bring fruit and produce from Church Pen. It wasn't much more than a token, as although Mama didn't have much she wanted Miss Sinclare to know she was doing her best to help with my keep. One day she came with a basket of yam and banana and cocoa on her head, as a present for my godmother, and the two ladies quarrelled. To this day I don't know what caused it, but my godmother could be so strict it wouldn't be too difficult to fall out with her. I heard them arguing, then Mama said, 'That's it!

Give me mi pickney *now*! I'll take her right away!' And she did! I was going back to Church Pen right then and there – never mind school or anything else!

Being tossed around like that is just what things were like, and while I'm sure such a practice today would be thought of as leaving a child seriously traumatised, what I remember most vividly is that Miss Sinclare wanted all of my pretty dresses back! She was a seamstress, like Mama, and would sew for me, thus out of school I wore the best dresses among the other girls of my age. But when Mama took me back to Church Pen, except for the one I was wearing I had to leave all of them behind.

After a few days in my auntie's yard back in Church Pen, I was moved again to yet another guardian and again a very different situation. She had a shop that sold all manner of produce for day-to-day consumption: hard dough bread, flour, cornmeal, sugar, sweets, saltfish . . . Her husband had a good job too, with the district authority, so they were relatively well off and my life was more comfortable than it might have been. There was always enough to eat, and I particularly remember the salted mackerel that was stored in a barrel of pickle in the shop – delicious! It was a real treat to be allowed to take one, which I used to think was a bit nuts, because other kids would ask for sweets when I wanted salted fish! It's stayed with me, though, because I still love that sort of fish today.

In spite of all this moving about I always did well in school, I was good at sports, I was a prefect, I carried myself well, I worked hard at my studies and, probably because of that, the teachers seemed to like me. I used to love school, too, maybe because I didn't have such a stable home life and school was a constant, wherever it was they were really all the same and I knew what to expect. Or maybe it was because of the other kids. I always was a bit of a loner by nature – I still am – but in school, in a class of twenty or so other kids of your age, you had to mingle.

I was well behaved, I was polite and didn't answer back because that was how Mama and the other adults in the yard had brought me up: I always tried to look clean and well turned out, and I only ever had one fight. It was in Old Harbour, I was nine years old or so, and this one girl was always trying to provoke me – 'You and your big mout', Marcia Barrett! Is who yuh t'ink you are?' *Needle, needle, needle!* I would never say anything, I'd just mind my business, because my biggest worry was my lovely uniform, a white blouse and grey skirt – I knew if I fought it would get crushed.

But this particular afternoon I'd had enough, so I faced her up in the street just outside the school, not even knowing if I was going to fight her. Straight away the other kids formed a ring round us like at one of those cock fights, then the other girl pushed me. That was the last thing she should have done, because it seemed to trigger something and I just thought, 'You've been taking too much from her, now you've got to be strong and *put her down on the floor*!' I flew at her, and we went down on the ground, got up, crossed the road, up on the banking, all over the place, with a couple of dozen kids crowding round us as it went. Eventually, when she was down with her skirt torn up and everything, the kids shouting, 'Marcia! Marcia!' I knew it was all over and I said, 'All right, now you've got yours! So leave me alone!'

That was the first and the last fight I've ever been in, I thought, 'Never again.' It was just too vulgar! I was a peaceful person then and I'm a peaceful person now, but sometimes, especially if you're not guilty, you have to go back into your reserve. And then I was ready to fight. Of course there was another reason not to fight – my guardian gave me such a beating when I got home. 'How dare you come home looking like this . . .'

School in rural Jamaica was another good example of how kids are more adaptable than people tend to realise: the school in Kingston may have been just over the road, but in Mount Charles and Church Pen it was a completely different matter. In Mount Charles my elementary school was in Mavis Bank, and that was about an hour's walk for us kids, there and back, which was cross country and involved crossing rivers on the way. These weren't huge rivers, but they were bigger than streams and the beds were full of holes that could sink a little kid up to their waist! At some crossings there were stepping stones, which we used to call jumping the rocks and that was a lot of fun, unless you slipped! On the crossings with no stones, you couldn't always predict where the holes in the river bed were, so we always tried to be careful to cross in the exact same places.

When I lived in Church Pen the walk to school was even longer, about four or five miles, it was made easier, though, because it was mostly on pavement, however that school had its own problem because my mother couldn't afford the school lunch. It cost what was called a 'quatti' in Jamaica – a penny ha'penny – but that was too much for Mama to pay for myself and Dorrett, so a lady who had a little shop a couple of minutes' walk from the school promised my mother she would feed us

– Mama must have been paying her something. She kept back some of the cornmeal porridge she would sell at breakfast time to give to us on the way to school, which we would eat for lunch. She would give it to us in an Ovaltine tin and by the middle of the day it was so cold it had set hard and we'd have to shake it out of the tin with our spoons before we could eat it! That was our lunch, which filled us comfortably, and even with that and the long walks we still did well in school – you just have to get on with it.

If I look at it from the outside – like now, or when I was in Boney M. – those early years seem very hard indeed, but when I was living that life as a little kid, I didn't know there was anything different. Nobody realises they are poor if everybody around them is too; you literally don't know what you're missing and as everybody I knew was in the same boat: that was my reality. Just like the long walks – in the country in Jamaica everybody else walked everywhere too! I worked very hard, with both my chores and my schoolwork, because that was what everybody else in the yard did and, as was illustrated when we went to wood bush to pick peas, if you didn't work you didn't eat.

So it didn't seem so bad. I've never been in any way resentful over my childhood or even had any regrets; I've always looked back on those times and been glad I had those experiences at the age I did. I learned that not having much to live on doesn't have to form a person's character, poverty might dictate what you are but it doesn't have to decide *who* you are. Where I grew up people might have been poor but they were still as proud as anybody else and conducted themselves accordingly. I learned to keep my clothes clean and pressed, because it didn't matter if your clothes were a little threadbare you still had to wash and iron them ready to wear – as a kid there could be no excuse for having a crumpled school uniform.

Those years taught me that you not only have to work hard just to get by, but you have to work harder still if you want to be special, and I applied that to every job I've had. Having lived in that sort of poverty keeps you down to earth, too, as you know what the other side of being a star and travelling First Class really is – you know that the cold cornmeal porridge that has set in the tin or five kids sleeping in one bed is never too far away! Also, in the time when my husband and I seemed to be struggling, I knew things weren't really that bad and we would be able to recover.

Living in the yards teaches you about respect for everybody, because you understand that we all have to contribute to how the whole community gets along, so nobody is more important than anybody else. Which means that, at my age and at this stage of my career, I can't look down my nose on anybody – just because they may not be so ambitious or didn't get my chances in life, whatever they do it doesn't make them any less than me, I'll respect everybody. All of this, I believe, is largely due to the way I was brought up.

Even moving about from place to place helped me, as I kept getting put into new situations that I had to process more or less immediately – I had to learn to cope, because I couldn't really see an alternative. I never ever thought, 'Why am I moving up and down like this? Does nobody like me?' Who could I protest to, anyway? I just had to go with the flow, adapt to the new kids in each school or home and make sure I wasn't left out of anything I wanted to be part of. I wasn't shocked when I had to move from one place to another, and I used to stay positive and think, 'OK, maybe this one will work out better than the last one and I can stay here.'

I believe that was the time I started to build up some sort of defence system that made me very self-reliant, almost self-contained. This was why I could adapt to different situations and could cope with all the stuff that was thrown at me during my career. Most of all, it made me a bit of a loner, I could retreat into my own little world, which helped me enormously when I had to look after myself in the entertainment business, but when I was a child in Jamaica it meant I never really had any close girlfriends. In fact, it wasn't until I came to England and we stayed in the same place that I ever made any friends.

There wasn't much affection shown in my family. My mother loved me, I know she did, but as a child I can't recall her ever hugging me or telling me that she loved me. As a young child I just thought that was how parents acted, because it was pretty typical of how things were in Jamaica back then. There were never those situations you see on television nowadays with parents telling their children, *Oh, honey, you know how much I love you*, and the kid yelling, *You're so embarrassing! Get out of my room!* Maybe that was because life was so desperately hard for everybody and children were expected to assume adult responsibilities around the place as soon as they could, meaning there was little time for them to actually be kids. Like with my sister: yes, I loved her and I was very protective of her, but there was never any real sisterly closeness or connection, because I simply never had time to experience that with her. From when I was seven or eight I was always *attending* to her, because I had to – as soon as I was able I had to take up all the burdens Mama wasn't able to, so I was looking after Dorrett, or Blossom as she was known – pretty much everybody in Jamaica has a pet name, a nickname: mine was Cherry, hence my younger sister was Blossom.

I wouldn't say I was at all bothered by this at that time, it probably contributed towards me becoming so self-contained, but I don't think it had too much of an adverse effect on me. In fact, I grew to be a very affectionate person, perhaps even over-affectionate – I feel therefore I show! Maybe I'm trying to compensate. That came on as I got older, as a teenager in London I would meet up with my best friend Elaine, we would hug, then walk to school together arm in arm. In the Boney M. days, when I came home off the road and went to hug Mama I'd feel her move away, just ever so slightly distancing herself. I would carry on hugging anyway, because that seemed to be the right thing to do.

Jamaican parents were more likely to go to the other extreme, and live by the maxim 'don't spare the rod and spoil the child', it was as if they didn't know how to discipline you by just talking to you and everything was a beating. When I said earlier that other adults in the yard or the village could discipline you if they caught you getting up to no good, I meant they could beat you and then when your mother or father heard about it they would beat you some more! It was a totally different way of thinking than it is today, and although it seemed to work – the kids where I lived were largely respectful and well behaved – I think the best way is somewhere in between. You have to have proper communication with the children, but at the same time children should have respect for their parents. Then, while a bit of fear can't do any harm, it's not a good idea to terrify a little girl like when I thought Mama was going to chop my head off! It might seem a bit comical now, but at the time it wasn't funny at all.

I was around seven years old and it was probably a Saturday because we weren't at school and we weren't in church. We were out playing, climbing trees maybe, and I can't remember what happened – maybe I fell – but I uttered the word 'Shit!' to my sister. Just to my sister – not to an adult or, heaven help me, to Mama – but when I looked round to see if Mama had heard, it was obvious she had. I took one look at my mother's face and I took off! Round the yard, down the hill, up towards wood bush, with my mother chasing me. '*What did you say?* Just wait till I catch you!' For about two hours, I don't know how she kept it up! Eventually she caught me, dragged me back to the yard and over to this big block of wood that was used to chop firewood and suchlike. Now I'm convinced she's going to chop my head off, because all I can see is a cutlass sticking up from it! There's other tools like a pickaxe and a shovel lying around, the sort of tools you'd find for everyday life in the yard, but I was so frightened I'm sure she is going for the cutlass. I don't know if she was just playing with my mind, but I genuinely feared this would be the end of my life! I'm thinking, 'Mi God . . . mi dead for sure . . . mi dead . . .'

The other kids were just standing around watching, and I was thinking, 'Why can't they help? Don't they see I'm going to die?' By then I was struggling like a mad thing, my feet were kicking right up in the air above my head as she carried me – it was like when you try to carry a chicken and it starts fluttering

its legs and wings to get away! I was in such a state I was frothing at the mouth and through my nostrils, and I was wrenching,
wrenching, wrenching. Finally I broke free! I couldn't believe
it – I felt as if I'd just saved my own life!

I ran and ran and although I say I slept in the gully all night,
really I didn't sleep too much! On the one hand I'm afraid to go
back in yard because I don't know what Mama is going to do;
on the other hand I know the longer I stay out there the worse
it will be when I do get home. Parents don't calm down, and
they definitely don't forget – as we would say: 'You can run
high, you can run low, but you're still going to get a backsid-
ing!' I came back the next day, probably because I was hungry
as much as anything else, and of course Mama was still mad, as
much because I had defied her and not come home that night
as much as for saying 'Shit!', and of course I got a beating. As a
child I never swore again, and to this day hardly ever. Ha, ha,
ha!

The worst thing about not being able to talk to other people as
is done today, is if you did have a problem there was nobody
you could turn to. More than once I was sexually harassed, and
although I didn't know anything about sex at that age – ten or
eleven – I knew that these advances made by adult men,
although they didn't succeed, were definitely inappropriate.
Looking back on it I'm pretty sure that it happened to other
girls too, but as nobody talked about it I thought it was just me:
that I was being singled out, as if it was some sort of punish-
ment. If my own feelings were anything to go by, we girls were
too embarrassed even to talk to each other and I certainly
wouldn't have said anything to my mother or any of my

guardians. In any case, I'm sure they would have just brushed it off and told me I didn't know what I was talking about. In fact, one of my attackers was the husband of my guardian at the time. If I was coming from the shops I would have to pass the pit toilet we had at the back and I would hear, '*Pssst!* Pssst! Cherry . . . Here, Cherry . . .' I had to fight that man off more than once as he tried to drag me into the toilet, but he never succeeded.

In Church Pen, when I was eleven or twelve and waiting to join my mother in England, there was an uncle of mine who used to come back drunk from the rum bar and try to rape me. There would be all the kids in the bed – I could be right in the middle – but he'd still find me and pull me outside. But because he was drunk and I was struggling he never actually penetrated me, and it wasn't until much later, when I found out about sex, that I realised he had been having orgasms on my leg. Another man I really had to fight to keep off was the husband of my guardian – he kept trying and trying, maybe five or six times, before he got the message. The worst thing was the morning after these attempted assaults when he would be out there shaving and getting ready to go to work like a proper gentleman, with his wife passing by, and I knew that if I said anything I'd most likely get a beating. Inside, though, I was thinking, 'Somebody please get me out of here!'

Another time I was walking past one of the big houses in Old Harbour that had bushes outside and I heard, 'Cherie . . . Cherry . . . You all right?' coming from these bushes. It was the husband of the lady who worked there as a maid. I said, 'I'm fine; I'm going home to sleep to go to school tomorrow.' He carried on calling me, then got bold and tried to pull me into the bushes with him. Again, I had to fight him off and run the rest of the way home.

I used to be so mad about all of this, because the way we children had been brought up we wouldn't ignore an adult when they talked to us – especially one that is known to you and your family. These men played on this, because once an attacker engaged you in a conversation he was halfway there. Then you'd physically have to fight, which I always did and nobody ever succeeded in raping me. I was only thirteen when I left Jamaica, so how old could I have been when this was happening? But these men just looked at us girls and simply because they saw breasts developing and the girls growing, they thought they could pluck us whenever they felt like it. We were children! All of these three men were old enough to have been my father. To see how much of it existed in my own little country made me feel worse! I thought the world was finished.

As a coping mechanism, I convinced myself that it was nothing to do with me, it wasn't any fault of mine, it was these men who were so wrong. I never felt ashamed of myself for what they were trying to do, I simply felt angry because they assumed it was their right to try to do it. However, because nobody succeeded in doing anything to me, and I fought them off until eventually they left me alone, I actually felt like a conqueror. But how many girls had that will or were as able as me to physically fight? That thought still bothers me, and it's why I get so angry when I hear about cases like this.

Not long after I turned eleven my mother left Jamaica to live in England to build a better life, and she had promised Blossom and me that she would send for us. Much as I loved Jamaica, and had heard stories about how different England was, I often used to think, 'Please, Mama, send for us quick, get me away from all of this.' It's probably the only thing that gives me bad memories about my beautiful country.

I was living in Church Pen when my father came to tell me that Dorrett and I were going to go to England to join Mama. Although we were so young when Mama left us in Jamaica, this wasn't such a big deal as people might think because, apart from the fact both of us had spent so much time apart from our mother anyway, it was a really common occurrence. Back at the very start of the 1960s the island was still a British colony, so Jamaicans had British passports and the same rights to live and work in the UK as any other citizen. Somebody from a family, usually the father, would go *a foreign*, as we called it, by themselves to prepare a secured living, then send for the others. Because of this automatic entry into what we were still calling the Mother Country, often there wasn't too much forward planning in these moves and people would just take off, *a go look betterment in Britain*.

Among the other children at school, I had long been hearing 'Oh his father's gone to England' or 'This one's auntie has gone to England', so it didn't feel strange at all. In fact, it was so widespread it almost felt you were missing out if one of your parents *didn't* go – like 'How come all their mothers or fathers are going to England and mine's staying in Jamaica?' So when it came time for Mama to go, I remember thinking how I was in that boat too, but also how her life had been so tough that moving to England *had* to be an improvement.

When Daddy told me we were going, naturally I was excited to be seeing Mama again; although the reality of living apart from her for so much of my life meant I hadn't missed her as much as I might have done, it didn't mean I wasn't keen to see her. I think it was comforting more than anything else, especially as we hoped it would be in much easier conditions. What I remember most, though, is feeling relieved! Relieved because she'd promised us she was going to send for us, so I'd been waiting for this moment for two years and it felt like all that time I was holding my breath and now I could finally exhale! I had put up with being tossed here and there and I'd made the best of it, but after living like that for so long you realise it's not what you want – I think that happens naturally as you get older. I was happy at the thought of not doing it any more, I was pleased at the prospect of going to England because I believed I would be settled.

The other reason why I was eager to go to England may sound a little strange, but when I was a little girl of nine or ten, I made a vow to myself to look after Mama, so when I was told I was going to England I figured that would be my opportunity to do so. This came about one day when Blossom and I were living with Mama in the yard in Church Pen and Daddy came to visit us.

As I've said, I rarely saw my father, maybe once or twice a year, but when he came round he'd always be in his full police uniform so well-pressed and starchy, which made quite an impression on me and I really used to admire him. This time when Mr Barrett was about to leave and Mama called us in, he stood there in his uniform and it was *kiss kiss, kiss kiss*, all very pleasant. Then Mama said, quite fiercely, tapping on the table as she spoke, 'Before you go, put something down for the pickney dem!' Daddy looked at her and said with contempt,

'*What?* Yuh mad, woman? Weh mi fi get dat?' And I was shocked! This was my father, a man I only ever knew as this dashing figure in a crisp uniform! I thought, 'Oh my God, did he really talk to Mama like that? How could he? What a rough man!'

Right there, I said to myself, 'Don't worry, Mama, I am going to take care of you. You won't have to rely on that sort of man again.' Which is exactly what I did. Of course I didn't know I was going to be one of Boney M., but I knew it was my responsibility to take care of my mother, and going to England to be with her would now make that possible.

Before I could go to England, however, my life being my life there was one more move for me in Jamaica. Daddy decided that Dorrett and I should spend our last few weeks in Jamaica together because we'd never really bonded as sisters. It meant we were going to move to Kingston to live with one of his other sweethearts and our half-brother and -sister, Winston and Dawn Barrett. They weren't our only siblings, Daddy used to say, 'There are nine of you that I know about, but I think there might be a tenth one out there somewhere!' Dorrett came in from Westmoreland and I came down from Church Pen and this lady Mrs Barnes became our guardian until it was time to leave. Although she had two kids for Daddy, she had too much sense to wait around for him to marry her and she had got married to Mr Barnes and they lived together with Winston and Dawn. Mr Barnes must have been a very tolerant man, especially as he had no problem with Blossom and myself staying there. The Barneses treated us very well, and we all got along fine: Dorrett and I had never really spent too much time together so this helped; plus it was my first time being close to other siblings, so that was interesting too and I've remained close to them as an adult.

All of this gave me plenty to think about – maybe that was Daddy's intention – and it meant by the time I came to board the flight to London I'd had no time to be scared or even apprehensive; more than anything else I was curious.

*Chapter Fifteen*

# 'A bus with two storeys!'

By the time we were taken to Kingston I was counting the days to the flight. Both of us had these matching suits made especially for the flight over, a dress with a little bolero jacket in aquamarine blue. That in itself was ramping up the excitement – I couldn't wait to put this suit on, because that would mean I was about to get on the flight. As a child of thirteen going on my first flight, while I like to think I thought I was all very sophisticated, really I was just so excited to see a different country and all I wanted to do was arrive to find Mama waiting for us at the airport.

Although the flight was a completely new experience, it seemed to go by in minutes! It was British West Indies Airways, and was very crowded. I sat by the window and to this day I will always ask for a window seat – since we've been married my husband Marcus has only ever sat by the aisle, and sometimes when I'm looking out over the clouds I flashback to that first flight to London! We got steaks for our meal, and Dorrett said to me, 'I don't like that!' She wasn't going to eat it! I was shocked, because getting meat in Jamaica had been so rare I couldn't believe somebody was going to waste it! Also, we were on an airplane and had to act like we belonged there; I figured the best way to do that was to eat what they gave us. I ate both of those tiny little steaks.

The stewardesses made quite a fuss of us – well, two girls in matching aquamarine suits with their hair done up nicely must have looked pretty cute! I was captivated by them too and spent a lot of the time watching them and thinking how beautiful they were. At that stage I thought, 'All I want is to be a steward-ess – give me the glamour!'

Mama didn't come to meet us at Heathrow, she sent a dear friend of hers, Mr Burnett, who had a van and would drive us into town. The funny thing was my mother never had any photographs of us because we had never had any taken so Mr Burnett had no idea what we looked like! Maybe Mama had been told about our outfits by letter, but when we came through immigration he had to come over and asked, 'Are you Cherry? Are you Blossom? I am your mother's best friend so I will take you to Brixton, where she's waiting.' And he walked us out to his van! It would be really difficult to imagine that sort of thing happening today and nobody getting arrested!

If it was a disappointment that Mama wasn't there, it was soon forgotten because this was like entering another dimen-sion. As we walked through the terminal I was looking round at people and thinking, 'What funny-looking clothes the people have on! Is that how everybody dresses over here?' I had no idea what a full-length coat was because I'd never seen one before – with these long things on I thought everybody looked like zombies! As soon as we left the building I understood. It was like a shock, because the linen dresses and jackets Blossom and I were wearing were useless against the sort of cold that hit us. It was March, and we had no coats! We were *so* cold! Living all our lives in Jamaica we didn't even know what being cold really meant; people had told us it was going to be cold in

England, but we had no context to put that in – for us it had only ever been some days and nights weren't as hot as others.

The drive from the airport to Kepler Road, just off Acre Lane in Brixton, took about an hour and a half, so by the time we got there my sister and I were freezing – so much so, my first memory of getting to the house is as much about how good it was to be out of that terrible cold as it is about running to Mama! But the door opened and there she was.

We girls went mad! 'Mama! Mama! Mama!' Then Mrs Clark came out to greet us – she was the landlady, who was also a long-time friend of my mother's from Jamaica, so she knew us girls. Soon the other tenants of the house came out to meet us and it was one joyous commotion down in the hall, a real celebration, with everybody talking and laughing. Mama held us both at arms' length and was amazed at how much we'd grown since she'd last seen us, especially me, as between eleven and thirteen, I'd shot up, and that brought it home to me how long it had been since we'd seen our mother.

After all the greeting – which took quite a while – we went up to Mama's room, up four or five flights of stairs because it was at the very top of the house. This was something else that was completely new to me – a house that was so tall! On the journey in from the airport I was fascinated by what I thought were great big buildings everywhere, not realising they were just average houses. In Jamaica I had seen very few houses that were even two storeys tall let alone three, so when we pulled up outside the house, my first thought was, '*What?* Mama lives *here?*'

The house was shared with three other families, all Jamaican, and the couple who owned it, Mr and Mrs Clark, lived on the ground floor, I guess so they could keep an eye on the comings and goings and they didn't have to climb any stairs! From where we were, we had to go down four flights to go to the bathroom and then it was 'Knock, knock' to see if anybody else was occupying it – if there was you had to just wait on the stairs. With the kitchen, which was down even more stairs to the ground floor, it was the same thing, because not all the families could cook at the same time, even though there were two stoves in there it was difficult trying to cook alongside anybody else. So there was very little privacy and an awful lot of waiting on stairs! There was a living room everybody would use – it had the only television in the house, which was always flickering. That didn't bother Dorrett and I; it was all so new to us and we loved it. Everybody gathered in there after dinner and we were allowed to join them for an hour before we went all the way up to get ready for bed, after which we came down to use the bathroom, then all the way back upstairs to go to sleep!

Mr and Mrs Clark were typical of many from the Caribbean who had come to England to work, maybe do more than one job and save all their cash to buy a house for cash – it would be difficult, if not impossible, for black people to get mortgages in England then. The houses they'd buy would most likely be in a rundown neighbourhood where prices were low, the kind of area where white English people didn't want to live – even less so when black people started moving in. Then, often while they still had their jobs, they would rent out rooms, usually to their fellow countrymen with whom they may have connections from back home. That's how Mama ended up in Mrs Clark's house, because they knew each other and she had contacted my mother to say she had a room to rent. This is a big reason why black people newly arrived from the Commonwealth put down roots in areas like Brixton or Peckham or Notting Hill – which wasn't anything like the upmarket area it is today – and why people from the same islands tended to live near each other.

Black landlords always had a big demand for rooms from black people, because it wasn't unusual for them to have difficulty finding accommodation on the open market – discrimination wasn't against the law back then. While property owners were pleased to be doing their bit to help other black people, it meant some got very rich – much later I heard stories of landlords renting rooms twice over to shift workers, who would sleep in the beds at different times! Many would buy another house with the money they made off the first one and so on and so on, all the while doing the job they got when they first came over. It was what was called 'immigrant mentality', it wasn't confined to Caribbeans either, and it meant the main reason you had come to England was to earn money, therefore you didn't mind working extra hard to do so. Most of the 'Windrush Generation' of arrivals from the Caribbean honestly thought coming to the UK was a temporary situation, so they'd do as much as possible to take as much as they could back with them.

Mama had this one little room, with one bed where all three of us slept, a little table on the side, a little bit of wardrobe, a single chest of drawers and a small window looking out at other houses. What gave me trouble when we arrived was this thing in the middle of the floor space that I thought was the stove. I asked Mama if she had to do the cooking in there, and she told me it was for warmth – it was a paraffin heater. This was before ordinary houses had central heating, and I found out that practically everybody else had these heaters – half the kids at school would be there with their clothes smelling of paraffin, I know mine used to! A man used to come round the streets in a van with a big tank of paraffin on it for you to go out, stop him and buy what you wanted in cans or bottles.

We didn't have a fridge, so Mama used to keep the milk outside that window on the sill, and when she used to make jelly for us girls for dessert she would put it out there to set. We used to think that was so funny, keeping things outside the window! At that point, though, I looked out of that little window at a grey London skyline, thinking about the sunshine I'd left behind to live in this one little room with a paraffin stove, and knew this is where my life was going to get *really* interesting, and that nothing was going to be easy. We went to bed and slept with all three heads together, rather than top-to-toe, and it was very comfortable, or maybe after the journey then that celebration, we were just exhausted. The main things were we were warm enough, as there were so many blankets, and we were with Mama.

The next morning I got up, looked out of the window and panicked a little bit because I thought there was smoke every-where! Mama explained it wasn't smoke it was fog, that it was just what the weather was like in London and I would see a lot of it. All of this just made me even more curious as it hit me how totally different life in London would be.

When we went out, it was so different from even the Jamaican capital city Kingston, let alone from how things were in the countryside. There were these big houses, and people all seemed to be walking so fast as they snuggled down into their coats and scarves and hats. The Jamaican countryside moves at its own *slow* pace, here it was a real hustle and bustle! The traffic was something else, too; there was so much of it, moving so quickly and apparently without any rules. That was another shock to me! Then, of course, there were the red buses, just the most fantastic thing I'd ever seen: *a bus with two storeys . . . And it's bright red! Wow!* If I'd ever seen a picture of one before I came to England I don't remember, and it would have been in black and white, now seeing them in their full glory I was spellbound and I still love London's red double-deckers. I vividly remember the post boxes and the telephone boxes, too, maybe because they were the same bright red as the buses so they stood out. In fact, that red was the only real bright spot. I had come from a country where everything was colourful – the sky, the trees, the birds, the flowers . . . even the people – now it seemed like everything was dark grey or brown and everybody dressed in these long dark clothes; there was a distinct lack of colour.

I was really fascinated by my new surroundings and trying so hard to take in the whole picture – it made my head swim. I knew right away I could get to like it, and thought, 'If this is the type of living I've got to get into then bring it on!' Of course I missed Jamaica – in this place there were no streams, no coconut palms, no ripe mangoes on the trees – but this was a different country, it was the Motherland, the land of opportunity, and I was determined to take every opportunity that came my way. I loved the buzz of London and the fact that London seemed a bit more serious. To me that was businesslike, I thought, 'This is our home now, so I'm going to learn to live here because this is where things are going to start getting serious for me.'

Coming to Brixton made things that much easier for me, because back then Brixton was Jamaican! When I went to Brixton Market it was like being back home: the foods on sale, the voices, the cussing and the laughter, being totally surrounded by black people . . . There was a little piece of home right there, so I felt less like I had been uprooted, which, I believe, made the whole process much less intimidating.

It was a couple of weeks or so before we started school because we had to go for an interview with the headmistress and to order the uniform – Mama had started the process before we arrived, as this wasn't like Jamaica where I would just be taken to a new school and be introduced to the class! Naturally I had my chores to do around the house, too, and soon fell into a routine. This was another good thing for us, as it was important my sister and I felt secure in our new environment and I believe children feel more assured about things if they have a stable routine, also it was something else we'd brought from Jamaica.

Mama had two jobs, which was how she raised the money for our fares – she had no help from our father with that. Her first job was as a seamstress in a nearby factory, then when she finished there she'd take the bus up to the West End where she worked evenings in a restaurant – washing dishes, I think. She was totally knackered by the time she arrived home, and she was never particularly domesticated anyway, so during those first weeks I took over looking after our little quarters upstairs, which I carried on doing after we started school. What became my routine was leave school at four o'clock, come home, do the house chores, get my sister's and my uniforms ironed and set out, if Mama wasn't there I'd serve the dinner for Bloss and myself, then maybe watch a little television downstairs before going to bed. That was it, pretty much the same every day. I never saw friends out of school, but then I never had time.

I took over the cooking chores from Mama, too, getting up earlier to make breakfast and a meal to eat in the evening. During the six-week summer holiday, Mama couldn't afford for us to go Butlin's or anything so I stayed busy by taking a job in the Sunlight Laundry on Acre Lane. The ten pounds a week I earned there made a huge contribution to the coffers, but the work was exhausting – this wasn't domestic laundry, but putting great big sheets in huge machines, real hardcore physical work. I've never been lazy, and back then whoever could add to the family coffers did so – I was proud to be doing my bit.

I started school at Parkside Secondary School in Clapham, I think in the third year, with what I thought was a very grown-up-looking uniform: a grey skirt and a grey pullover. I was so looking forward to starting school in London, so walking in on that first day to see all the other girls was really exciting. It was about fifty-fifty white English girls and black girls who were the daughters of immigrants from all over the Commonwealth, with quite a few from Jamaica, and everybody seemed to get on well together. In the early 1960s it was commonplace for girls from overseas just to turn up in schools, so everyone was used to it and I was made to feel very welcome. I worked hard to fit in, too. I knew I shouldn't dwell on how my life had been; I had no idea when I would be going back to Jamaica – although initially I assumed I would be – so I just had to move on in the here and now. School was a straightforward example of having to adapt to the rules and regulations of a new system, so that's what I did. Also, it was in Mama's thinking that her coming to England could offer us girls a better education, so I wanted to make sure I got the best out of it.

It was at the first recess I got among the others and hit it off with my classmates immediately, that was when I met Elaine Tracy, Veronica Woodhall and Valetta Duffus, and we formed a little clique more or less straight away. Elaine is Jamaican, two months younger than me, and had a very similar background and route to England and we took a liking to each other which has stayed there over the years.

The teacher introduced me in front of the class I was joining, and that was about the only similarity between school in London and in Jamaica! It was indoors, when most of my other schooling had been outside; I found it unusual to have to go to different rooms and be with different teachers for different subjects; but the biggest difference was the discipline – it was completely unlike anything I had experienced. Jamaican teachers were very, very strict, and they would beat us with a belt to achieve the sort of discipline they expected. It surprised me that if kids at Parkside misbehaved the teachers used to just say 'No!' or maybe the girl would lose a point towards being a prefect, or, at the very most, they might get a little tap on the hand with a ruler – in England they would take teachers to jail for what was everyday in Jamaica! The English way seemed to work, although, ironically, in recent times more and more parents are sending their London-born children back to live with relatives in Jamaica so they can go to school there because now they're saying the discipline in English schools is too lax. Back then my Jamaican schooling meant I had no problem with that side of things, indeed I think it was because I was well-disciplined my form teacher took a liking to me and whenever she had to leave the classroom she'd tell me, 'Marcia, you take charge while I'm away.' I'd have to stand in front of the class behind her desk. I loved that, because there would be no chatting, no gossiping, no fooling around, and it showed me then I was to be a leader not a follower!

I was a good athlete at school, I used to love the straightforward running races, and for me the crowd of girls shouting 'Come on, Marcia!' was every bit as good as winning! I liked most subjects because I was always very curious and keen to learn, my favourites were English language, history and geography and of course I loved the arts – music and drama. Really, the only thing I wasn't too keen on was maths, which, as we'll get to later, got me into a lot of trouble.

One of the first plays we did at school was *Macbeth* with me in the role of Macduff, and we were doing rehearsals on this great big stage where I thought I really had to act it out. I came charging on with this big theatrical voice and '*Horror! Horror! Horror!* This is beyond words and beyond belief . . .' My classmate who was playing Macbeth looked terrified! I think she thought I was going to kill her! She said, 'Marcia, you look crazy; it's only a play, you know! You don't have to get so involved!' But I was really enjoying myself, and I think other people enjoyed it too because I was always getting roles and have been pretty theatrical ever since.

Miss Tetley, our music teacher, would take the whole class up to Sadler's Wells Theatre in Islington every month, and we would see fantastic productions of classic operas such as *Madame Butterfly*, *Carmen*, *La traviata*. I was totally captivated! I would sit there in the dark thinking, 'Oh my God! That's me! *Really!*' It

185

was the acting and the singing. Together. By the same people! It was such an inspiration, because with the acting in the school plays and singing in assemblies that was what I wanted to do – act and sing. One of the great things about Boney M. was how we'd get into the songs like we were playing roles and act them out as much as singing them – I'm even more like that these days with my own songs. It's still one of my remaining ambitions to act on stage; I'm still healthy and I still look good, I'm sure I could do some roles.

Miss Tetley was really encouraging; she wanted to make sure we girls knew about all sorts of music and singing, not just what was on the radio. This was one of those things that you might not value at the time but in the years that follow you're glad you have that knowledge or experience. I really appreciated what she did by opening up my thinking about music and would love to see her today and talk to her about it. Some years after school, Elaine wrote to me and told me that she had met Miss Tetley on a bus, and the teacher had told her she was getting married and she asked Elaine to sing at her wedding. Then she asked Elaine if she knew where Marcia Barrett was because she'd like the two of us to do it. Elaine said, 'Haven't you heard? You know the group Boney M.? Well, Marcia's one of them!' Miss Tetley was shocked, but then she said she'd always thought I would succeed at something.

It quite surprised me that Miss Tetley would pick me out like that so long after I finished school, because what I remember most about her dealings with me was her telling me not to sing so loud! In music class when we were singing the rounds and doing harmonies it would be, 'That was very, very good, but, Marcia, your voice is overpowering the other classmates. Could you take it down a little bit, please?' It had been the same when I was singing at school in Jamaica, with the other thirty kids turning round to look at who had the voice louder than anybody else! Even as an adult in Boney M. I would be in trouble with Frank Farian who was always telling me, 'Marcia! Why does your voice have to be so much louder?' and I would take two steps back from the microphone. This wasn't my fault; I just have a very well-developed diaphragm because I used to cry so much as a baby! I didn't know anything about this, until one day in Jamaica I was walking into the village and one of the neighbours said, 'Good morning, Miss Miserable!' That confused the hell out of me because I didn't think I was at all an unhappy child, so I asked Mama, who told me when I was a baby I did nothing but cry! She said, 'Cry, cry, cry, cry, cry, and there was nothing that would quieten you down, so the whole neighbourhood would hear this baby crying, non-stop, and they started to call it Miss Miserable!' Really this turned out well for me, as once I learned how to sing properly and could control my voice I had all the power I would ever need. It can be a bit of a curse, too, as I hate squashing my voice down even when I am talking – I believe my voice to be my freedom and I've never been a whisperer! However, it means I can't carry a mobile phone because if I start talking on the street people will stop and turn round!

I did well at my studies and Elaine, Veronica and I were great scholars because we used to enjoy learning and reading – maybe these days you'd call us nerds, but I think we all had the same curiosity. I was sixteen years old, I was on course to do my O levels and I might have gone into the sixth form, or gone to

Pitmans Secretarial College, but before I could get that far something happened that would change my life for ever. I had a baby, and nobody was more shocked than me.

I didn't know I was expecting, I didn't really know too much about conception or pregnancy, and I genuinely don't remember it happening. I've seen a TV documentary about other young girls who didn't know they were pregnant until they gave birth and they talked about how they must have blocked out what happened to them, and maybe it's the same with me and I've pushed it out of my mind, but *I cannot recall any part of how that child was conceived.* I wouldn't even say I was in a haze or anything like that, I simply have no memory at all of the event. I have read about something called 'repressed memory syndrome' where an event can be so traumatic that the mind can push all recollection of it down so deep that until it surfaces – which it might never – there is no memory of it at all, like it never happened. I think that's what I must have because obviously it happened, but it's as if I know nothing about it. What was in no doubt is who the father was. I had no boyfriends or anything like that – again, I had no time – and the only man I came into contact with was Wesley Demercado who was at least ten years older than me and was helping me with my maths for school. He never denied it, and even seemed to know what was going on with my pregnancy before I did.

He was a friend of my mother's from a Seventh-day Adventist church she used to go to in Piccadilly, and a truly brilliant mathematician because if I did any homework with him every girl copied it the next day – 'Marcia, Marcia, let me have a look . . . Oh, so that's how that is!' He always seemed to present himself as very nice, a gentleman. Mama said she had warned him not to try anything on with me, and she trusted me enough to let me go to his rooms in Upper Brixton for tuition. Whatever happened must have happened during one of those visits; it definitely wasn't as if we were having any sort of affair and I was complicit in it, I cannot summon up any memory at all of having sex with him but it must have taken place because my son Wayne is now over fifty years old.

It was a very strange beginning for my life as a mother, and although Wayne and I were very close while he was growing up, our relationship wasn't really what many people would call 'conventional'. I was so young when I had him I still had to finish school and make my way in the world, then I was away much of the time, both in Boney M. and before that, so really my mother brought him up. And that made sense to me because that was how I had been brought up – my mother went away to England to make a good life for us girls and we were in the care of relatives back in Jamaica. I had Boney M. as my way to make the best possible life for my son and my mother.

Wayne was a very happy and much-loved child. He travelled with me whenever possible, and we both cherished our time together when I was home from touring. Mama, Wayne and I were a good, tight family, and although it may not have been to everybody's choosing it was a structure that served us well, just as it had served countless other Caribbeans.

However, the circumstances of Wayne's birth were so extraordinary I don't think anything could have fazed me after that.

## Chapter Sixteen

# 'Baby? What baby?'

It was a Sunday morning and I had been up early cooking a real Jamaican Sunday breakfast – callaloo, saltfish and fried dumplings – for my family and Wesley who by now had moved into the house we lived in. I don't know whose idea that was but presumably it was to save on our rent and make more money for the landlady, as our room had been partitioned in two with a curtain and a bed and some basic furniture for him on the other side. I had just taken him his food, and began to feel bad. I hadn't been feeling one hundred per cent for a week or so, but now I suddenly came over really weak with a terrible pain in my stomach. I didn't know what was happening. I felt dizzy – as if I was going to pass out – and I was starting to panic. Wesley put down his paper and said to me, 'That's the baby yuh 'ave!' I thought he was trying to be funny, but it was getting so bad I gasped for him to call for an ambulance on the one telephone in the house.

The most remarkable thing about this was my mother was at home, she was in our room when I was in such pain in the kitchen. She was so disengaged from what was going on with me that either she wasn't aware of the commotion that was going on or she chose to ignore it. But that was my mother for you.

Thankfully the ambulance came quickly, with a driver and a nurse, and by then my heart was beating so faintly they called it a fatal heartbeat as they carried me into the back of the ambulance on a stretcher. The driver started to pull away and turned on the siren but he didn't know where to take me – they were asking me where I was registered as an expectant mother and I didn't have a clue what they were talking about. It simply didn't register with me because I didn't even know I *was* an expectant mother. So the nurse asked me directly where I was going to have my baby.

*Baby!* That was the first I'd heard about any baby. I'm telling them, 'What baby?' So now they're confused too. The nurse said, 'Let me feel your tummy.' Then she said, 'Yes, you're definitely having a baby, and it's going to be a boy.' I still couldn't accept it: '*What?* A baby is in there? *Really?*' I was beyond shocked, I nearly rolled off the stretcher and I couldn't speak any more because I was too weak.

They drove me to the nearest hospital, which was in Clapham South, and I was in such a bad way they rushed me straight in for blood transfusions – the baby I didn't know I was carrying had taken practically everything from my body and left me almost too weak to go on. The staff were so worried about me they watched over me the whole time. The pains I had been feeling went on all day, labour pains, and lasted until my son was born at three minutes to eight in the evening.

I was absolutely terrified. I was a sixteen-year-old girl – a *kid*. Earlier that day I'd been merrily going about my business cooking breakfast for my family and for Wesley – he paid me a few pounds a week to do his cooking; the next thing I know I'm in agony and having a baby I previously knew nothing about. The pain was like nothing I'd experienced before, and I was convinced I was going to die.

I had not been to any antenatal classes so I had no idea what was happening to my body and I hadn't been taught how best to deal with it. I can't remember the delivery – just the pain. I was in a daze until I was back on the maternity ward and they brought my son out to me: 'Miss Barrett, you have a lovely baby boy!' That was enough to bring me straight back to the reality of my situation. Suddenly it was as if the world was spinning around and I could see no conclusion of what is going to happen. I'm thinking, 'What am I going to tell Mama?' Then, because I was so young and had always been very ambitious, I'm thinking that I'm just a girl, come from Jamaica three years ago, looking to make my way in the world, and now I've got a son – this isn't me, it can't be. What am I going to do? I want to be a stenographer. I can't be finished already, but this child is going to hold me back.

Everything was going around in my brains, and if it sounds as if I was being selfish, it was because I just couldn't really comprehend what was happening to me. All my dreams and aspirations had disappeared and I had no idea what I was going to do next. When they handed Wayne to me I looked down at this tiny little thing all wrapped up, with hair all over his head, and said, 'He's mine, he's my son.' I knew I was his mother and I knew I was going to keep him. I even wanted to give him my name – Wayne Barrett – although that was not to be.

That evening when the nurses took all the babies away, they let me keep Wayne with me for an extra half-hour, which caused a few complaints from the other mothers, but they said that was because I was so young, that I was just a child myself.

I appreciated that because I still needed to come to terms with the fact I had a baby.

I was kept in hospital for about two weeks, because I was anaemic and they wanted to make sure I was getting enough rest. For the first time in my life I literally had nothing to do all day, so I was able to reflect on my situation. The thing I thought about most was how could I have been carrying that baby inside me and not known or not have had the tummy to show it? Back then we used to wear our girdles to pin up our stockings, they were a little elasticated so that might have helped, but Wayne was seven pounds at birth, which was considered big in those days, so I couldn't understand where he had been. Right up until the week before the birth I had been doing sports at school, netball and rounders and running, in fact the only thing I can remember as different was drinking so many of those little bottles of milk we used to get for free every day at school. It is said the body will let you know what you need and I was always thirsty for the school milk, but that was the only extra nutrition I was getting. Maybe that was what saved me.

I hadn't had any morning sickness, and I'd even been to the doctor when my monthlies stopped happening, he'd told me everything was fine and if he knew I was pregnant he didn't mention it. I was so naïve at that time because in those days, especially among Jamaicans, girls' mothers wouldn't talk to them about becoming a woman and the changes that will come over them – I think one of the reasons there used to be so many pregnancies among the young girls is because we were so ill-prepared. My mother wasn't there in Jamaica during those most important years and nobody else was going to teach me about growing up, and Mama certainly never spoke to me about it when I came to England. This isn't a personal thing, it's just how it was, and the only bits I really knew were what I had talked about with my friends, which wasn't much. I had so little understanding of what had happened to me when I got out of hospital I was afraid that if a man came and stood beside me for too long I was going to get pregnant! Each time I saw a man I was like, 'Oh, horror! The same thing's going to happen again!'

Wesley had no such naivety, though, and what he had said to me before he called the ambulance now made sense – he knew what was going on because he knew what he had done to me. In Wesley's mind there was never any doubt he was Wayne's father, and he was the only person who came to visit me in hospital. He only came once, but that was enough as none of what he had to say cheered me up.

When Wesley came into the ward, the first thing he asked what why had I named the baby Barrett; I should give the child his name because we're going to get married. He is in love with me. *What?* As if I didn't have enough on my plate already? I didn't know anything about love, especially not with this man who had known I was an innocent and taken such advantage of me – he had never been my boyfriend, there had been no affair, I had never slept one night with him, so why would he assume I was going to marry him? That was the worst thing he could have said to me, because at that time of my life the word 'husband' used to scare the living daylights out of me. At school I'd been the only girl without a boyfriend because I never thought I needed to have a man as soon as possible to be fulfilled,

I had had my plans and I knew I could carry them out for myself. I had never seen my mother with a man – Daddy was only a visitor – and although things were far from perfect she had got us to England by herself. Now I've got this grown man proposing marriage to me and all I can think is, 'Help me, Jesus; how am I going to get out of this?' In the end, to calm him down, I agreed to give the baby his surname, which is why he was never Wayne Barrett, yet even after all that fuss he didn't contribute a thing to Wayne's upbringing or give me any kind of support in the early days.

The other piece of unwelcome news was the message Mama had given Wesley to bring me: that it was all right for me to come home but I had to leave the baby at the hospital for adoption. She couldn't take the disgrace. For Mama it would be too shameful; her friends, like Mr and Mrs Burnett downstairs, would be saying things like, 'What! Cherry just come to England, get pregnant already and have baby? Oh my God!' I understood that, but I didn't even think about it, I told Wesley to take the message back that it was OK, I would find somewhere else to live because I couldn't leave my baby.

When I left the hospital I went home because I couldn't think of where else to go. I had Wayne in a shawl, I knocked on the door, boom, boom, boom, and after what seemed like ages Mama opened the door. She took a long look at me, showed no emotion, just stepped aside and I walked in. She closed the door, and just disappeared without saying a word, leaving me with no idea if I was going to be allowed to stay there or not. I went into our room. Wesley was staying out of the way too, and Blossom just looked at me and said nothing. Then as I was putting the baby down on the bed the three of us shared, Mama pushed the door ajar, came in and handed me a bowl of beef soup. I said, very meekly, 'Thank you, Mama', and the tension went right out of the room, suddenly it's like Bloss could speak again and I could breathe – Jamaicans fix everything with beef soup, so I knew she was going to let me stay. Whether she had forgiven me or not I still don't know, but it was the most positive thing to have happened to me since I'd had the baby.

She didn't speak to me again that day; in fact, she didn't speak to me about the baby, how I might have got pregnant or anything like that – *ever*. Up until the time she passed in 1996 she never told me what she thought about that whole situation, she didn't even pick the baby up for about a month. If he was crying she would call me to come and pick him up – never mind if I was all the way down in the kitchen cooking, it would be '*Cherry!* Come and pick up the baby!' After that first month, though, she relented and started to love Wayne – however angry she might have been with me she couldn't resist him, and the two of them became very close.

All through this my mother's treatment of me was harsh, too harsh really, and a bit frightening at the time, but I've never harboured any ill feeling towards her. I looked after her until the day she passed and once I was doing well with Boney M. she never wanted for anything. Except for the one thing I couldn't help her with – my father, Mr Barrett. As I got older I realised how he had broken her heart in a way I wouldn't wish upon anybody and she never fully recovered from it. He had hurt her so deeply and I think she associated me with that. I remember once, when she was telling me off for something, she said, 'Look at your face, you look just like him!'

The man was a rogue, he was already married, he had sweet-hearts all over the place, yet he let Mama think there was a chance of something meaningful. As I've said, I never saw her with another man because she was waiting for him. In London she had this trunk she kept in the shed in the garden. In it she kept all these glamorous negligées that she was saving for when she went back to Jamaica to be with him. It was so sad, and my heart went out to her.

Through all of this I had to organise the practicalities of having a baby in the house. There was no space for his cot in our room, so it was put on Wesley's side of the curtain. That was another weird one, because he never picked the baby up either, if Wayne was crying I would have to push the curtain aside, go in and settle him or pick him up to take him back to our side of the curtain. If Wesley was in the room or in bed he would completely ignore me. I would have to wash Wayne's nappies and his clothes in the basement, which was a real chore. There were no Pampers back then, it was only terry-cloth nappies, which had to be soaked in a bucket before I hand-washed them with bleach then hung them up outside.

I had to learn quickly as I went along, but what I really wanted was to go back to school. Although I knew that would make my life so much harder I also knew if I wanted to make a life for my son I had to carry on where I left off before Easter and finish my exams. I had my baby a week before the Easter holiday ended, and a couple of days after Bloss went back to school she told me that the headmistress, Madam West, had said she had heard from the hospital that I had had a baby. She told my sister that she considered me a brilliant scholar and a credit to the school in other ways, so I could come back to do my exams if I wanted. The only condition was that nobody was to know that I had a child, which I was quite happy to go along with. I arranged with Mrs Burnett for her sister to look after Wayne, I could cover that with what I earned from doing the cooking. I dragged out my uniform and started ironing like crazy!

When I went back the other girls were all, 'Oh Marcia, where were you?' I told them I'd had really bad flu: 'It was terrible, man, had to go to the hospital and everything!' It didn't work out very well, though. I was *so* tired all the time: Wayne was less than four weeks old, and when Elaine came to call for me in the morning I'd already been up for hours, washing nappies or cooking food for the house. By the time I got to school I was nodding off – the teachers were always shouting at me: '*Marcia, pay attention!*' Once again I was drinking the free school milk like crazy, but it wasn't enough to get me through this because as well as the tiredness I was constantly worrying about the baby. I couldn't concentrate in class because I was thinking, 'Oh my God, I wonder if he's crying now?' This went on for a few weeks and it was so strenuous I couldn't go on. I had to leave and it was that decision, with Wayne in mind, that marked the end of my school days.

It wasn't the end of my education, though, whether I had a baby or not I didn't leave school just to sit at home – I had seen what happened to so many girls who had left school because they were engaged or they were pregnant, then I'd run into them in Brixton and it was as if the spark had gone out of them. I'm not saying there is anything wrong with this if it is their choice, it simply wasn't mine; I had things to do. I booked in at a night school on Brixton Hill, Mama or Bloss would watch Wayne, and I finished my qualifications. I also took a stenographers' course and came out of there with shorthand and typing speeds of eighty words per minute. It hadn't been easy, but I was on my way and really excited about it.

*Chapter Seventeen*

# 'My first taste of real show business'

As a sixteen-going-on-seventeen-year-old, with the short-hand and typing speeds I had, it wasn't difficult to get a job in an office, so I did what most girls did and signed on with a secretarial employment agency in London's West End. The first job they placed me in was in Newman Street, just off Oxford Street, where I learned how to do stencilling and filing, but because I was the young girl in the office, all I seemed to be doing was making tea and coffee, not using the skills I'd learned at night school. I know everybody's got to start somewhere but you know how it is with teenagers: they want to run before they can walk. All I could see for my future at this firm was 'Marcia! Can I have a cuppa tea, luv?' or 'Two sugars please, Marcia!' because there appeared to be no chance for progression. But this was the 1960s, before word processing and when there was more or less full employment in London, so there was a constant demand for typists and office girls – if you worked hard and you were pleasant and presentable you could always find a job.

I decided to do temporary work, which was so popular: being a 'temp' was like a proper career and moving from job to job every couple of weeks meant I never got bored or frustrated in any environment. Then because I had Wayne at home and was a bit of a loner anyway, I didn't worry too much about the social side of being in the same office long term. The work was mostly filing or taking dictation in shorthand then typing it up, but I did get to do all sorts of different things at different companies, learning skills I'm still using today to run my own office and keep my business efficient. The job I enjoyed best was working on reception; although I haven't formed many friendships I do like meeting people and it was always good fun to be the face out front. Sometimes I would have to answer the phone, always sounding like I had a few plums in my mouth, which wasn't difficult because Mama, like most other Jamaican parents in London, emphasised how important it was to be able to speak English without a Jamaican accent outside the home.

After a couple of years of temping I knew I was doing OK, because I always had a job to go to and several offices asked for me to come back, but I also knew it wasn't for me. I wanted more out of life, although I couldn't just pack it all in because I had Wayne to support and Mama counted on my contribution to the family finances. But my world was changing.

There was so much pop music around it was impossible to ignore. We might not have had too much of it in our home, but it would be on the downstairs television and so many of the offices I worked in had the radio playing. I loved it! I was a fan of The Beatles, The Stones, The Monkees, Eric Burdon and The Animals, Joe Cocker . . . all those English guys. That was the pop music I grew up with, I've always loved it and it has probably influenced my approach to my music more than anything. I didn't really know anything about Jamaican music even though it was really coming into its own about this time because I'd never been exposed to it in Jamaica, then in England I'd only heard what was in the charts. I knew about Desmond Dekker and Jimmy Cliff because they'd had hits, but that was about it. It was only when, at age seventeen or eighteen, I started going out locally that I found out anything about reggae or soul music.

I wasn't any sort of raver because of my commitments, but I was starting to go out once in a blue moon. Sometimes I would go out with Mama and her friends to those old-time house parties, where you paid a couple of shillings to get in, and the same price for a drink or a plate of food after that! The atmosphere would always be very nice, it was Jamaican music or soul music, they'd have Jamaican curry goat or patties, and all of us ladies would drink Babycham or Cherry B! Everybody knew each other, they could talk about home, there was hardly ever any trouble and I used to go home feeling really good.

I think it was at one of these parties I met Dandy Livingstone, who was a big recording artist in Jamaica and was popular in Britain among white kids as well as black. He and his friends, one of whom was the recording artist Count Prince Miller, started taking me to clubs every now and then. I was the only girl in the group – it was like a boys' night out with Marcia! – but nothing untoward ever went on. They were fantastic, they were my *friends* and they knew it; in fact, they looked after me so much I always felt safe wherever we went. Mama knew Dandy, and would tell me that I was going out with very protective men.

We would go to clubs in Brixton or Peckham or Streatham, very nice places and sometimes we'd see some big-name soul or Jamaican acts live, which always fascinated me. Then one night

Dandy said we were all going north of the Thames to a place called the Q Club in Paddington, which was the premier black club in London. We were going to see Jackie Edwards, who was a big Jamaican star – he sounded like Nat King Cole – and a good friend of Dandy's. As he was living in England at the time Jackie became part of our clique, and we'd go to the Q Club with him quite often. One night I was down there dancing and a space cleared on the floor around me, which was unusual because normally the place was too packed for anybody to have too much room to dance. The music was always so good down there and I had got lost in my own little world, started to cut loose and really go wild! People were clapping and shouting, then afterwards Jackie said to me, 'I didn't know you could dance like that! Have you thought about dancing professionally?' Of course I hadn't, but he said he was signed with the Stigwood Organisation, they were booking dancers for dates in Germany and maybe they could fit me in. I agreed to go along for an audition, and it turned out to be the best decision I have ever made.

The company was run by Robert Stigwood, who would go on to produce the stage musicals *Hair* and *Jesus Christ Superstar*, and the movies *Saturday Night Fever* and *Grease*, but at that time he was big as a talent manager, tour promoter and record label boss. I knew and trusted Jackie, so I figured I had nothing to worry about and went for an audition. Although I didn't have a conscious ambition to get into show business, I wasn't happy doing office work even though I was qualified for it. I had been inspired by the operas I went to at school and now by stars like Shirley Bassey, Barbra Streisand and Dusty Springfield. I'm pretty certain I knew I wanted to do *something* on stage, because I could still remember the thrill of conducting the school orchestra in Jamaica, or playing Macduff, or singing in the choir, I loved how I would get butterflies before the performance then goose pimples afterwards when the people applauded. I believe up until then I had kept these ambitions hidden even from myself, because I had no idea how to get started – that's why I would always ask questions about the artists we saw in the clubs. But this audition was a real opportunity, and I knew it.

I got through the audition in London, which meant they sent me for another audition in Belgium, because if I got through it they would want me to work on the Continent. I had to leave for that audition practically straight away, and as you couldn't really ask for time off as a temp, I quit the job I was doing sooner than expected. They were so lovely to me, saying, 'Oh Marcia! Don't say you're leaving us already? What if we give you another couple of pounds . . .' I had to explain that it was nothing to do with them, and they wished me all the luck. I was a little bit sad, and a little bit apprehensive, because quitting the job wouldn't go down at all well with the agency, so was I burning a bridge I couldn't really afford to? The bottom line in a situation like this is a person has to make that leap: if you don't you'll always wonder about what might have been; and you could just as well lose your job working in an office as dancing in a discotheque and still have to start again. If you want to succeed at something you have to fully commit to it and not just dip a toe in the water. Here I was at near enough nineteen years old, and fate had put me in the right place at the right time with all the right moves so I had to at least give it a try.

★　　★　　★

The audition was at the Casino Knokke, in a seaside resort near the Dutch border, and the Stigwood Organisation had booked me on a flight from Southend Airport to Ostend, which was on one of those small planes that got tossed around so much I honestly thought I wasn't going to make it. I was so frightened, and I could see how bad it was because of the nervousness on the stewardesses' faces – one of them kept taking her hat off and putting it back on again! I was silently praying to myself, 'Oh please God, you can't take me now, I have to get to this audition!'

I practically kissed the ground when we got there, but what was to come was almost as daunting. The audition was for a month-long dancing gig in Greece, and it was to take place onstage in the nightclub they had in there, but it wasn't to take place while the club was closed, it was as part of that night's show, in front of a full-house audience. Talk about being thrown in at the deep end – I had never danced onstage before! Several other black girls would be dancing that night, and I was told they were from Paris, which didn't help as I was just dressed in an ordinary trousers and top – like I was going to the office – and I assumed if they were from Paris they would be very exotic and dressed in all the latest fashions, showing me up. As it was, when I met them they turned out to be very down-to-earth girls. By the time the show started I had relaxed as the place and everybody in it was so nice – we each had our own little dressing rooms, which was a relief, then the manager told me because he'd seen the others dance before he wanted me upfront. More pressure!

The band did one number and then we dancers came out, took our places and just got into it with no choreography or routines, just freestyle with us looking as good as we could while we were dancing. The band was excellent – very funky, with horns and everything – so it wasn't difficult to get into the music, and *boy* did I get into it! I was giving out so much energy that one of the other girls danced over to my spot on the stage and said to me, 'Better you don't use so much energy right now; you need to save some because we're up here for an hour and that is going to seem like a long time!' I was so carried away and I really wanted to impress, so I said, 'No, it's OK, I'll be fine,' and I got crazy again.

This was my first taste of real show business, and although I remember it as being every bit as exciting as I'd hoped it would be, I wish I could remember more of it! We danced and danced and the people applauded and applauded, and suddenly that was it – the hour had gone by in what seemed like seconds! Back in my dressing room I was still on a high, then there's a knocking at my door – my locked door – and I hear, 'Marcia, Marcia!' quite urgently. It's the boss of the casino, saying he wants to see me and my mood changed instantly: I'd been told I would be notified in two weeks' time if I'd got the job, so this must mean I'd not made the grade; or he wants to try and take advantage of me . . . either way it was not good. I approached him with great trepidation, thinking about how I *really* didn't want to go back to temping, and he told me, 'That's it. You're in. You were fantastic and you're going to Athens with the rest of the girls.'

So now I had got a proper professional job; I was officially a *dancer*, not just an office worker who liked to dance. When I went to Greece I was so relieved, I was completely sure I had signed with the right people, which was so important, especially for somebody as young as myself. The reality of what I was doing fully sank in, and I began to feel that this was me, this was truly my thing.

I was dancing in the nightclub of a big Athens hotel, in front of a seven-piece live band, the J.J. Band, who played mostly cover versions and would really cut loose on all the excellent soul music they played. There were several of us girls and we'd take it in turns to go up on stage in groups of two or three and dance a few numbers – for about half an hour. The dancers would carry on when the band was taking a break and the disc jockey was filling in. This was perfect, because it was a very energetic show and we could give it everything when we were up there and not get tired out. I was never nervous, I don't know why not – this was my first job and I had every right to be! Maybe because I was on such a mission all I could think was, 'OK, you've reached this far, now don't fall on the next step.' It also helped that I wasn't comparing myself to anybody else; that will always make somebody nervous because they'll be worrying about living up to what it is they see. It didn't matter to me how the other girls were dancing; in fact, they were all excellent but their moves might not be right for me, so why compare myself? All I ever did was go up and do my best – it was the same all through Boney M. and it is today, that way you have much less to get nervous about. Anyway, the crowds seemed to love it and we always got great rounds of applause when we went off stage.

It was really the best introduction to this new world, as it was all relatively easy and straightforward. It was one month at one hotel with one address, so there was no packing and unpacking or spending hours on a bus, and none of the anxiety that might come about from always wondering what the next gig will be like, what sort of state the next hotel will be. Being at one place gave us extra security too, because we were there long enough to get to know the staff in the hotel and in the nightclub, which made our lives run a lot more smoothly. We had room and board provided by the hotel, and the pay was about three times what I was getting as an office temp. Life was pretty good for a teenager just six years out of Jamaica!

It was simple to get into a routine, because when I was done in the club it might be as late as two in the morning, then I'd have to take off my make-up before I got into bed, so most of the days were taken up sleeping! I'd get up at about one o'clock, get dressed and ready, get something to eat and then head to the club. I always liked to be there early, because I don't like drama before a show and things are far more likely to go wrong if you're trying to prepare in a rush. Also, I quickly discovered the best thing for me was to sit quietly and take time to get into myself before going on stage, something that became more spiritual as my career went on. These pre-show routines of keeping things as calm as possible haven't changed up until today.

I found it easy to get along with the other dancers, and because it made sense not to move about this foreign city by myself, we would look around Athens together on our days off. It was a fascinating place, but so was the window shopping! It was still fashionable to wear fur in those days and the city was full of furriers where we were told the coats were much less expensive than they were in London, but still none of us could afford them! We were just feasting our eyes, standing in front of the shops nudging each other and going, 'Ooh, look at that one!'

Going back to London wasn't the comedown it might have been, my hard work and dedication out there had paid off as everybody in Athens had said they were very happy with me and the Stigwood people had told me there would be more bookings. The only problem was they didn't say when, so rather than spend the money I'd saved while I was away I signed on with another temping agency. I didn't feel as if it was a step down to go back to office work; in fact, it was so much easier than when I'd just left school, because at that point I didn't know where I was going and so I couldn't see anything else. This time I knew it was exactly what the agency called it – temporary!

Of course I could go back to office work, even the constant coffee-making, because I knew it would just be what I did and not what I was. What I was was on the first rung of what I knew would be a pretty tough climb. Having that sense of direction in my life was, to me, as good as actually making it – I knew I wasn't any sort of star, I knew I was just at entry level, but because I could already see the rewards and the progress my hard work was bringing I was sure that little by little I would get there. I wanted more and it was only a matter of time.

In the meantime, however, I felt pretty proud of what I had done, I'd gone away by myself – I was still a teenager – and I hadn't let myself down in this new professional environment. Importantly, as I still had responsibilities, I had come home with a very healthy bank account – it cost me hardly anything to live out there, I didn't go out partying and there wasn't much time to spend money otherwise, so I'd saved quite a bit. When I came back from that first trip Elaine was really excited for me, she gave me a compliment that to this day is one of the nicest things anybody has ever said to me: 'Marse! I know you like the back of my hand, and that you've just gone off and done so well is no surprise to me.'

Now it was just a case of waiting to see where the Stigwood Organisation took me for my next step towards my goals.

## Chapter Eighteen

# 'I grabbed the mic and started singing'

My next job was in Germany, at the Top Ten Diskotek in a place called Harburg on the outskirts of Hamburg. I travelled over there by sea from Southend, which took a couple of days and was quite an experience – I'd never been on a ship before! I was there for four months at a time, returning to London in between for a bit more temp work before going back. The pay was good, and it was the same deal as I'd had in Greece – the discotheque had ten rooms upstairs where the dancers and other performers lived and a restaurant where we all ate – so I was able to save nearly every penny I made. By the time I went home after the first stint, when I put my earnings together with what I'd saved from Greece and a little money Mama had put aside, I had enough to buy a flat for us in Peckham: two bedrooms and a living room, for cash – £2,750.

Immediately I became Miss Houseproud, and every time I came back from Germany with some more money I would organise some improvements to the place. It was the first time we'd had a home of our own, and as it was really just a house split in two the first thing I did was make it self-contained by putting in our own front door downstairs and another new door leading into the living room. Then I renovated the kitchen.

And so it went on, patiently doing a bit each time for the next few years until it was exactly how I wanted it. It was around this time that I could afford for Mama to stop work. She had worked so hard all her life and it used to break my heart to see her coming home from the factory with cotton in her hair and looking old before her time. Now it made sense for her to be at home, because I was away so much, Wayne was growing up fast and the two of them were devoted to each other. It wasn't a perfect situation, but if you consider how I and so many others I'd known had grown up it was what I knew and what I knew to be something a child could adapt to – second to his mother, who better to look after Wayne than his grandmother?

The Top Ten Diskotek had two shifts: the first, Teenage Dance Party, began at four in the afternoon and was for youngsters, literally *teenagers*, which was a lovely idea – the kids would come and dance, hang out, listen to the music and even go outside where there was a beautiful lake – I'm not even sure if they served alcohol. I would be there for between two or three hours, sometimes dancing on the podium or sometimes the kids would move back on the floor to give me space to come down and dance, afterwards they'd applaud and move back on to the floor to do their own things, it was a bit like *Soul Train*. After eight o'clock the club was for the older folks. I'd get a break then and come back about ten o'clock or so, and what I did was more or less the same. We all got a couple of days off during the week, when it was quiet – Thursday through the weekend to Sunday was packed in there, but the beginning of the week was much calmer. The work was hard, but who was I to complain? I was fresh and I was young, and it was all so enjoyable that I threw myself into it, which must have impressed the management because I was the only girl that kept being asked back.

There was no live music at the Top Ten, it was only a DJ and records, with two or three different dance acts that rotated during the two shifts, but although the vibes were always very good in there, there wasn't that *live* music feel and I must have thought things needed shaking up. Although I don't remember planning anything, one night I was dancing up by the DJ, and I thought, 'Enough of this crap!' I grabbed the mic that was next to his turntable. The Edwin Hawkins Singers' 'Oh Happy Day' was playing and maybe it was the spirit of that gospel took me, but completely spontaneously I started singing along with it. I began by joining in that big chorus then really got into the song itself. If the crowd in there looked shocked, the manager and Uwe the disc jockey looked like they might pass out!

I finished up to a really good applause, and it was when the manager came over that what I had done hit me. I had no idea what he was going to say, but I was still on a bit of a high so was ready for anything. It was like a replay of Jackie Edwards in the Q Club and all he said was, 'I didn't know you could sing like that!' Then he spoke to Uwe and went away. From seeing the reaction, the boss was sure he had something that would bring the crowds into his club, so he asked me to do my Teenage Dance Party dance stint, then to come down later on, in my evening dress, and sing two or three songs. It was brilliant! I decided on a little repertoire, which I remember had Jackie Wilson's 'Higher and Higher', 'Land Of 1000 Dances' by Wilson Pickett and 'Get Ready' by The Temptations in it – I knew the lyrics to practically every soul song because I'd been dancing to them for so long. For me, this was fantastic, because it gave me a little opportunity to practise and to learn what I had to do to fulfil my dreams – by that point I knew I wanted more than just dancing, which may have played a part in me picking up the mic like I did.

Harburg is not very big, so it didn't take long to get round local entertainment circles that there was this hot new girl from Jamaica singing at the Top Ten. One night after a performance, I was approached by this guy Ernst Harnell, who managed local groups and said they were always looking for singers. He said he would like to do some management for me, how soon could I start? I felt really flabbergasted – this was it, this was what I'd always wanted, and here it was being presented to me.

After that, everything happened so quickly: I had been coming to the end of a stint at the Top Ten, so there wasn't any problem with the Stigwood Organisation, and maybe a week later I was meeting the bands Ernst had contacts with and rehearsing a little bit with them. They were bands like The Tornadoes or The Vallendras, who were pretty big on the club circuit in Germany, and I would go on the road with them either doing a few numbers with them or opening for them with taped backing. I'd do a few promotional things too: setting up in a shopping centre and singing a little ditty in praise of some product or the other, like a living advert! I was sent to Switzerland to sing a little jingle for Camel cigarettes, even though I didn't know anything about them because I've never smoked. However, that didn't stop me setting up in the shopping malls with two dancers beside me and singing about the joys of smoking: *Camels are great fun! When I first wake up in the morning* . . . I'd do a few gigs, then go back to London for a couple of days, then back to Germany and back on the road.

The money wasn't fantastic – I made more as a dancer – but I was working more so that balanced out; I could spend four or five hours in a day travelling but I was getting to see a bit of Germany; and I really felt I had moved up to another stage – I hadn't made it yet, but I was obviously going in the right direction. Pure and simply, I loved it.

Once more it seemed as if I was in the right place at the right time, had met the right people and was ready to work hard at what I was doing – if you take the definition of luck as 'what happens when opportunity meets preparation', then I was very lucky. At that time in Germany soul music was a really big thing, so there was a fashion for black girl singers and dancers, many of whom were like myself, coming from England and of Caribbean descent. I was being billed as the Beauty From Jamaica or the Hot Chocolate From Jamaica – this was the 1960s, remember! I had good people looking after me too, which was very fortunate as everything had moved so quickly I hadn't had time to think about it too deeply. From day one, with Ernst Harnell, the bands, the promoters, the venue people and so on everything was correct and I was treated with total respect. I'm sure there were sharks out there, but looking back over forty years in the music business I do believe, in general, it was much more civilised back then. I was never scared and I was never approached improperly; in fact, people went out of their way to make sure I felt comfortable.

This manager was ready to invest in me, so pretty soon after I started on the road he sent me to a vocal coach for technique training – I won't call it 'singing lessons' because I don't believe anybody can be truly taught to *sing*, but everybody can learn techniques that can improve *how* they sing. I went to the Edie Hofner Schule in Hamburg for three months, which at first was a little daunting. One of the things Edie did was to put her fingers into my mouth to feel my tongue, which was worrying enough, but she had a little dog that was running around the place and all I could think was, 'Did you wash those hands after you petted the dog?' Edie taught me to understand my voice, how it worked and how I could get the best out of it. We did breathing techniques, how to hold a note, how to bring it back into another note, how to emphasise specific notes in a sequence, breath control so notes began and ended exactly when you wanted them to, or how to sing quietly with power and loudly without screaming or shouting. I also learned how to sing and dance at the same time, which might sound obvious but you have to know what you're doing if you don't want to miss notes or be panting for breath after two or three numbers.

Through Edie I learned how to portray a song exactly the way I wanted to, and, most importantly, how to do it with minimum effort or strain – that way your voice will hold up better during a show and will last longer over your career. That's the only training I've ever done, and it was over forty years ago, yet I'm still benefiting from it today as I'm still sing-ing like I was in the Boney M. days and I've had no setbacks with my vocal cords, even after having a tumour removed from my oesophagus – thank you, God! Too often I see people who started around the same time whose voices are completely shot because they're worn out. I tell my young backing singers if they're serious about a career, they should invest in some training.

Gradually I got better known and got to meet more people in the German music business. I was opening for all sorts of acts in Germany and other European countries, plus I was doing my own club dates. A German record producer, Joe Menke, had prepared backing tracks for me of instrumental arrangements of numbers like 'Get Back', 'Whole Lotta Love', 'Preacher Man', 'All Along the Watchtower' and 'Smilin' Faces Sometimes', recorded specifically for my voice, and I would swap them around in my set. I used to pay him a little bit for the playbacks, and I had invested in my own reel-to-reel tape recorder, so I was totally self-contained – I had a sound engineer so we could just turn up at a nightclub, plug it into the sound system and I was away.

I was building my own audience, which meant going beyond the cover versions, and I wrote and recorded both sides of my first single which came out in Germany in 1972 – 'Could Be Love', with 'It's Time To Go' on the B-side, produced by Joe Menke. I wouldn't say it was a chart topper, far from it, but it got very good reviews and taught me a lot about how the record business worked and what needs to be put into it as regards marketing and promotion. I learned that no matter how good the music might be, it's only a part of it! It was during that period that Joe and another German songwriter/ producer, Drafi Deutscher, wrote the song 'Belfast' for me – they wanted to send out a positive message about the troubles in Northern Ireland, and originally it was called 'Londonderry', but they couldn't make the word fit neatly into a chorus! I never recorded it, but it became a really popular part of my live show. I used the very same backing tape for the absolute first Boney M. stage show, and as soon as Frank Farian saw how every audience loved that song he decided to take it for the group!

I stayed like this for about five years; I never became any sort of big sensation – before the Internet or MTV nobody became a star overnight – but I was out there! I was active, I was moving forward and I was earning a few bucks – at one point I had over 100,000 German Marks in my bank account, over $40,000, which was a huge amount of money in the 1970s. Recording and working with Joe Menke had given me hope there was something bigger and better out there.

I was even dating a German man at this time who I'd met at the Top Ten. I would stay at his flat in Hamburg while I was working in Germany, but even though I kept clothes and other personal effects there, I wouldn't have said we ever really lived together. He was seven years older than me and seemed like a very nice person at the beginning of our relationship, which didn't last very long. He was a stockbroker employed by one of Hamburg's big banks and we stayed together into the Boney M. days, when, unfortunately, I allowed him to manage my earnings, knowing he was a qualified banker. Back then, although he used to treat me well, it was never going to be serious because ultimately all I wanted was to do my job properly and get back home to England as soon as possible to a set of responsibilities that didn't concern him and would always take priority in my life.

I'd go home as often as I could and stay for as long as I could, usually around a week, and each time I'd organise something else to fix up in the flat, and make sure everybody had everything they needed. That end of things was straightforward, what

# ROOT

Britain's biggest Black ma

DEC · JAN 1980/81 75p

**JAMES BALDWIN writes on jazz**
**PROFESSOR PANKHURST on**
**Pushkin's ancestry**
**Xmas food and drink**
**Plus: Fashion, Reviews, People...**

Such a privilege to get on the cover of Britain's first black fashion magazine, *Root*.

Steigenberger Airporthotel · Postfach 75 04 29 · D-6000 Frankfurt 75 Flughafen

Flughafenstraße 300 - 304
D-6000 Frankfurt/Main 75
Telefon: (06 11) 6 98 51 · Telex: 04 13 112 aiho d
Telegramm: airhotel frankfurtmain
Bankverbindungen in Frankfurt/Main:
Commerzbank AG, Flughafen
Konto-Nr. 7 417 355 (BLZ 500 400 00)
Dresdner Bank AG
Konto-Nr. 967 506 (BLZ 500 800 00)
Hessische Landesbank - Girozentrale -
Konto-Nr. 11 836 004 (BLZ 500 500 00)
Postscheckkonto:
Frankfurt/Main, Konto-Nr. 411 81 - 609 (BLZ 500 100 60)

Ihr Zeichen    Ihre Nachricht vom    Unser Zeichen    Hausapparat    Tag

A Birthday Message    16th May, 1981.

To:- Mama
From:- Cherry B.

Mother Of Mine
My love Devine
Sincere friend of a Life time
You are my only Valentine

Sitting here alone on your birthday
Wondering what makes a hard day
Mixing with people who are meanless to me
Life seem to be deciding for us
Thus! indeed in eachother we trust

Your inspiration, inspires me
Your warmth, glows over me
Your modesty, soothes me
Your beauty, satisfies me
Your character, powers and enchant me
Mother Of Mine
Oh! Lady of a lifetime
You loving me, ever and ever
The loving you, a pleasure forever
Mother Of Mine

A. Steigenberger Hotelgesellschaft AGaA
Sitz der Gesellschaft: Frankfurt. — Persönlich haftender Gesellschafter: Egon Steigenberger. — Vorsitzender des Aufsichtsrats: Max Greifele. — HR: B 8297
Weltweit kostenlose Buchungen durch den Steigenberger Reservation-Service

A poem I wrote for Mama on her birthday, Frankfurt, 1981.

Singing in my self–produced solo show at the Drury Lane Theatre, November 1981.
*(Photo by Peter Bischoff/Getty Images)*

Marcus and I frying fish in Eddy Grant's yard, 1983.

Marrying the man of my dreams on our beautiful island of Jamaica, 20th August 1984.

With producer Joe Menke in 1990 –
he worked with me pre-Boney M.,
and co-wrote 'Belfast'.

Whilst undergoing
chemo, I used my bald
head to my advantage
rather than covering
it up.

(above) The magazine I published, to celebrate my battle
with illness.

(right) Boney M. champagne presented to me in Moldova
– the champagne's long gone but we still enjoy the bottle.

At home
1996.

Our beautiful waterfront Florida home, with my baby, Sasha – she was such a comfort to me during my illnesses and really helped me when I had to learn to walk again.

Marcus and I today
– still happy and still
looking good!

Touring as a solo
artist – no more
Boney M., but the
road is still the road!

was difficult was leaving Wayne because each time I had to say goodbye it really tore me up. I was reassured to know that he was in good hands, as now Mama was there to take care of him full time and because of the love she showed for him now I trusted her completely. That allowed me to prepare for and do my shows without worrying about what was happening to my son, who was growing into a young man by this point, but it didn't make the moments when I had to walk out the door any easier.

By the middle of the 1970s, I felt as if I was standing on the threshold of Marcia Barrett, solo star. I knew I still had a way to go, but the prospects were tempting and the idea of a solo career suited my loner mentality. The last thing I wanted to do was become a permanent member of a group. Or so I thought, because this was when that lady Katja Wolfe got in touch, representing Frank Farian and looking for black women to join a group called Boney M.

We've already looked at how that would totally transform my life, but no matter how successful or glamorous the group became it did nothing to protect me from what life would throw at me when I left Boney M.

*Part Three*

# PERSEVERANCE

## Chapter Nineteen

# 'We were just having fun and feeling brilliant'

Boney M. had dominated my life for almost fifteen years, and much as I had enjoyed most of it and it went a long way towards making me the woman I became, it was a huge relief not to have to rush around the world at someone else's beck and call. Yes, it left a great big Boney M.-shaped hole in my life, but I saw that as much more of an opportunity than something lacking – I was looking forward at what was going to be, rather than back at what wasn't any more. I would no longer be around people that I knew didn't have my best interests in mind: from that point onwards I would be surrounded with love, peace and optimism, which was such a nice feeling. Without having to concern myself with the day-to-day running of the group, life got very simple for me. I had only two items on my agenda: 1) live a proper life with my husband; 2) get my solo career going. Luckily, they overlapped and could best be achieved from my lovely house in Hobe Sound, Florida.

I had the house built in 1980 just after Boney M. were at their peak. I picked Florida because it was easily accessible from London and it was only a short flight to Jamaica. Hobe Sound is about seventy miles up the coast from Miami, not far north of Palm Beach, and like all the towns along what they call the

Treasure Coast it sits just inland from the Atlantic Ocean across the Intracoastal Waterway, a wide stretch of water that runs all the way down America's east coast. We were on the mainland side of the waterway and there was a causeway bridge that led over to the beach and the ocean. The German architect who built the house was somebody I found through the German stockbroker I was dating at the time, and he recommended that town as he had connections in the area. He couldn't have picked a more idyllic location.

I bought two adjacent lots of waterfront land, with the Intracoastal flowing, literally, along the end of the garden. I had two boat docks and a low wall that I could sit on and fish or just watch the boats sailing past. I had the same view through the big picture window across the rear of the lounge, too. Marcus and I have seen it all on that stretch of water: the biggest yachts, private fishing boats, seaplanes landing, tourist party boats . . . sometimes it was our evening's entertainment! The house was built to my specifications – a single storey built around a big patio that led down to the garden and the water, with three self-contained suites, one each for Mama, Wayne and me – mine had a sauna built in. Then there was a big living room that was always filled with light. I had a lovely big modern kitchen put in so I could indulge my passion for cooking, but because this was Florida where so much of life is lived outside, there was also a big area for barbecuing – as soon as Marcus saw that his face lit up and he bought one of those enormous grills with the chimney, a smoker!

Marcus loved that house; he says if we ever get another built it should be exactly like that – I still have the plans – and I'm in agreement on that. However, while he still dreams about it, I don't. Not because I want to forget it, because they were fantastic years down there, but because the way we lost it was so upsetting, and I don't want to remember it like it was a loss, but we'll get to that later on.

Including the cost of the land, by the time it was all fitted out and furnished with antiques from Worth Avenue in Palm Beach, it set me back around $400,000, which back then *really* wasn't cheap, but it was a very important purchase for me. To be able to buy it for cash like I did was a definite symbol, to myself, that I had made it. For the first couple of years in Boney M. I could *feel* the success coming in slowly and I had dreams of how I would live when we finally made it, now this purchase proved to me I was getting to where I wanted to go. A bit later on I bought a third lot adjoining my property and the neighbours were all trying to look over to see what would be built, and some of them were more than a little grudging as this is the biggest piece of land around there and it's owned by a black woman!

The Hobe Sound house was also so important to me because it was a holiday home, a getaway where I could remove myself from all the Boney M. stuff and live a natural life. This is why I took so much trouble and expense to get it just right, because when you come off the road you need to unwind – totally. Also, nobody in Florida knew who Boney M. was, so I was never going to be recognised and could just go about my business. I could dress how I liked and there was no pressure on me to always look immaculate – that was my usual appearance anyway!

It was my retreat from what I did the rest of the time, a kind of haven where I could get a proper rest and recharge my batteries before getting back into the Boney M. fray. It was this sanctuary aspect of being in Hobe Sound that I was looking for after leaving the group. This period immediately after Boney M. – the beginning of the 1990s – was as much about personal regeneration as it was about professional growth.

Marcus and I had been married for about six years at this point, but I had been away with the group so much it felt like the start of our married life, and it was lovely. Straight away we were having the quality time together we'd never had before, and in many ways acting like a couple of kids!

On a typical day in Hobe Sound we would go about our sports; early morning, we'd go over the bridge onto the beach, then maybe go jogging around the island, or we'd ride our bicycles down to Jupiter Lighthouse. That's about ten miles each way, and we'd race each other, laughing and giggling – we were just having fun and feeling brilliant. This was the restorative power of that part of the world, the air, the sunshine, the beach, the ocean . . . You even love the rain in Florida! It was all so natural, sitting on the wall with our feet swinging over the water, catching fish and putting them straight on the outside grill.

Even when we went out to eat, the seafood and fish restaurants on the Treasure Coast were amazing, but again it was mostly straightforward cooking – grilling or steaming. There was this lovely crab restaurant in Palm Beach, Charly's Crabs on South Ocean Drive, where we'd go for anniversaries and birthdays and I used to eat a 3lb lobster by myself! Just grilled with melted butter. Now we live in Berlin, and I really miss eating like that. The only thing the same as in Florida is the size of the portions – I don't know who eats more the Americans or the Germans! We go to some lovely restaurants, though, and we've even got a couple of little grills outside on our patio here, although I don't remember them being used in seven years.

Looking back at those first few years in Hobe Sound it's a wonder we never got on each other's nerves, as we were in each other's company pretty much twenty-four hours a day, we did everything together with practically no disagreement. We didn't have disputes about anything big, indeed the only thing we always seemed to differ on was going jogging in the evening! Marcus would happily come with me in the morning but couldn't keep pace with my programme, so I couldn't get him out of the chair in the evening. I'd say, 'Come on, you ate today, didn't you? Let's go and shake it off!' And he'd tell me to take the dog! You know if that is all you've got to argue about then life has to be pretty good.

Gradually, once I'd got as much of Boney M. out of my system as I could, we started making music together. We didn't force anything, we knew we had time and wanted to let it happen naturally, which was fantastic for me after so many years of schedules and not having time to think about what I was doing. If any ideas came to Marcus he would go into Wayne's room, which we'd set up as a music room because he was hardly ever there; we had a little four track mixer in there and it's where Marcus kept his instruments. He would be in there, and I'd hear his riff playing through the house and would think, 'Aha! What is that?' After a while it might give me an idea so I'd go in and say something like, 'What about trying this?' Or I might get an idea for a lyric, or what I'm hearing might even fit with a lyric I've had in my head for a while, so I'd go in and we'd talk it through.

Most of the stuff we wrote together was written like that. The connections I enjoyed the most would happen if I was in the kitchen and Marcus was in Wayne's room, which meant we were opposite each other across the patio. Because we were on the water we'd make the most of the sea breezes and open the windows instead of running the air conditioning, so music would float from one room to the other, with the natural background of the rustling of the trees or the lapping of the waves. In the evening that could be magical. When Marcus was composing like that I would be particularly inspired to come up with my own contributions. I drop everything in the kitchen, run across to Wayne's room and start singing my melody or running through my lyrics. I know I've let a few pots boil over because I've got involved in the tune Marcus was working on!

Once we'd put our ideas for a song down on tape we'd sit down together, usually on this bench right on the waterfront, which was the perfect place, or in the living room if it was getting late, and go through what we'd done to start to put the tune together. Once we had the bass line, we'd put the melody on, then start adding the riffs to flesh it out. We'd work around with that for a while, then take another session on another day to add the lyrics. It was a real fun process, because we were both involved with every bit of it so it was always a complete collaboration – we even thought about working as a duo, and did a photo shoot with that in mind!

Sitting outside by the water was a real gift for us because it was so inspiring. I wrote the song 'Man in the Moon' out there because one night we were looking up at the stars and

I saw what looked like a man in the moon. I know it had to be something else and Marcus claims he never did see it, but it was so romantic out there you could think you saw practically anything! On another occasion we had been working in the studio with the guitarist Jimmy Haynes, he came back to our place that evening and after dinner started playing 'Amazing Grace' over the water. It was magical, the three of us just sat there as his beautiful playing rang out across the Intracoastal; my spirit was so moved by it I started singing. I don't know what tongue I was singing in but it seemed to fit the music perfectly – Jimmy said it sounded like Arabic, I don't know any Arabic but it could be so mystical out there who knows!

This is what I always imagined my solo career would be like, very laid back, very creative, with ideas developing naturally and with no outside interference. Also it meant we were keeping it all 'in house', which was very important for us after what happened to my previous shot at going it alone: I had cut a solo single for Boney M.'s label Hansa, but it had sunk without trace through no real fault of my own.

Back at the very end of the 1970s, about three years before my work with Eddy Grant, I thought it was the right time to launch a solo career, keeping it under the Boney M. banner but obviously my own thing. The group was at its height, which would work for me, and I believed another aspect to Boney M. wouldn't do them any harm either – I always felt there was plenty of space for everybody. It all started off brilliantly: I had met this beautiful composer and singer in London, Kelvin James, who was fascinated with my voice and the person I was, so had written some tracks with me in mind. I had taken on representation to get the solo thing underway, and the guy who was managing me, Derek Stirling, introduced me to an English producer, John Edmed. Of course he was keen to work with me – I was a big star! – but we hit it off really well and he produced three of the tracks Kelvin had written for me. The songs were entitled 'You', 'Breakaway' and 'I'm Lonely'. We recorded them in London, completely away from Boney M., and they were rockier than people might have been used to from me, but that suited me fine.

All of us were very pleased with the results, and I was really excited to get a solo single out there, so I took Kelvin and John to Germany to meet Frank. I thought the guys could do with the break and that this whole thing is going so well that we can branch out from such success, and everybody will benefit. However, Frank's a producer and constantly on the look-out for new talent, so he immediately put Kelvin in a studio, asked him to run through the songs he had written, accompanying himself on an acoustic guitar. He listens, says, '*Ja, ja, das ist gut,*' but absolutely loves 'Breakaway', the song that was planned for the B-side of my first single. There and then he says he wants it for the next Boney M. album *Boonoonoonoos*, and of course Kelvin isn't going to say no – a track on a Boney M. album for a young, budding songwriter, it's manna from heaven? To me, though, it was a big loss and I can't say I wasn't a bit resentful because I was so looking forward to doing that song as part of my solo launch. It did cross my mind that Frank might have taken it just to show me who was in charge. However, I chose to trust him and took it at face value when he said that he should have it for the group, telling me, 'Oh Marcia, you *know* this is a Boney M. song,' almost as if he was doing me a favour taking it!

At the time I didn't get too hung up about it, I just said, 'What the heck! Frank's just being Frank.' I figured I've still got the two other tracks and there will be plenty of others after this. I had already spoken to Frank about what I was doing; he knew I was really interested in a solo project, and how I was keen to put it under one roof. He seemed agreeable: 'Oh, *ja*, I'll do that . . .' So I went ahead and recorded the other two tracks with John as the producer, then 'You' came out on Hansa, with Frank overseeing it because, thanks to Boney M., he had clout at that record company. Things didn't work out well, though.

It wasn't publicised or marketed or promoted properly, and I can't help but feel that wasn't by accident because there is no way, at the very beginning of the 1980s, there's going to be no interest at all in the first solo single from the lead singer of Boney M. – even if the record had been terrible, which it wasn't! The record company fixed up virtually no press for me at all; I couldn't believe it and they just kind of stonewalled when I tried to find out about it. 'You' was a very good record and at the time the public deserved to hear it, but it got no push whatsoever and I believe it was only released to keep me quiet – there you are, it's out there, what more do you want? Then this lack of success could be used to tell me there was no point in me trying to go solo because the public didn't want it.

This is typical music industry politics: I suspect that it wasn't in their interests for me to build a solo career because it might have spelled the end of Boney M. and there's a good chance I'll take myself to another record company. Record companies spend so much time thinking about what could go wrong, it wouldn't have taken much for them to think that my single could kill their golden goose. I'm sure Frank was never too keen on somebody else producing one of *his* Boney M. girls!

I felt like this had been a little sham of a release, but the way I had to look at it wasn't that I had been stopped, merely that I had been set back: I was still determined to develop a solo career, I just knew that I would have to do it by myself. It was really valuable to learn the lesson that I shouldn't assume everybody has the same outlook as I, also on the plus side I'd met Kelvin and John so I could start building up my own posse, away from Frank.

I thought the best way forward would be to introduce myself to the world on my own terms. In November 1981 I put on *The Marcia Barrett Show* at London's Drury Lane Theatre, a big-time, full production to show what I could do away from Boney M.

Putting that show together was a real experience, and really enjoyable but very demanding as I was out of the country for so much of the time. I wanted to do it in the UK because I needed the physical distance between myself and Frank and Boney M. I picked the Theatre Royal as it was where we performed for the Royal Variety Performance so it held a great memory for me, plus I remembered its acoustics were fantastic. I hired the venue myself, for a Sunday night; I paid for all the musicians and technicians and for the promotion, so it wasn't exactly cheap. Derek Stirling got some great promotion for me: he got me on TV programmes like *3-2-1* and my show was even advertised on the sides of London buses, which was a real thrill! Tickets went on sale, but it didn't sell out. I made no money but that didn't matter, I invested in it because I wanted to show what I could do and I had realised after the experience with 'You' that I was going to have to take all responsibilities myself. It was a showcase that was less about selling tickets than the invited part of the audience – the music industry and the press. Even the advertising on buses and so forth was more to alert the industry to me as a solo proposition.

I engaged Boney M.'s touring band Black Beauty Circus, supplemented with a string section, to provide my music, because I knew I could trust them to give me the best possible show and if I was free for that date they would be too! When I asked them there was no hesitation at all, no arguing about money, just, 'Of course, Marcia, we'll be there for you!' That was really heartening. I auditioned dancers and singers, with the one condition that they were jobless at the time because I wanted to do my little bit to help the young and unemployed in London; my criterion was 'It doesn't matter if you don't have employment as long as you have talent.' Eddy Grant helped me choose the six singers I needed, because I'd met him when I had to present him with an award and we'd stayed friends. To this day I applaud his patience with those auditions because he sat there with me while we sorted through ninety girls, but that's Eddy Grant for you – if he says he's going to do something he'll always see it through. It turned out so well, the singers we selected were brilliant, one of them was Caron Wheeler who went on to huge success with Soul II Soul.

Rehearsals were hard but great fun because I knew the band so well, and it was so exciting because this was *my* project. It all had to fit in around Boney M.'s schedule so when I knew I was coming back to England I would set up a rehearsal date and because time was so precious my big memory of those days is jumping into my Mini Cooper to go out and get buckets of Kentucky Fried Chicken for everybody so the band didn't have to stop! It was worth the hard work, because the show was fantastic, the Jamaican reggae artist Count Prince Miller, who I knew from the old Q Club days, was the compere and he did a great job because he's as much a comedian as he is a singer. Kelvin James and his band did the first half, then after the interval Black Beauty Circus opened proceedings and I came on with a full line-up of six dancers and six backing singers. It was a true spectacular, and gave me such a feeling of freedom, able to take things in any direction I wanted – it was the kind of show I'd love to be putting on now, and I'm sure one day I will.

There was a lot of rock in the show – I did covers of 'Hey Joe' and 'All Along the Watchtower' – it was a real mixed bag because I wanted to show my versatility as a soloist. It was designed to be a little taste of everything people could expect from me and while some of it may have surprised people, which was my intention, it was very well received by the audience, the critics and the industry in general. Of course I invited Frank and the others in the group and their families but I didn't really talk to them too much about it.

Bobby couldn't make it because he had stuff to do in Holland, and I think the others were surprised at my commitment to a solo career and without wishing to appear rude, I wasn't really looking for their opinions or their endorsements – although Maizie was very nice about it! I wasn't looking to leave Boney M. either, this was purely for me to say, 'Hey, listen here! I'm not only in Boney M., but I am a soloist as well and this is what

I can do!' I believe the show achieved exactly that, as the tracks I did with Eddy Grant — the sessions at which I met Marcus — came about because CBS Records were one of the several record companies that took note of that show.

CBS wanted to sign me on a solo deal, and at the first meeting with them they asked me if I had a producer in mind. I didn't but I suggested Eddy Grant. They loved the idea, and went as far as wanting him to write some songs for me, which couldn't have suited me better. Eddy was perfect for the artist I wanted to become because as well as being so talented I believed he perfectly understood the combination of pop, rock and soul I wanted to do and, most importantly, he has always been his own man and was never intimidated by record companies. They were willing to pay for three songs to be done at his new Plantation studio in Barbados, then it took the best part of a year for work on the recording complex to be completed and to coordinate our schedules. Eventually I flew out in early 1983 to get to work.

Although, as I've admitted, I was more than a little distracted after meeting Marcus, the tracks turned out great, Eddy did a brilliant job and the record company were very satisfied and wanted to go ahead with me. Or at least they did before one of the head representatives in their London offices decided that releasing Marcia Barrett solo material would be a waste of time because I would be too busy with Boney M. to promote anything. As things stood, that was right, but there was no reason at all why something couldn't have been worked out. It's long been my suspicion that hints were dropped to CBS that there could be problems ahead and the last thing record companies want is problems, especially expensive high-profile ones. Whatever went into it they seemed to think I wasn't worth the risk and just pulled out of any further interest, which is why nobody's ever heard those tracks I did with Eddy. However, he's still got them, they even survived a fire at his studio, so who knows . . .

After all the pettiness and selfishness that had been standing in my way for a full ten years, being in that beautiful Florida location, with my lovely husband, making exactly the music we wanted was like a great big weight being lifted off my shoulders. This was true freedom for me to resume my solo career. I say *resume* rather than launch, because it had always been my plan to go back to it – it was really just on the backburner while I was in Boney M. Even when Frank was keeping me down over it I kept myself going by thinking, 'Don't worry. Don't lose heart. You know you can do it and someday your time will come.'

Now it had. At last I could get my fingers on the stuff we'd been putting together over the years. Marcus and I would put ideas together in our little demo studio then take them out to studios there in Florida to work them up further, because we were getting to meet the local musical community. We were finding studios and finding people in the business in neighbouring towns, and every appointment left us with hope that we were moving forward. There was one studio, Avalon in Port St Lucie, where the guy knew I was a big name and when he heard what we had he believed in it so much we figured we had a chance to start up there in America! We did a lot of recording there and in Palm Beach. It was simply wonderful.

Those first few years out of Boney M. were probably the

most relaxed and contented of my life to date: we lived in paradise; we ate well; we kept fit and healthy; the music was coming together nicely and I was looking forward to finishing off my first solo album. Then Marcus and I went to Jamaica for a holiday and to take in a music festival; by the time we returned to Hobe Sound my life would be changed out of all recognition.

## Chapter Twenty

# 'Cancer! The word jumps out of the sentence at you'

While we were living in Hobe Sound you could safely describe me as a fitness fanatic, because I knew I would be going back on stage at some point and I wanted to be ready for it. As well as the jogging and the cycling, I was going to a nearby gym a couple of times a week, where I had a personal trainer and was really getting into an exercise regime. I would do an hour on the treadmill just to warm up – Marcus would only usually manage thirty minutes! – then get on the bicycle and the ski machine for half an hour each – the ski machine was my favourite! Then there was the stairmaster . . . After a good aerobic session I would do weights – five forty-five pounders on each leg for three reps. More than once the people at the gym tried to convince me to compete as a bodybuilder, but I wasn't interested, I was just doing what I needed to do.

A couple of times a week, after about four hours in the gym with Marcus – by which time people were asking if we didn't have a home to go to – I would go into the dance room and dance like crazy on my own for an hour. People would be peeping in through the glass in the door and asking, 'Who is this woman? Where is she from?' So it was all fitness, fitness, fitness, I was thinking how ready I was to get back on stage and

I'd never felt better. So when I went for one of my feminine check-ups down in Palm Beach and I was told everything is fine but your cells are changing, I didn't think anything of it. I didn't really understand what it meant, but that was the only explanation that was offered. I didn't feel sick in any way and because I was fit I assumed I was healthy too, so we went on with our lives.

We went on holiday to Jamaica, staying at Bath Fountain, a spa hotel with hot springs in St Thomas, and something definitely wasn't right as my monthly was coming on at entirely the wrong time. That was very worrying because that never happened and it was much heavier than usual – one time Marcus had to walk behind me because there were spots of blood on the back of the white dress I was wearing. Still I had no other symptoms and felt good in every other respect so it became as much a mental as a physical issue because I didn't know what was going on at all.

As soon as we got back to Florida I went for a check-up at Jupiter Medical Center, because I wanted a second opinion. They examined me, ran some tests and took some X-rays, and told me they had to admit me because I had a tumour on my ovaries. I didn't have a clue, so I asked, 'Oh really, what does that mean?' That's when they told me I had cancer.

That was a very strange moment. When a doctor says you have cancer and you actually hear the word it jumps out of the sentence and hits you like a blow – *cancer*! I felt as if the word had doubled up like an echo in a big room: cancer . . . cancer . . . cancer! That word is literally all I could hear for a moment or two, then I kind of calmed down and my immediate emotions were of shock and confusion. I didn't know the medical stuff or how the immune system works, so it was as if I'd just been told something that couldn't be possible! All I could say was, '*Excuse me? This body? Cancer? Ovarian cancer?*' I couldn't understand how, with a body as fit as mine, this disease could ever enter. I was glowing. I thought I was untouchable. *Really!* I honestly believed the way I looked after myself, the exercising and healthy eating, would protect me from anything. To put it bluntly I thought cancer was something that happened to other people and I had never even considered it. The doctor explained to me it could strike anybody, that it really is a great leveller, and although I was fit and healthy in every other way I was never going to be immune to cancer. Nobody is. Now, when I do talks about getting check-ups for cancer, especially to women, I always stress this point: it's pretty much out of your control if you're going to get it, so the best thing is that it is diagnosed early, hence the importance of regular testing.

Things were happening fast, although for a while Marcus and I were probably still processing the idea that I had cancer and in a slight state of shock, but once I started thinking clearly it was all a matter of, 'What's the treatment? What happens next? We have to get rid of this . . .' There was no throwing up my hands in despair and wailing because unless you've been in that situation before you don't know what to do so you have to start asking questions. I've always been a very practical person and that side of me took over. The doctors impressed on me that the sooner they started treatment the better, and I was lucky – relatively speaking – inasmuch as mine was in its early stages. The Medical Center told me they were going to take me in straight away for surgery. To remove the tumour they would have to take out my ovaries, fallopian tubes and womb. For any woman that's a really big operation – psychologically as well as physically – but for me it wasn't presented as an option, the specialists told us that a high proportion of women didn't conquer ovarian cancer – this was back in 1994.

I felt I had nothing to worry about, I was sure that I was going to be OK. But that wasn't quite the vibe we got from the doctor who came in to run some tests before I went up for surgery; he looked doubtful and made a point of telling us there were no one hundred per cent guarantees in matters like this.

This was unsettling, but it didn't shake us; we are two strong believers and because we put our faith in God we were not afraid. In fact, it became a bit of a challenge for me, and I've never backed down from a challenge in my life! As I waited to go in I was thinking, 'I'll show him because I'm coming out of this.' It was very important, at that moment, for Marcus and I to believe that we would go home from this hospital and the minute we got in I would drink a glass of wine, ask Marcus if he'd caught any fish and start cooking for us . . . We had to remain positive that life would go on normally.

We had absolute faith in the doctors and nurses there; we had good feelings about all of them, even the doctor who looked unsure, Dr Schneiderman, who is now a good friend of ours. It wouldn't surprise me if hospital regulations required him to let people know there was a possibility of things not working out. We made sure we let them know how much we believed in them and how much we appreciated them. Before the operation we would always say to the doctors and nurses we had no doubt they were going to do it, sentiments which came from the soul and I think those good vibes gave them a little spark too.

The operation was a success, and the surgeon felt confident they had got all the cancer, which we had never doubted. As it turned out the worst thing about it was having to stay in hospital for three weeks afterwards, some of that time was on the recovery ward where they keep a close eye on you, then in my own room. I had to have blood transfusions, because I have always been anaemic, which were more uncomfortable than the operation because I was wide awake throughout! As I was lying there watching somebody else's blood flowing into my arm, it brought it home to me how in this life you can't be prejudiced. I didn't know whose blood this was; all I knew was that it was a match to my blood type and the donor could be any race or religion, so how could anybody hate when maybe the group they hate is saving their life? As my life continued I would have so many blood transfusions there's a good chance the donors have come from all over humanity's spectrum!

After my body had recovered from the shock of the surgery, they kept me there doing tests to establish the programme of chemotherapy I was going to be put on. This would last for about a year, I would be an outpatient coming in once a month for treatment, so they had to weigh up what I might need to get rid of any cancer that remained against what they thought my body could handle.

I used to get very impatient and would tell the staff, 'Come on. Give me my chemo! I have things to do!', but it was particularly hard on Marcus when I was in there. There was all the toing and froing as he came to visit me twice a day every day, then he was at home by himself with just our dog, Sasha, for company, and although he was always so positive I knew he still worried. Initially he was even more baffled than me about it, and when we first were told all he could say was, '*How? How could this happen?*' But all through the hospitalisation and the treatment he was a real source of inspiration because he never had any fear, he was never afraid that I would be anything other than well again. He would tell me that we hadn't even started what we had planned, and what would happen to all that music we'd been getting together? It couldn't go to waste. Marcus had great support from his family, too. He would pray for me as did his brothers in England and his sister in Atlanta who is a minister, she organised a prayer group to come to Hobe Sound and pray for me. It was such a show of love from them, I had to be all right!

When he wasn't visiting me he carried on as normal, looking after the dog, taking care of the house, fishing, composing and working on our music . . . This was so good for me because I could talk to him about everyday things as if nothing was wrong. He made me laugh when he told me neighbours would ask him, 'So how are *you*, Marcus?' And he'd tell them, 'Oh, I'm fine, but it's just Marcia that's in the hospital – she's the one that's going through it!'

When I left hospital I felt really hopeful about my life; I knew I had been in good hands and given the best possible treatment, I could feel the prayers that had been going around from family members, friends and fans, my room had filled up with flowers . . . I felt protected and cared for by people who loved me. There was only one thing I was disappointed in and that was every time the door to my hospital room opened I hoped it would be my son Wayne. But no, it was either a nurse or Marcus. I didn't even speak to him on the phone until I got home and then I'm not sure who called who. It was such a shame, but I had to get better, I couldn't let that throw me off.

As soon as I left hospital I did my best to get back into normal life. The minute Marcus brought me home I was in the kitchen cooking, rooting through the fridge and the pantry asking 'What do we have?' There was lovely music playing and I was dancing in the kitchen while I'm working. I'd even asked my oncologist if I could drink a glass of wine and she told me, 'Well, as long as you don't drink the whole bottle!'

The next day I asked Marcus what he was composing, he went down and started playing the tracks and when I heard anything that inspired me I'd drop what I was doing, run down to Wayne's room and straight off start singing a melody . . . I was back in the groove!

In the first days I had to go to the Medical Center every day – even Sunday. This isn't like back in Europe – nobody knows me so I don't have to dress up – but I thought, 'Why not? Make the effort to show how alive I am.' After the first week I was sitting down taking my chemotherapy and the doctor said to me, 'How many different outfits do you have in your wardrobe? Every day you've come here looking completely different!' I told him that's just my character. This was the thing: they never saw me with a long face, because why should I take my burdens down to other people? It's not their fault I have this illness, so why would making them feel uncomfortable help anybody? Everybody else has their own cross to carry, this was *my* cross and I would deal with it in a way that suited me and suited the people around me. We were all there for the same reason – to help me recover.

★    ★    ★

The course of chemotherapy lasted about a year, and after that initial period I'd go back to the Jupiter Medical Center once a month and they'd put a needle in my arm and I'd sit there for two hours while the chemo flowed into my veins. The frequency of the visits varies for different people, they monitor patients carefully to make sure they're not reacting badly to it, but the thing that affected me most about it was how tedious it was! After completing the chemo I had to have a one-off radiation treatment just in case there were any cancerous cells still hidden in there, and that was the only time I had a bit of an episode! I was preparing myself for it, the machine's red light was on and it was starting to whirr, they told me to breathe in and breathe out and I had a mild panic attack: 'You're not going to put anything near to my throat, are you?' They seemed a bit surprised – nobody knew I was a singer – and assured me, 'No, no, no, no! Nothing is going to be near your throat!' That was the only time I got alarmed, because I've always been very protective of my vocal cords. After that I made sure the doctors knew I sang for a living, and I really didn't want anything to spoil what I had planned for the future, especially after coming so far in beating that cancer.

There was no question of me refusing the treatment, or even not wanting it, because, like the chemo, it's going to save my life. The last thing I wanted was for the tumour to have the chance to build itself back up because I heard that could happen and, as I said before, I had things to do.

I couldn't wait to get back to my regular life – or as regular as it could be with the chemotherapy. Essentially I had to rein in my plans a little because of having to go to treatment or be available if one of the specialists wanted to see me, also it could leave me feeling a bit sick and woozy. But that was a small price to pay for life. It was psychologically important for me to get back into as much as I could as quickly as possible, because I was sure I would heal faster if I felt normal and people treated me as such, not like some sort of invalid. A big part of that involved going back to the gym because I'm convinced that the fact that I was so physically fit played a big role in my body fighting against the cancer. Now I figured getting back to exercise and weight training could only help with my recovery. The medication they give you is fine, but, I believe, it will only take you so far and then it's down to the patient – they have to add their own contribution, physically, mentally and spiritually, to the healing process.

The other reason for getting back to the gym was far more mundane – I had actually put on weight! Most people lose weight under those circumstances but I was starting to get a little plump! Not *fat*, just a little fuller, and I'm not sure if that was from the medication or because I was no longer working out. While it didn't bother me, it was an obvious reminder that I was missing the gym.

Within a couple of months we had found another gym in Jupiter, which was much closer to our home, and I threw myself into it, doing spinning classes and everything! Taking up exercise and weight training again gave me so much drive because I could feel myself getting stronger and each time I got on a different machine I was thinking, 'Right! This illness has no idea who it is messing with! If anybody thinks I'm going to succumb to it they are making a sad mistake!' I would be there pumping this and lifting that or testing the treadmill to its limits, then I'd finish up feeling so good, like 'Mission accomplished' and it was another round to me in the fight against that cancer. Marcus could tell you I would put so much into it sometimes there'd be a puddle of sweat under my machine and I'd come out of the spinning room shaking with my face so pale! I even convinced him to join me in there: at first he was reluctant because he thought it was all women, but I showed him there were men there and when he realised he didn't have to go mad like I did but could start gently he absolutely loved it.

My doctors were shocked at what I was doing so soon; I'm sure in the beginning they didn't approve, but when they discovered how fast I was healing and how well my body was reacting to the treatment, what could they say? They were surprised by my demeanour throughout the whole thing, they would compliment me on my positivity and I would tell them that because I had embraced my life once more it was impossible to be anything else. I'd do my thing in the gym, head into the steam room for a sauna, then we'd drive home from Jupiter to Hobe Sound very slowly, taking in what a beautiful part of the world we lived in. If Marcus hadn't been fishing we'd stop and buy two fresh fish or crabs straight from the boat, then we'd go home, light the grill, open a bottle of wine and life really was like paradise. If I find it hard to relate this to recovering from ovarian cancer at the same time, that's because there was so much joy and beauty in our lives the illness would recede into the background, where it was much easier to overcome.

Of course my hair fell out during the chemo. I was prepared for it as it's one of the things the hospital briefs you on, but the way it happened took me by surprise. When I left Boney M. I still had the long braids that had become something of a trademark,

247

but after a couple of years living such a natural lifestyle in Florida I wanted to grow dreadlocks like my husband. In order to keep my head looking neat, I had left the braids in but been locksing up underneath them for some time; my intention was to let the dreadlocks grow to shoulder length then cut out the braids. The locks were growing quickly and were several inches long, although people wouldn't have been too aware of them because I still had the braids at the end.

After the first couple of chemo treatments one or two locks fell out with no warning, and I wasn't sure what would happen next so I took to wearing a scarf around my head like a band around my hairline with my hair coming out through the top. Then quite a way into the chemo treatment, when my sister Blossom and one of my half-sisters, Dawn, were staying with us, I took the scarf off and my whole head of hair came off! I won't even say it fell out because it wasn't like that, it peeled right back like rolling up a carpet back on a floor – because it was locksing it held together and just came off all together like a cap. No scalp came away, just the hair and – bam! – I was left looking at myself in the mirror totally bald.

Although I was pretty sure it was going to fall out, I expected it to be more gradual, one dreadlock at a time. There is a lot of cultural significance in many black hairstyles and through-out our history wearing them is an expression of who you are, a source of pride and identity. Our hair can be much more than just something that is just to be styled on your head. I think I would have been even more shocked if I'd known that morning had been the last time I'd look in the mirror and see myself with my own hair for ten years, which we'll get to in a while.

I confess I did freak out a little bit because my whole head of hair just peeling away like that gave me quite a jolt and I started shrieking. '*I'm bald! I'm bald!*' Once that subsided, though, I took a long look at myself and 'I'm bald! I'm bald!' was replaced with, 'OK, so you're bald. What are you going to do about it?' Marcus was even more shocked than me, but I said to him, 'It's just my hair.' If keeping it would have helped to cure me then I would have fought to hang on to it, but that wasn't the case, so I let it go. It was something you are born with, you are used to, but if you have to lose it in getting better then what is the most important? Having my hair wasn't going to make any difference to what I had to do. I can completely understand why women cancer patients get very upset when their hair falls out, because it's a very visible sign that they are not well, but I think to come to terms with it avoids a great deal of stress, which in itself can hinder recovery. When I looked in that mirror I knew I was still Marcia Barrett of Boney M., regardless of whether I had hair on my head or not!

I thought about a wig, which would have been the easiest solution for my hair, but my eyebrows and eyelashes had gone too, so there was nothing to mascara and I would have to draw the eyebrows on with the pencil. And then I realised that my bald head actually looked pretty good, so I began to work out what I could do with it. I had to pencil some eyebrows on, which took a bit of practice; I did my make-up more or less the same, perhaps a little different around my nose; then it was a case of lovely bright lipstick, big colourful, dangly earrings and sometimes a bright scarf. Occasionally little wisps of hair would appear and I would shave them off; otherwise the only mainte-nance required was to keep my scalp greased, and very soon I got to love my bald head. I felt one hundred per cent confident when I went out, and other people took to it too, as people I met didn't know I'd had chemo so they would assume it was a style. They'd tell me how much they loved my head and would advise me not to grow my hair back!

Being proud of what had happened to me because of the chemo was another way of bringing it into my world instead of the illness bringing me into its world. I am sure it was things like this that helped me to feel like I was in control, which went a long way to keeping me optimistic.

After the full course of chemo and the radiation, when I was told I was clear it was more than just a relief, it was a fantastic piece of news. Although we had no doubts this is how it would end up, it was still such a joy to be in the office with my oncologist who looked through her book that made up my file, going 'Mmm . . . hmm . . . Mmm . . . Mmmm . . . Hmmm . . . And you're feeling fine?' I replied I was, and she told me, 'Well, that's it then!' After a year out of my life, it was all over. The most recent round of blood tests had found no more cancerous cells, so although I'd have to go back for tests every so often for a few years, I was free of it. That meeting almost seemed like an anticlimax after the year we'd been through – 'OK, that's it, you're done!' We joked that there should have been some sort of ceremony or at least a bigger announcement.

Not that it mattered; the key word was *free*. We were free of this weight that had been on top of us for so long, and after having life on hold for a year we were unchained, and it was such a beautiful feeling. We could reset our goals as composers and artists, pick up the pieces and say, 'OK, *now* this is it!' We had been very active during that time, turning our ideas into basic tracks, but all of sudden it was time to go into our demo studio and get some backings done. Just the act of doing this was so liberating it made the previous twelve months disappear. I've never liked dwelling on the past so that was a big part of getting closure on this.

After I had been given the all-clear I started to think about how my experiences could help other people; and because of my optimistic approach I was asked to talk to those with the illness and hopefully inspire them. So I shared my view that it was important to stay upbeat and not to give up, no matter how disheartening things might appear. I would say, 'Do you enjoy life? Do you want to live?' I'd say that although we go through hard times, and in something like cancer there can seem to be no hope at all, there is still no reason to be afraid. I'd tell them if they were afraid they would lose hope and without hope there could be no belief. That was the key for me, so I would impress upon them it should be the key for them and motivate them to have that belief. I'd ask them if they *wanted* to believe they would get better, which of course they did, so then it was a matter of encouraging them to do so: belief in themselves and the powers of their bodies to heal; belief in their physicians. Most importantly of all, I would urge them to believe they were not finished yet, that they had a life to enjoy. If they registered all of that in their hearts, their souls and their brains, then nothing would be able to stop them.

I would also advise them on the reactions of people around them, helping them to avoid the sort of negativity that could come their way and be damaging to the positive vibes. Marcus and I told as few people as possible what I was actually suffering from, only if it was absolutely necessary, especially in the early days, because as soon as you say the word 'Cancer' they start to dig your grave! It's usually just unthinking rather than anybody wanting to do you down, but although people are trying to be sympathetic the expression on their face or the tone of their voice can be very discouraging. It's natural because there is so much pessimism around cancer and people tend not to focus on the success rates – when I told my own son Wayne that I was clear, he seemed doubtful and told me, 'Cancer is cancer.' That word strikes so much fear in people. Of course those close to you will pull you up about it when they do find out: 'Why didn't you tell us? We're family!' However, after what we had been through that was relatively easy to cope with.

I really had faith in that sort of positive thinking, and would hold myself up as the best example I knew of somebody who never had any fear, never had any doubt and had come out the other side to be back at the gym lifting weights! Little did I know that I would have to use these motivational skills on myself: three years after being given the all-clear from cancer in my ovaries, the disease struck again – this time in my right breast.

## Chapter Twenty-one

# 'How could I start feeling sorry for myself?'

When I was first told that I had breast cancer to say we were stunned would be a huge understatement. We couldn't believe it! Our immediate reaction was '*Again!* How could that *possibly* be?' I thought cancer was like getting mumps or the measles: if you've had it once and you've been pronounced clear you have some sort of immunity and can't get it again! We were in such a state of shock when we left the Medical Center that Marcus pulled out of the hospital car park and he turned the wrong way and was driving on the wrong side of the road. We were heading into the traffic, cars were coming down on us hooting, with drivers waving and shouting. That was what focused us, because it was so frightening to see those cars bearing down on us, we had to pull off the road and get ourselves together.

I had detected a lump in my breast a week or so previously when I was in the shower, called Marcus and he said he could feel a lump, too. At that point I was just thinking what could it be? Somewhere in my mind I was thinking, 'Well, I *suppose* . . . perhaps it *might* be . . .' I had never heard of anybody getting cancer twice. I was so naïve I thought after all that chemo and radiation that would be the last thing that could happen to me. Perhaps, like the first time, I was a bit over-confident because I was so fit at the time and I wanted to believe I had completely killed it off – I remember getting a bit sharp with my half-brother Winston when I told him I had recovered from the first case and he said, 'You mean you are in remission?' I told him, 'No! I'm clear! I beat it! I won't have cancer again!' But in spite of what I thought I knew, I was also aware that the earlier these things are identified the better so I had to confront it.

I was due for my twice-yearly check-up the next week, so when I went in to see Dr Reich, my oncologist, I told her about the lump and after feeling it she took some tests that confirmed it was cancer. Once what she was telling me had sunk in, I really didn't have time to feel resentment like, 'What have I done to deserve this? Why can't this cancer leave me alone?' I've never been the sort of person to feel sorry for myself, and I don't know if I might have started then because it was a pretty low moment, but what I knew was I *had* to start planning for the treatment I needed. That was when I heard the doctor telling me, 'You'll beat this, you've done it once, you'll do it again. Now go and get better as soon as you can, because I have no doubt you will.'

Obviously we were still really shaken up when we left to go home, but nearly getting wiped out in a head-on collision did a great deal to calm us down and make us think about how precious life is. I wanted to take the same approach to the disease: 'OK, this really is a pain in the arse, but we're going to have to deal with it. *I've got things to do!*' My aim was to go into my reserves, to have faith in God, have faith in the doctors who were going to take care of me and have faith in myself. I would stay strong, not worry and look at it straightforwardly: 'OK, what's the next step?' The medical bills from the first treatment had more or less wiped us out: every doctor and every surgeon needed paying, then there was the out-patient treatment costs and the cost of my hospital stay – the bill was itemised like a hotel bill! I had stopped receiving royalties by this point, so we had nothing coming in and had been burning through my savings. I was still a British citizen and I had my blue passport, so I decided I would go back to London for treatment and stay with my sister Blossom in Croydon.

When I phoned to tell her about the illness, first of all she freaked out a little bit – '*Lawd mi God!* Why dis cancer don't leave you alone? What is it? A plague on you now?' But she agreed that we could come and stay, and as she and her husband weren't together at the time she said we could have her room. Getting treatment would not be a problem: as Marcia Barrett, British citizen, I could just turn up at the hospital – back then everything was far less complicated, you didn't even need to be registered with a GP, you just needed to be sick.

Although we were going to be staying at my sister's we still needed to raise some money to finance the trip – we would be away for eight or nine months – so we decided to sell some of my antique furniture. We didn't want to, but my health was far more important and we couldn't see how else we would get the money to go to England. There was a couple we used to see when we jogged around Jupiter Island in the mornings who were always very pleasant to us and we knew they had an antique store. So, Miss Brazen, I knocked on the door of their house, introduced myself – they said they knew who I was, which was very nice – and told them I was ill and needed to raise the money to go to England for treatment. I said I had some antiques at home, and asked if they would be interested in buying a couple of pieces. My plan was that when I got back on my feet, if they hadn't sold my pieces, I would like to get them back and pay interest on the money. We called it mortgaging the furniture and wrote it into the contract.

Two days later she came round, walked through the hall, the living room and the bedroom and selected a marble-topped French commode, a little chest of drawers in our bedroom and a piece of silk carpet. I was looking at Marcus and thinking, 'Oooh! This is going to work!' because although I knew the value of those pieces, it was all so spur of the moment I hadn't really known if they would be interested. She said she would give us $30,000 for those three items. So that was it. We booked the airline tickets and we were on our way.

I went to the Mayday Hospital in West Croydon for my operation – it's now called the Croydon University Hospital – it was local to my sister's, which I was using as my address, so the arrangements could be made very quickly and I was admitted more or less straight away. I was operated on there, then I was to have the chemo and radiation treatment at the Royal Marsden Hospital in Surrey. There were two beautiful teams of people in those hospitals and I was very well looked after in each case.

I didn't tell any of the staff there that I was Marcia Barrett of Boney M., I was just Marcia Barrett-James the cancer patient, but eventually they worked it out and some of them would freak out a bit when they got it: 'Boney M.! Boney M.! Oh my gawd!' Sometimes I'd catch other patients looking at me like, 'No, I can't believe it . . . is that her? . . . No . . . It can't be . . .' But they wouldn't approach me because we were all patients there, all with our own health issues and nobody needed any extra pressure. The staff and Professor Yarden were great; I told them I didn't want people to know what was happening to me because that would attract interest from the press and I couldn't handle having newspaper people coming around while I wanted to concentrate totally on my health. I wanted to get over it and then I could talk to the media about how I beat it. In spite of that old saying 'there's no such thing as bad publicity', talking to the press about what I was going through definitely wasn't what I wanted. I could only be negative because the only way any newspaper article would come across at that time would be like I was feeling sorry for myself or trying to milk the situation. Nothing could have been further from the truth, so we made sure we kept it hush-hush and the hospital people really knew how to keep a secret, because although they were aware of who I was they kept it strictly to themselves.

I got really tender care in both of those hospitals, everybody there made all the patients feel like *you* are getting their best care, even though you know they do that for everybody. Because they were very kind, very gentle, and you could see in their eyes they had no fear that what they were doing wouldn't work, it made me feel so much stronger in my recovery. When I gave them praise they knew it was coming from my soul, and of course there were always the jokes Marcus and I were cracking. In both the Mayday and the Royal Marsden it was a situation where the teams and I inspired each other because each of us putting everything into making the treatment a success. I never had any doubts at either hospital.

The operation was a complete success, they removed all of the tumour without my having to have a mastectomy – it helped greatly that I had identified it early and acted quickly. I was in there for about two weeks, then started my chemo, which was once a month and this time it gave me no side effects at all – I didn't feel weak or get any nausea or anything, and I still didn't have any hair from the last time so it couldn't fall out! I would go for my treatment, come home, drink a glass of wine, go into the kitchen, cook a meal for whoever was there – I just carried on as if nothing was happening.

That was my method; we even made an outing of my trips to chemotherapy. We would set out quite early, take the bus and the train from Croydon to the Marsden, then stop at the café next to the hospital and treat ourselves to a full English breakfast each. We *loved* those breakfasts, and I could never understand why so many people talk about them as being so terrible! Maybe because I was brought up on *proper* breakfasts, I thought it was all good stuff. Perhaps I was so keen on them there because you can't get them like that anywhere else in the world, so that became our routine and reason enough to look forward to my chemo.

We were determined to apply the same attitude as we had last time around: to stay away from negative people, to continue to be positive and not to dwell on any setbacks. The reality was this second cancer was a massive setback for us, but we couldn't keep looking at it like that. There were still good, fun things happening to us so we would concentrate on them. It's like if it's raining one day, think that it will be sunny tomorrow – have hope – because if you put it in your subconscious that it will be sunny tomorrow you will have a sunny time. It's like setting your mind to work for positivity because you have to fulfil all your dreams. They do come true, mine did.

One morning, after breakfast by the Marsden, I was walking in the hospital and saw a really humbling sight – all these little toddlers with bald heads. Toddlers. They couldn't have been older than two or three, being treated with the same chemo as me because they have some cancer. How could I possibly have anything to complain about? These are babies! I've been alive for years, I've had fun and lived a great life; these little toddlers were battling with the same disease at an age when they've got *everything* in front of them. I felt really blessed and lucky that I didn't have something like this hit me when I was their age.

This gave me another perspective of wanting to survive and not feeling sorry for myself. If these little kids can go through that and I'm a fully grown adult, forty-odd years old, then I'll take my blows and I'll get over it. I can think even better than these toddlers because I can reason what life is all about and come to terms with it, they don't know what's happening to them, yet most of them didn't seem unduly upset by it. So how could I start feeling sorry for myself? Deal with it as it comes at you, otherwise you are going to end up damaged.

Because I only had to go to chemo once a month, we had time on our hands and we didn't want to hang about at Blossom's all day. I'd never stayed in anybody's house for nine months, even if it is my sister's. We wanted to give her some space so we'd go out first thing in the morning and often come back quite late in the evening. Sometimes we were so late my sister would ask me where we'd been!

I wanted to keep as active as possible, I would do a lot of cooking for the whole family because my sister was fostering two boys from Afghanistan and she had a special needs son and her daughters there, that way she could get a bit of a holiday. Marcus and I would go to Surrey Street Market by Crystal Palace or Maple Road Market in Penge and buy food – Marcus even got a backpack for the first time in his life! That was so funny, but the West Indian provisions we used to buy – yam, green banana, dasheen and so on – were quite heavy. I had been told to eat a lot of liver and kidneys because it would be good for my immune system, my blood and my haemoglobin levels, which was fine with me because I love liver and onions. I'd cook really wholesome food – fish, liver, onions, steaks, mashed potatoes, plantain, yam, sweet potato – we'd come in from the market and I'd start cooking straight away. Everybody seemed to enjoy it. And it must have been working, too, because I never felt ill at all.

Some days we'd just go walking, we'd walk all over the place often not really knowing where we were going or where we'd been. Or we would just sit in the park, usually Crystal Palace Park, and talk and read. We'd put the world to rights on a daily basis, or we'd just talk about life in general and make plans for our future. If it was raining we'd still go to the park, just open up the umbrella – we must have looked mad to anybody walking past: two black people sitting in a park in the rain, probably roaring with laughter. Those were lovely days, very relaxing and thought-provoking, quite a bonus coming from the fact I had to be in England with nothing to do.

We would read Norman Vincent Peale's book *The Power of Positive Thinking* aloud to each other and talk about it. We found that book a real source of inspiration, and we had already experienced, with my first cancer, that it does work: don't think on any negativity; think on the positive; and if you are attacked by negativity pick the positive out of it because there will always be some somewhere in there. That book became our guiding light, the force that we live by, and I would write quotations from it out by hand and put them in the rooms of our house when we got home. Number one, I can do all things through Christ who has stayed with me and is strong with me; number two, I don't believe in defeat; number three, the rough is only mental, the positive approach is a smooth handle; number four, if I think victory I get victory. We were so inspired by that book and how it seemed to harmonise with the way we tried to live our lives; it articulated so much of what we'd always thought, I used to give it to people as a present. I think what sums up our time in London and at the time pushed us towards not giving up or even faltering was the quote: 'life cannot deny itself to the person who gives life their all'.

I really feel that during this period we reconnected with London. We would ride around on buses, something I never could have done in the Boney M. days and I've loved London buses since I was a little kid: 'Come on, Marcus! Let's go upstairs!' I loved it! We'd go up Regent Street, along Oxford Street, round Piccadilly, get off and walk around Covent Garden or Soho or Hyde Park down to Knightsbridge . . . sometimes we'd stay out all evening and go to a restaurant or to Ronnie Scott's. Or we'd get the bus from Upper Norwood to Brixton, which was like reliving my schooldays, then sometimes we'd get another bus up to Victoria. We'd take taxis too, because Marcus loved the black cabs and he would always comment on how he had so much room in them. We went all over the place, and I really enjoyed reconnecting with London again.

Although I would hear Boney M. on the radio every so often, I didn't get recognised all that much as it was a good few years since we'd had hits in England, and anyway, I'm sure nobody expected to see one of the Boney M. girls on the top deck of a London bus. We'd often hear Boney M. playing in Alders in Croydon and just smile at each other and occasionally get a raised eyebrow or a sideways glance from somebody old enough to remember the group. There would definitely be a few 'Is it? . . . No, it can't be!' type of looks! Then we would get people staring because of the way I was dressed. Even though I wasn't on stage or anything I didn't dress down: one day I would go out in my tartan coat and my tartan Dr Martens, so I would get looks on the bus or on the street – even one day my sister looked at me in the hall and said, 'You would go 'pon the bus like *that*?' I replied, 'Of course, dear!' I was having fun! It was important for me not to hide away, but to get up and dress up and be *me*, in spite of what I was going through. Yes, I am having treatment; yes, my hair has fallen out, but I still need to feel good when I go out. When I looked in the mirror I wanted to see nothing less than Marcia Barrett of Boney M.

We got the chance to hang out with friends and family – that is Blossom's and Marcus's families, as I only saw Wayne once when he visited me in the Mayday hospital. We would see my old school friend Elaine, and we'd just sit talking like we'd seen each other two days before. She would come round to Blossom's to see us and once when we went to her house she prepared cow foot for me because she knew how much I loved it. It was so nice, because she had been like a sister to me when we were teenagers. Then there were Marcus's brothers and sisters who would come over to see how I was doing, and we would go and visit them, so that aspect of being back in the UK was fantastic too.

The only thing missing from our time in London was music: we did go into a studio to finish off a couple of tracks, but I think we were too distracted to do much more and it was pretty expensive so we had to put the rest on hold. It meant I was really impatient to get back to Florida and get back to work, because this was now the second time we had got close to having something ready only to have to put it on ice for the best part of a year. So when I got the all-clear from the Royal Marsden I was even more excited than I was the first time – it was like, 'I've beat it once and it came back, now I've beat it again!' I felt absolutely invincible, so proud of myself, of Marcus, of the teams of doctors and nurses, because together we'd licked it again. That was *such* a good feeling.

We had been away from our home for the best part of a year and we were homesick – we missed our dog, Sasha, so much that we would try to talk to her on the phone! She was staying with our neighbours and we would phone saying, 'Sash! Sash! How are you?' All we'd hear is panting coming from the other end, so I'd say, 'Sash! It's Mummy and Daddy! Hello, Sash!' Bear in mind, this is from England and back then transatlantic calls cost a fortune, yet all we could hear was more panting! Then we'd tell her, 'You know we're coming home soon?' and there'd be even more panting! It was so funny. We missed our house because we'd just left it locked up for all that time, the gardening contractor came to cut the grass and keep the shrubs trimmed, so I guess we would have heard if anything had been seriously wrong, but we were starting to feel we'd been away from it for long enough.

Then there was that thing they say about house guests being like fish, that if they hang around for too long they start to smell, and things weren't as comfortable for us at Blossom's as they had been in the beginning. At first it was a real novelty because Boney M. would still be on the radio or quite often featuring on television rerun shows and Blossom's granddaughter would be dead chuffed: 'Look, look, there's Auntie on *Top of the Pops!*' Over time, however, it became a strain for all of us and we knew it was time to go home.

This was a small concern compared with the bigger picture: I had beaten cancer once again. I had known all along that I wasn't ready to go anywhere, that I loved life too much. Besides, what would Marcus do if succumbed to that illness? He's like a lost baby without me – and vice versa, I'd better add! Once we were ready to go home, it felt like somebody had once again been pressing the pause button on our lives for nine months. We had things to get on with, we had music to put out there, and we could hardly wait.

## Chapter Twenty-two

# 'My legs were like two pieces of dead meat'

It seems almost impossible to imagine that cancer could come for me again, five years after the last time. Really! What crime had I committed in another life that led to this sentencing? This one was a complete surprise, too. Not because I wasn't vigilant – I was – but because it came in a totally unexpected area. I knew about breast cancer and cancers of the internal organs, but we had no idea you could get it on your spine. Nobody explained that was a possibility, so because I was performing all the regular tests I could do on myself, when I started showing what were symptoms caused by the tumour as it grew, cancer was the last thing on my mind.

As before, I was eating healthy, natural food and I was just as much of a fitness fanatic, going for long walks or running every day on the beach with the dog and going to the gym. It was in the gym that I first noticed something might be wrong: I was still pressing huge weights with my legs and was noticing that my right leg seemed to be losing its strength – I couldn't do as many reps with that as my left. I resolved to work it harder, but rather than that leg getting stronger, the other one started weakening too, and that definitely wasn't right. I also started to get a kind of tingling in my lower back, which would come and go but was getting more frequent and starting to regularly develop into a pain if I was sitting down for too long. Things came to a head when Marcus drove me down from Hobe Sound to Miami to do a radio interview; it's almost two hours in the car and by the time I arrived it hurt so badly I could barely hold my back up straight. The only way I could sit on the stool in the studio was to wear one of those big weightlifter's belts to support my lower back.

I still had no clue it might be cancer, I assumed it was movement related, or even something like sciatica, so I went to see a chiropractor. He couldn't find anything wrong and didn't do anything to ease my discomfort either. It was getting worse by this time because I was starting to walk with a limp just to ease what was now a pretty constant pain. The chiropractor suggested acupuncture, and at this point I would try anything so I went for a treatment that didn't have any effect either, although it was then I got the first inkling that something might be seriously wrong. The acupuncturist examined my back and while he wasn't saying anything, he was looking *extremely* worried, which left me thinking, 'Why isn't he looking joyful if there's nothing there he can treat?' His body language seemed to indicate whatever was wrong with me was beyond him and he was giving up. It wasn't the kind of positive approach I was hoping for, so that was the point at which I started to consider my condition in a much more disturbing light.

I started to think back to an incident that had happened when I was doing that radio interview in Miami. It was a Sunday morning and they had a church session on the radio, which included these two spiritual women, an elderly woman and a young girl, both Jamaicans, who would pray for people over the airwaves, people with ailments – I guess they were modern faith healers. They said they would pray for me because I was obviously in such bad pain with my back, so they put their hands on where it hurt the most, then they actually jumped back! They looked *frightened* and were saying, 'Oh no, it's too much for us . . . we can't do anything about that!' I don't believe in that sort of stuff – I'm all for positive thinking but I thought this was hocus-pocus so I didn't think too much about it at the time. Now, however, when this acupuncturist was showing the same fearful mannerisms, I began to think there might be something serious going on.

By this point I am starting to get very concerned, not because I was scared – I wasn't, I've fought cancer twice! – but simply because nobody seemed to be able to tell me that there was anything wrong, let alone what it actually might be. I knew I wasn't imagining things because when I thought back I realised I had been deteriorating for weeks, now the pain was getting worse as time went on, and without knowing what the problem was there was no way on earth I could do anything about it. I still hadn't considered cancer.

One morning I was starting to brush my teeth over the sink in the bathroom and I simply couldn't stand – I collapsed on the floor, not because I'd passed out or anything but because my legs simply wouldn't hold me up. I shouted for Marcus, and we didn't panic; we just knew he had to get me to the hospital as soon as possible. I still couldn't stand, so rather than carry me to the car Marcus put me in the computer chair from the office, because it had wheels, and tried to push me out of the house. It was then things got really freaky. When he was wheeling me it was as if I couldn't find my legs! They weren't just numb, or pins and needles, I couldn't feel a *thing*. I literally had to look under the chair for them, where they were being dragged along underneath it like two pieces of dead meat and I had to pull them out with my hands to stop them getting run over! Now I was panicking, because this is quite simply the weirdest thing that's ever happened to me and I still don't know what's causing it. Marcus had to load me into the car – like cargo! – and what was going through my mind was, 'What has happened to me? Am I going to be sitting in a wheelchair for the rest of my life?' For me, that was probably the worst thing that could happen to me because since I was nineteen, my whole adult life, I've been on stage dancing and singing and I couldn't accept that had come to an end in a manner I didn't understand at all.

I had to stay in the good old Jupiter Medical Center for several days while they did all sorts of tests on me, resulting in them finding a tumour growing on top of my spinal cord, about the size and shape of a coffee bean. *Another attack of cancer!* I couldn't believe it. Until they told me that, nothing could have been further from my mind! I'd had cancer before – *twice!* – I didn't think I'd get it again. I was so naïve I actually thought that was me done with cancer – as if I'd had my turn! Also, that was the first time I'd heard of cancer of the spine, although I later found out it isn't uncommon for previous cancer sufferers, especially breast cancer patients as the condition can migrate to the spine. Although nobody ever wants to hear they have cancer, in some ways to be given such a diagnosis was reassuring: prior to that I simply didn't know what was wrong; now I knew that it was cancer and I also knew I'd gotten through that twice before and could do so again.

This one was going to be tricky, however, because the operation to remove it was a far more delicate procedure and the doctors wouldn't know exactly what they were dealing with until they opened me up. They told Marcus and I that they might have to put a metal pin in my back and that there was a possibility I wouldn't walk again. At that point they couldn't tell us too much for definite, so it left us alone with our faith – faith in God, faith in the surgical team and faith in my capacity to take on cancer yet again!

In fact, the surgery to remove the tumour was relatively simple and they were sure they'd got it all, but they'd had to remove four of my vertebrae to do so. I thought if that was all then that was fine. I'll be a little bit shorter than I used to be and with a slight hunch in the back, but who cares? I'm still alive! I said to Marcus, 'If that's the case I'll just have to wear taller heels!' Then they told us: 'Although the operation has been a success, at this time we cannot guarantee you will be able to walk again.' My immediate thought was, '*What!* I thought you said it was a success?' But it was explained to us that when a tumour grows it damages some of the nerves in the spinal column, and these nerves control your legs – that is why mine were like two pieces of rubber when Marcus brought me in. I would have to retrain those nerves by learning how to walk again. And even then the damage might be too much to retrain the legs.

I didn't know all of that at that moment, but I knew enough to look at Marcus, who looked back at me, then I turned to the doctor and said, 'You know what, Doctor? I *will* walk again.' He couldn't really say anything to that, other than a very non-committal, 'Hmmmmm . . . yeeeeaaahhh.' In fact, he looked a little embarrassed: while he clearly didn't want to discourage me as I'd just come out of surgery, he was sceptical to say the least and obviously didn't want to give me any false hope. As far as I was concerned, after being told that, I was determined not to allow this paralysis to take over my life because the only thing I wanted to do at that moment was go back on stage and sing – sing and *dance*. Because that's what I do, I'm a performer. It was as simple as that.

Not once did we dwell on the idea that I wouldn't walk again, because there was no way I was going to be sitting in a wheelchair for the rest of my life. We didn't even think about what *might* happen. Once again, it was all about belief and the power of positive thinking. I told myself that if I could get it set in my mind to *believe* I'll make it through this and that I would walk and dance again, then so it would be. Yet again I had to have no fear, and, believe me, I had no fear at all. Marcus is of the same character, which was every bit as important because he believed the same as me and he had no fear either. However, when we presented this united face to the doctors, they looked at us as if we'd come from outer space. I don't think they had ever come across two people who appeared to be completely ignoring qualified medical opinion, just because they *believed* they knew better. But they'd never met Marcus and me before.

I'm still not sure if fighting like this for a third time was easier or more difficult. On the one hand I knew the surgeons had done their job with this tumour and that chemo and radiation had been successful in the past, also I knew how to put up the fight needed. On the other side, though, I was having to dig even deeper into my reserves to come up with what was needed for the battle. I didn't doubt I could do it but I knew it was going to be tough, but at least this time I could get involved as I physically taught myself to walk again – this was crucial, as I felt it put me in charge of my own fate. In all of this I was feeling very sorry for Marcus and sometimes I don't know how the poor guy got through another bout of cancer. I could feel what was going on in my body so I knew what I had to react to and fight against, but all he had was my word for things and he had a fantastic force of will to stay there alongside me fighting something he could only imagine. That's how strong his love is.

I was in the hospital for nearly a month, and after about a week's rest to recover from the surgery I became the busiest patient in that hospital. I knew I had work to do, but it was work I had to do by myself because I wanted to be back on my feet as quickly as possible, which was definitely not to the hospital's schedule. I couldn't let anybody know what I was going to attempt, not even Marcus.

As soon as visiting hours were over I would roll out of my hospital bed, crawl into the middle of the floor in the room and do push-ups – that's how I started to build up my strength in general. Then I began to pull myself upright on furniture, eventually getting over to support myself on the wall. It was a frustratingly slow process, especially for somebody like me who wants to see results quickly, but I was thankful for those gym workouts, which gave me the strength in my arms and body to get up on the wall where I could start taking steps. Boy, was that tough at first! I got to understand what teaching my legs to walk again truly meant, as I had to think as hard as I could about doing something I could never remember having to think about before. I would have to completely concentrate on something as straightforward as trying to lift my legs and move them forward – the muscles were there, I just had to focus my mind to control them.

For somebody as impatient with themselves as I am, improvement seemed to be taking ages, and while my legs were definitely getting stronger for a long time I couldn't feel anything in my feet. They were numb, my toes were all twisted, the veins were showing, they always felt cold and sometimes one foot would just swing to one side. It wasn't nice, but after just having a tumour successfully removed from my spine, did I really have anything to complain about? No, I did not. I kept on. At first my feet dragged, so all my energies were put into trying to lift them, but it was working and soon I was able to make it all the way around the room holding on to the walls and furniture. When I felt I was steady enough on my feet, I was ready to go into the corridor! I started taking very slow walks around the corridors; I'd often have to stop to rest then carry on holding on to the wall, and it was a busy place so nobody paid any attention to me as long as I didn't look in pain and was back in my room at meal times. Sometimes I'd do it at night, because I didn't want anybody on the floor to know I was practising walking because they had their physiotherapy plan worked out for me and this wasn't it.

I carried on for about three weeks, I was doing my leg exercises, taking my strolls around the corridors and I was making definite progress; I could feel myself getting stronger and stronger and I was really looking forward to surprising Marcus with what I'd achieved. My confidence with how far I could walk had been growing and one evening I got a bit carried away and went too far, Marcus had arrived to visit me and found I wasn't in my room. Nobody knew where I was, so now there's a panic on – apparently I can't walk but I've gone missing somehow! Naturally Marcus was very worried, he started dashing around the corridors looking for me and had come back to my room when I finally saw him. While it's not really fair to make fun of what he must have gone through in those moments, when he saw me coming towards him with one hand on the wall and the other pulling one of those tall spindly trolleys with the two drips attached to it, his face was a picture! I think he was too shocked to speak or even move, and I walked past him into the room with a breezy, 'Hello, darling, how are you?'

This meant my self-rehabilitation was no longer a secret and the doctors were going to find out about my walks. This worked to my advantage as they were so impressed with what I was achieving, they decided to let me go home almost immediately. Obviously I would have to come back for chemo and radiation. While I was delighted at the prospect of going back to my own home after a month or so away, like the other times I can't look back at that period in hospital with any negativity at all. All during my stay, even when I was dragging myself around the floor of my room, I never once felt sorry for myself. In fact, my room was always a joyous place because I used to tell the staff jokes every day. It started with a couple of the nurses who were Jamaican and we used to talk in our patois, and it was obvious there was some sort of fun going on in there so others, the Americans, would come around to my room. It got to the point they used to say if anybody was looking for anybody they'd try my room first because that was where they'd most likely find them.

My room was the sweetest room too – there were always fresh flowers and I always had some nice perfume on, so they'd say they liked to hang out there instead of other rooms smelling of hospitals and disinfectant! While they were there, the nurses used to tell me their problems . . . *their* problems! I'm supposed to be the sick one in hospital! But I'd talk to them about whatever it might be and they would listen, then tell me how things worked out. So it was as if I was motivating people from my hospital bed.

When it came time for me to leave the doctors asked me if I wanted therapy at home, and I said 'No!', I'd come this far all by myself, I knew I could do the rest and now they believed me.

As we prepared to leave my room it was a real joyous occasion, quite a few doctors and nurses had come to see me off, all excited about the progress I had made. Behind the smiles, however, I had private misgivings. My oncologist was the last to leave, and just as she turned to go through the door I called her back to tell her: 'I don't know if my assumption is right, but I did feel a lump here . . .' She felt my breast, at the side, and looked very grave. She told me there was definitely something there, that I wasn't going anywhere that day, and they kept me in that same room to send me for tests the next day. It was another tumour.

The culprit for my fourth attack of cancer was a tumour growing in my lymph node on the left, so I'd had two different tumours growing in my body at once! I had first felt this little lump under my left breast about three weeks before but I didn't share my discovery with anybody because I was in there for my back and I wanted to deal with that first, as I knew I could. Then, after the operation the most important thing became teaching my feet to walk again, so I knew if I told anyone about a new lump in my breast it would only distract from me getting back on my feet. Because the doctors didn't know I was doing my own version of therapy I would just have been put in for the operation and the recovery time would have set my rehabilitation right back. Hence it was important I got so far with it before I talked about the other issue. However, I didn't want to actually leave the premises, I would rather stay and have it treated because it would be too dispiriting to have to come back in. It would have weighed on my mind too much when I would have had other things to get on with at home.

Marcus, of course, was shocked, but he understood why I had kept it from him, and also why I wanted to get it done straight away without going home, even if it meant another week in hospital. Once again it was testament to the strength of the man's character that he didn't lose his mind at this point. Yet there he was, joking about how it's typical of me – getting a two-for-one deal because I'm always looking for a bargain!

The operation to remove the lump was another total success, and because it came so close to the one on my spine the same chemo and radiation would be effective in both cases. The only thing that came close to a complication was later when my breast started gathering fluid and they had to pump it off. This continued after I was discharged and I had to go in once or twice a week for a few weeks until the doctor told me they wouldn't pull off any more fluid because it might be too much and lead to infection – for a while I felt like I was leaning to one side because this breast was so heavy! The fluid went after a short time, but it left a little lump there which is benign and has been nothing to worry about since. The things I had to go through after two *relatively straightforward* operations!

In America, when you are discharged from hospital after surgery they take you to the front door in a wheelchair. I could walk, with some support, but if that is what they wanted to do then it didn't really matter to me. I was taken down to the car, and as I said my goodbyes to the staff – *again* – I saw Marcus folding up the wheelchair and putting it in the back of the car. 'What's *that*?' I asked. I told him we had perfectly good walls at home for me to hold on to when I walked around! He tried to reason with me that I might need it to get around and we ended up with a compromise that it would come home with us and if I didn't need it he would bring it all the way back without complaining!

In the end I sat in it twice: once when we went to the supermarket because I could hardly walk along holding on to the shelves, but I thought that trip was a disaster; and once when we went to a private beach in Hobe Sound which has an entrance fee – and when the guy on the gate saw me in the chair he said, 'Is that permanent? If it is you can come in for free.' That really affected me, I don't know why. Maybe it was hearing the word 'permanent' in relation to me being in a wheelchair, but it shocked me. When we got home I said to Marcus, 'Right, that's it! It's going back first thing tomorrow.' So two days after I was discharged, Marcus and I are back on the I-95 taking this wheelchair back to the Jupiter Medical Center! I wasn't even going to think about using it. I was getting ready to go back on stage and that certainly didn't involve a wheelchair.

When we arrived back at the hospital with it, at first they were a bit baffled. They saw Marcus arrive with it, and when we told them we were there to give it back their reaction was, 'But you've had it less than a week. How are you going to manage without it?' Quite matter-of-fact, I told them I was going to walk and when I was doing so I'd rather not even see the wheelchair. Then they realised that I had walked into the building, and there I was *standing* next to Marcus, and we all had quite a good laugh about it. I told them thank you very much, they took the chair away and that was the last I saw of it!

I know wheelchairs are absolutely vital in a great deal of cases, and I would never ever belittle anybody who uses one, but with me it was symbolic – I had to walk again and rejecting the wheelchair when it was offered was all about pushing myself forward and not letting the cancer even imagine it was having an effect on me.

I would keep up my walking, from room to room, supporting myself by the walls, or leaning on the counter if I was in the kitchen. I could feel myself getting stronger and more confident on my feet day by day. Then one afternoon Marcus and Sasha were fishing from the back yard, I was doing some walking and found how sturdy I had become, I could walk the length of a room without needing any support! I was so excited, I could hardly wait to let Marcus know, but instead of shouting to him I opened the doors very softly and walked slowly and silently to the middle of the lawn. I called to them and these two heads turned round in perfect synchonisation. Marcus looked really alarmed and said, 'No! No! No! Don't walk any further!' And his voice had so much concern in it, it stopped Sasha in her tracks and she didn't know whether to run over to me or stay where she was. I told Sasha to sit, and Marcus to stay where he was and, carefully of course, walked over to where they were and sat down with them. 'See, I told you I would walk again!'

From that day on, literally, there was no turning back! On the oceanfront, every morning, Marcus would drive to the beach so I could walk on the sand or in the surf to make these legs stronger. I think the only reason I could do it was because we had that Range Rover as my back was still healing and it meant I didn't have to contort myself into some little low slung thing, then I could sit up comfortably keeping the pressure off. I would walk down the beach and into salt water and I was like a soldier marching through to get vengeance on the enemy! That was the spirit I was in – I was strong, I was going to beat this! It wasn't easy walking on the sand or up to my shins in the waves, but I walked and walked, with the dog running next to me and Marcus struggling to keep up! 'Wait for me! Wait for me!' is what I used to hear!

It was fantastic to feel my legs building back up. I fell a few times but the sand was soft so it didn't matter – I fell off my bike a few times as well when I started cycling again – and eventually I started to run. Not running like I used to, not immediately, but I was getting there. I knew I was getting back to my old self and I had done it through sheer belief and strength of will. Sometimes I look back at all that I went through in those years and honestly believe my body must be something else.

It wasn't all smooth sailing once I got home, though, and once again I was blessed that Marcus is the man he is because during those first few weeks I really do owe him my life. Because of the operation on my back, they had made quite a long incision down my spine and the last five centimetres of it refused to heal up and looked as if it might be turning septic. It needed to be redressed every morning, which wasn't a particularly pleasant job but it became Marcus's job. The nurse showed him what to do, gave him a supply of the medicine, cotton swabs and dressings and told him to get on with it! He would say he was terrified in the beginning because it was a bit tricky to swab out the wound without hurting me, then put the plaster on so it wouldn't come off as I moved about, he so didn't want to get anything wrong and make things worse. I was never worried. From the very start he did it perfectly and after a few days was telling me how the infection was going down because the cut didn't look so red, then how it was slowly healing up and getting smaller and smaller. I was so relieved I had somebody as steady and as unafraid as he was to look after me in that instance.

Getting over these two cancers was exhausting, especially after the first two. This is how I was starting to feel with my health now – I'd been attacked in the ovaries, both breasts and my spine, and now I was just plain *tired* of being ill. I'd had enough! Just leave me alone now and let me get on with the life and music my husband and I have got planned for ourselves. But life's tribulations weren't finished with us yet.

## Chapter Twenty-three

# 'We got out of the cab and our beautiful home literally stank!'

When we finally got back from England after my successful treatment for my breast cancer it was such a relief. Our lives had been put on hold for nearly a year and finally we'd been given them back, but this time the joy from getting the all-clear was tinged with the beginnings of real financial concerns that would dominate our lives for the next ten years. That things were no longer as comfortable as they could have been was made clear to us in possibly the most vivid way imaginable: when we arrived home, we got out of the cab and our beautiful home literally stank!

Just before we travelled to the UK, while I was getting everything ready to go, Marcus had done little other than sit on our wall and fish – and it was as if he could do no wrong! The fish were practically jumping into his bucket! It seemed like every time he threw a cast he pulled it out with a sheepshead or a drum or a perch. We packed them in bags and stored them in the big freezer in the utility room, and were so looking forward to them that the last week or so in London we were actually talking about how we were going to cook them! But because an electricity bill hadn't been paid, the power had been turned off and you can imagine what a chest full of fish in Florida temperatures for a few months is going to smell like! We had to throw out the freezer as well because we knew it would never be right again – the gardeners said they were worried because they thought there might be somebody dead in there. We had left the air-conditioning on low too – as is the practice down there to stop damp – but because of that unpaid bill it too went off and a lot of my clothes were ruined by this strange yellow mould that was growing on them.

It was a real pain and a half, but nothing really compared with my health, so we cleared everything up and just got on with it. However, it made us realise exactly how precarious our situation was. The bill was only just over a hundred dollars, but getting back from England after my nine months' treatment, we were not on time to pay it. As I said earlier, the first cancer had virtually bankrupted us, and I had sold some antiques to pay for our trip to England for the second. The third and fourth were treated for free at Jupiter Medical Centre, because they have in their charter this rule that nobody will be turned away, whether they can pay or not: I paid the first time because I could afford it – just; the next time we had no money, they treated two cancers for me and I have never paid a penny. Each time I received *exactly* the same level of care, which shows how wonderful those people are. I literally don't know where I'd be if it wasn't for the Jupiter Medical Center.

We were so hard up because, quite simply, we had no money coming in but we still had our day-to-day expenses, which were relatively small, and we were investing in my new career. Up until I left the group in 1990 I was being paid for live work – not as much as I was sure I should have been getting but it wasn't too bad by that point. When I left the group, I wanted to make a clean break so I chose to go to America where I was sure I would be able to launch myself as a solo artist. I deliberately turned my back on the whole multiple Boney M.s thing. This meant I missed out on immediate and guaranteed income, because there was still a demand for Boney M. in most parts of the world, especially Europe where the others were all based. They might not have been earning huge amounts, but at least they were earning. We took a gamble on my solo career in America, but never got the chance to find out how far it would have gone because my illnesses kept interrupting any progress we felt we were making.

A large amount of money went into making my first album – at least $50,000, because we wanted to keep control of everything and make our own decisions – just like Eddy Grant does it. We had masses of songs to choose from as we'd been writing together for ages, and we started demoing songs at Avalon studios in Port St Lucie and Saturn Studios in Palm Beach, with these really great local producers Joe Betura and Scott Christina. It was shaping up very well, until the first cancer interrupted what we were doing, and although we got going again afterwards, recording finished versions of the songs, the whole process took much longer than we anticipated and we didn't have a finished album until 1996. We decided to call it *Survival* and wrote a title track to match. We tried to do deals with a couple of different guys who promised all sorts about what they could do with the songs, and there was a lot of running back and forth getting things ready for them or putting down new things or new twists on what we had. They seemed genuine, and we were getting so excited, but each time it came to nothing – in one case a guy took our music and we never heard from him again.

This took up more time, and wasn't getting anywhere so we decided to sell it ourselves on Amazon. We got the artwork done and the CDs made and we had a good network through the Boney M. fan clubs whose members were always really interested in what I was going to do. That was *really* hard work! We shifted quite a few copies – in fact, we still get people contacting us for it – but the two of us had to package them up, address the envelopes, and take them to the post office ourselves! It seemed like we were constantly buying stamps and padded envelopes too! The existing hardcore fans were buying it, but because we didn't have the music business machinery behind us and the independent people we'd gone to had let us down, we couldn't get beyond that market to sell enough to make any money.

This was very disappointing, even I will admit that. It wasn't just that we were losing money we couldn't really afford, but also that I was debuting Marcus as a songwriter and musician and I wanted the world to hear his talents. After all, he'd waited on me for so long. We picked ourselves up and said, 'Aha! Maybe this was not the right time for us. So let's just carry on.' We had learned an awful lot from the experience, both in the studio and in the business, and we had a massive catalogue of songs, so we hadn't come out of it too badly.

Although the delays to that album really messed us up as regards any potential for earning, the main reason we had no money was because my Boney M. royalties virtually dried up in the mid-1980s, while Marcus and I struggled to pay for getting me healthy again. When Frank stopped working with Boney M. in the beginning he would perhaps send out the odd cheque here and there, if I got in touch to nag him about it, and for a short while he was sending out a regular sum each month. It seems like a great deal, but it feels like nothing compared to what I think I should have earned from all those compilation albums and the radio airplay Boney M. was still getting. Then the cheques stopped coming altogether, around the time Frank had moved from Germany to Miami – Fisher Island, no less, where Oprah Winfrey and Julia Roberts had homes. When I called his office I was never put through to him – I am convinced that as soon as his staff heard my voice on the phone they would either hang up or tell me he wasn't there.

After he moved back to Germany it became like a game of cat and mouse because we used to get up at four or five in the morning to phone from Florida to catch him, but we could never get through. Then when we moved to Germany, Marcus and I found out where he was and went to see him at his old studio, the place where we made so many Boney M. records. He greeted me with huge enthusiasm, like I was his long-lost sister, and told me it would all be sorted out. Of course nothing was – the most I got was a cheque for a few thousand euros.

I often get asked why I haven't taken this further, and my answer is always the same: I'd rather save my precious energies for a more positive and satisfying future! The thing that upset me most about that meeting was when I went into the studio's control room and vocal booth, and there was nothing there except a few dangling wires. Everything was gone, all the equipment, and while I wouldn't have thought I would be so sentimental about those days, it hurt to see such a big part of my past had just been ripped out.

I made a nice profit on the sale of my house in Croydon, which had given us a start, but with nothing coming in after leaving the group and the first cancer treatment costing so much, by the time we returned from England after the second, we had to refinance the Hobe Sound house. This meant borrowing money against the value of the house and paying it back as a mortgage, with the intention of repaying the sum borrowed when we were flush again. Because it was built for cash and had gone up in value quite considerably this wasn't too much of a problem, but it was only a short-term solution.

It was also a bit distressing for me because that house, perhaps more than the house in London, was a real bricks-and-mortar illustration of what I had achieved with Boney M., regardless of official recognition or financial reward. And that I had designed it and had it built without having to borrow a penny made me very proud – remember, I am from Mavis Bank, Jamaica, where we used to sleep five to a bed. To have to go the mortgage route at this stage, when I thought things should be getting easier, was disturbing. Sometimes I think part of the reason I was hit with the third and fourth cancers was because our situation was nagging at me and I wasn't happy or fully relaxed. The way I looked at it in the end, though, was it was only a house: if refinancing or selling it gave us the chance to survive this bump in the road and move forward, then so be it, maybe that was always its purpose in our lives.

We refinanced more than once, raising a considerable amount

of money but reducing our equity in it, so we knew this couldn't go on for ever.

Things were looking very tight during my third and fourth cancer treatments, and just after I had recovered the house was put up for auction twice, which was quite an experience and not one that I would recommend! The first time the sale didn't happen because, I think, the people bidding for it were looking to steal it and bid so low it didn't get sold that way. On the next occasion something bizarre came about: one of Frank's employees phoned me to ask the date of my property's auction because Frank wanted to know! I must have told him that we had our house up for auction when I was trying to get my royalties out of him. I don't know if he even bid for it, but he certainly didn't buy it, so why he'd want to know when it was going under the hammer is anybody's guess.

Our auctioneers turned up not long before our sale and said the house needed to be cleared, immediately. I asked him how we could possibly do that and he suggested we put our possessions on our third lot because they needed to be outside the gates! Like a flea market! We didn't, and as it turned out it didn't make any difference, but I think these characters from these firms just like to throw their weight about even though they know the householders are in distress.

In the end, the second auction never went ahead because we met a lawyer who offered us another way out. He had a lovely house in Crane Creek, in Stuart, which was empty and we could live in it; he would take the monthly rent from the profit we would receive after the house was sold. He even said we could buy the house if we wanted to, once we got straight. If you look at it from a strict financial planning point of view, again it wasn't ideal: he wasn't a charity so we would lose out as he made his money, but by that time we had little choice – we owed about $100,000, couldn't refinance the Hobe Sound house any more and had no income.

We looked at it as another blessing that would work towards getting us on our feet again, so we moved up to Stuart, which is on the coast about twenty miles north of Hobe Sound, and things started off very well. The house was so beautiful: huge kitchen, lovely living and dining area, big master bedroom suite, an office, a computer room and a huge swimming pool, which was fantastic for me as we didn't have a swimming pool in Hobe Sound, so now I could catch up with my swimming by doing laps in the backyard! What I particularly liked was it was part of a gated community so people couldn't just pass by and if anybody was coming to visit they call you from the gate to check they are expected. This made us feel very safe, and we immediately felt comfortable there. We moved our furniture in, made it beautiful to our taste, we had the breathing space we needed and were happy again.

We'd been there for under a year when a miracle happened, or something we looked on as a miracle because it was something we couldn't have predicted in a million years. A former neighbour of ours from Hobe Sound – a German woman married to an American – was on a cruise in China. She got talking to one of her fellow passengers, a German journalist, and mentioned she was friends with Marcia Barrett of Boney M. Apparently the guy near lost his mind! 'Where is she? What is she doing? We all thought she had vanished . . . She needs to get over to

Germany and get to work on some music . . .' As soon as she got back to Florida she put us in touch with him, he had a wealth of contacts in the music business over there and two weeks later we were on the plane to Germany to start work on what became the *Come Into My Life* album.

At that point it was the move that made the most sense to us, as it was proving too difficult to get anywhere in the USA because if you're unknown, which Boney M. was, and you haven't got a record company behind you, you can't break through on the radio – this was well before the Internet was making such a difference! Also, my illnesses kept breaking things up so I couldn't even build my own momentum. In Germany, however, I had an audience it seems had been waiting for me to show myself again. Maybe I did know this at the back of my mind but was wary of the Frank Farian influence over there and I just wanted to avoid any possible unpleasantness. Of course the first thing he said to me when we came back was, 'What are you doing in Germany?' I told him I was picking up the pieces of my career and that was that as far as I was concerned.

I had wanted to distance myself from the various Boney M.s on the road as that was nothing to do with me but could be confusing if I was looking to build an audience. I really think I wanted a completely fresh start and thought, 'Americans have ears too.' But to listen to Germans we were meeting it was as if I'd been deliberately hiding in Florida for almost fifteen years.

The thing about the Germans is they will never forget you. It doesn't matter if you're not recording any more, or you're no longer considered *fashionable*; if they loved you once they will love you for ever, and they loved them some Boney M.! Behind

James Last we were probably the biggest international success to come out of that country, and by then the forty- and fifty-year-olds who are working in TV and radio and making decisions had been teenagers when we were at the top and they were still hooked. They are still keeping the group alive – right up until today Marcus and I turn on the TV and we're getting reruns of Boney M. – and of course their kids are hearing the songs and loving them because they're good songs and there's still a lot of pride about us being a German group.

So this was by far the best situation for us. The journalist who got it all rolling got me back in the media spotlight, which spread to other northern European countries, allowing me to reconnect with my original fan base. We could get to know promoters and agents again so the prospect of doing some live work began to build up, and the producer I was working with, Mario Sixer, seemed like a good guy.

We became transatlantic commuters, flying over to Göttingen to work with Mario for a while, then returning to Florida for a bit. The album was for his own label, Sixstein, so he was putting up the cash to make it and I think working like this was more economical as he could break off to do other stuff. We didn't mind, because we knew it was getting done and as it wasn't long since I'd fought off two cancers at the same time I didn't really want anything too intense. I had written or co-written nearly every track with Marcus in Hobe Sound, already in demo format, and a couple of others whilst recording the album. We both produced the CD with Mario and Thömas Korber, the owner of the studio. The only problem was the accommodation – it was diabolical! Not even when I first came to England from Jamaica had I seen anything that bad.

When we were doing the deal we were told that the studio had living quarters, so we knew it wasn't going to be a hotel, but we were expecting something along the lines of Eddy Grant's place – not as grand but with that sort of comfortable vibe. When we got to the studio, it was in quite a small building but they told us we would be staying upstairs. We looked at each other quizzically, then went up to this attic room with a stained mattress on the floor, like some sort of squat. Their idea of a kitchen was a little two-ring thing in the corner, and the bathroom was downstairs shared with whoever was working in the studio. And it was all so filthy we didn't even want to drink a cup of tea in there! But what can you do? We had nowhere else to go, and after all that had happened to me such was our drive to get that album done, we bought rubber gloves, cleaned everything up as best we could and stayed there until we got to move into a little apartment nearby. The next time we came over we stayed in a house that was offered to us by the same lady from Hobe Sound who had told the journalist about us – she owned a small house in a village just outside Frankfurt, which wasn't such a bad journey to the studio.

The recording sessions were going very well, Marcus, Mario and myself were very happy with what was being done; we even took time off to go to Hanover to stay with my friend Dagmar, who made all the Boney M. outfits. We were far more relaxed now, maybe *too* relaxed, because one of our visits ended up with me on the operating table in a local hospital.

We were up there taking a few days' break from recording, and it was during one morning my stomach started to feel funny, getting steadily worse. At first I thought it was the effects of all the bread and cheese and cold cuts Germans eat for breakfast – and Dagmar loved to feed her guests. I thought I was just having a reaction to coming back to the German diet after years of healthy eating in Florida, so I would have to go back to a laxative or a wash-out and everything would be fine. Until the pain became unbearable, so serious Dagmar called an ambulance for me.

They took me into hospital and after the examination told me I had a twisted intestine which was stopping food going down and they would have to operate immediately. I'd never even heard of twisted intestines! We were thinking, 'Oh no, here we go again! Why won't these illnesses leave me alone? This time they're even finding new conditions for me!' It wasn't an easy operation, I was in surgery for more than three hours, during which time they cut out this and that and removed a piece of gall bladder – I really didn't want to hear what they'd done! I didn't need to – I'd been through cancer four times at this point so I had total faith in the medical team there. It wasn't anything I would have chosen, but I honestly thought it was going to be easy compared with what I'd already been through. It was Marcus I worried about because they kept me in for two weeks, he spoke no German and Dagmar spoke no English and he was staying at her apartment!

It was another setback, taking a little toll on me, but when it was over it was over, with nothing like chemo or radiation afterwards. Such was my desire to get back to the album I think I willed myself better, and a week or so after I was discharged we were back in the studio.

★　　★　　★

As soon as we had something to talk about Mario started arranging PR for me. This was important because Frank was still doing his thing, Liz was doing her thing, as were Maizie and Bobby, so they were always somewhere in the spotlight, but I had been away a long time and now I was back with my bald head! In the beginning he got me little TV and radio shows, then once the ball started rolling people were very keen to talk to me. It was lovely because many of the people who I knew from the Boney M. days were still doing TV and radio, or people that were just assistants back then now had their own shows, so it was like getting together with old friends. One guy, Pit Weyrich, who had directed so many Boney M. videos, was now the producer/director of a very important Sunday TV show called *Fernsehgarten*, and they called me on there, and I sang the album's title track and did an interview.

Everything felt good. This was 2005, the album was due out later that year, there was plenty of advance interest, tracks were already getting radio play and we were booking gigs in Germany. There was plenty of interest in me as Marcia Barrett of Boney M., so I felt I was really moving on, until everything started falling apart back in Florida.

We loved the Crane Creek house and we hoped to buy it, which was part of the agreement we'd made with the owner. Now it looked like things were going to happen for me in Europe that was becoming a distinct possibility. We left for Germany, to finish things off with the producer, told the neighbours we'd be away, locked up and headed to the airport. Little did we know, we would never spend another night in that house.

Before we left for this trip, the owner had told us he would be doing some repairs to the roof while we were away, so we should make sure everything was put away or locked up. Fine, we thought nothing of that. We parked the Range Rover in the garage, I locked all our private papers in this lovely black crocodile box I used to carry my jewellery in when I travelled with Boney M. and put my jewellery in a combination lock box in our bedroom. Other than that, it was all tidy but just left the way we were living there. Before we returned I phoned to ask how the repairs had gone, to which he replied that they were doing some redecorating inside and not to rush back. I thought this was a bit odd, but no alarm bells went off until he told me not to worry about anything because his wife would pack our things up, and she was very good at packing. They're going to have our belongings put in storage. *My God!* I didn't want people handling my things and putting them away in storage, because I have a lot of antiques and expensive custom-made furniture – this stuff was very valuable and most people won't know how to handle it and can ruin things. Like the Hobe Sound house, I knew what I had to work through to get where I am and being able to buy lovely things was a symbol of what I had achieved. I was also devastated because I am such a private person – the thought of somebody else handling my things behind my back was horrifying.

We were booked to come back about a week after this conversation and couldn't get a flight any sooner; by that time he had told us where our stuff was in storage and to meet a lawyer at the unit to get the key. First we went to the house to pick up the car, and our first thought was that he was doing the place up for himself and not for us to buy or even move back into. Maybe his wife, who we never got on with, saw how nice we had made the place and wanted to live in it herself. We had arranged to stay with my cousin Dorothy in nearby Palm Beach, and when we drove up to the storage facility, which, of course, we were going to be billed for, our worst fears were realised.

We opened the unit door and I thought I was going to have a heart attack. All our possessions had just been stacked in there without any coordination, crammed in up to the ceiling – it was like a puzzle. Marcus had to climb up what looked like a cliff face just to see what was packed where. I couldn't see much, but I could see my beautiful white leather chair with the kitchen bin on its seat and that was enough for me. I said to Marcus, 'You know what, baby? I can't go in there. I cannot even look at this.' It was as if my life had been just chucked in this great big storage unit with no thought of what it might mean to us or how distressing a situation it would be for us. We locked up, turned around and went back to Palm Beach.

It took two or three more visits before I could bring myself to start doing anything about it, and on that last trip up there I told myself how running away from it wasn't going to help, that I had to stay strong. I looked to summon up the same strength I'd used to conquer my illnesses, because compared to that, this was nothing. I told myself I had to sort my furniture out and I had to sort my life out too, even if we had to start from scratch somewhere new, because Florida wasn't working for us. We decided to clear out that storage unit once and for all, which was symbolic as much as it was practical – we were making a new start and we didn't want to bring any of this burden along with us.

We had to take a much smaller unit as an interim measure but would get rid of a great deal of stuff, as we knew we wouldn't have another house that grand to go to – we hadn't ruled out getting one in the future but immediately we would have to trim down pretty drastically. There were time constraints on us too, because this big unit was really expensive, we didn't want to pay any more than we absolutely had to and if we'd left it and gone back to Germany and fallen behind with the payments the storage company would have auctioned it all. We wanted to give stuff away to people we knew – and some people we didn't – and we allocated a single day to do it in. My half-sister Dawn who was living in Fort Lauderdale came up, my cousin Dorothy was there, even Marcus's ex-wife and her husband came down, and his two daughters were there . . . everybody got stuff, even some strangers we met along the way, like the girl on the reception at the hotel we booked for Marcus's girls! Everybody entered into the spirit of things and although we'd said take what you want there was some stuff we wanted to take to wherever we were going, so if we said 'No, sorry' then that was fine. Only Marcus's ex-wife and her husband were a bit overwhelming, grabbing this and grabbing that.

It worked. We cleared that unit out, left my crystal and other fragile items with the storage company to pack up properly and put with the other stuff we were keeping, and we were done. The guard at the gate to the facility was amazed; he told us he thought there was no way we would clear all that in that time! Mind you, Marcus worked so hard that day – we called it Transaction Day – it affected the rheumatism in his fingers and they swelled up a bit and I would tease him that he was getting gout because he was living the good life too hard. We both had a good laugh about that.

★   ★   ★

We had decided to head back to Germany and make that our home as my audience was obviously that side of the Atlantic. We'd given America our best shot and for one reason or another it hadn't happened, but in Germany I had a record coming out, I was doing live shows and my profile as a solo artist had established itself. We weren't sure where, exactly, in Germany we would base ourselves, but after the accountants had picked over the sale of the Hobe Sound house and we'd settled up in Stuart, we were left with a cheque for $80,000, so we had a bit of leeway to find our feet.

The most important thing was we felt we were being proactive. After the bruises and blows life had dealt me during that past decade, sometimes I felt like a ragdoll, being bounced off one wall, caught, and then bounced off another! That period was very rough as it often felt as if we had no control over what was happening to us; now I felt we could put ourselves in charge again and move forward.

## Chapter Twenty-four

# 'I borrowed money from the gardener to bury my mother'

During that same period of financial troubles and the problems with my health, my family life was going through similar turbulences, and I used to thank God every day I was blessed to meet Marcus. He stood by me when the others who could have been supporting me were adding to my difficulties.

My sister Blossom and I were never particularly close, but that didn't mean she wasn't family so I always wanted to do my best for her. From when I was a young teenager I looked on myself, my sister and my mother as a tight unit – remember, we all slept in the same bed for years! – and the monies I earned from working in the laundry were to help take care of all of us. I wanted Mama to give up working hard as soon as I was able to support us; then as soon as I was doing well with Boney M., I was happy to share what I had. Later, I virtually adopted Blossom's daughter Samantha, from the time she was a baby, Mama and I brought her up as part of our family – she and Wayne became inseparable, more like brother and sister than cousins. But it wasn't easy as I was on the road so much of the time.

I could see how my lifestyle might have left an impression

that I was made of money but I understand how financial pressures can stress people out and resentments can build up. After a few issues that was finally enough for me and I have to admit I decided 'Right, this is it!' That was over ten years ago and Blossom and I haven't spoken from that day to this. I know it sounds terrible, but I don't want to ring her unless I know that we can both put the past behind us.

It was during that period, in 1986, that my mother died. Although it wasn't that much of a shock as she'd had a small stroke, was suffering from dementia and just seemed very tired, it still hit me hard. Since I had come to England in 1963 I had always lived with my mother – even when I designed the house in Hobe Sound she had her own suite in it for when she came to stay. Although ours may not have been the most demonstrative mother and daughter relationship, in fact sometimes it seemed downright distant, we were close.

I was in Hobe Sound with Marcus when Wayne phoned to tell me Mama had passed away; it was just before I had to go on the road with Boney M. Bobby and Maizie were supportive, and I got through the rest of the tour before returning to Florida so I could go down to Jamaica to arrange her funeral. She had been living in Jamaica for two or three months, as she was always adamant she wasn't going to die '*inna Hinglan*' but wanted to spend her last days back home. I was all for her seeing her life out in Jamaica as that is the intention of so many people who left the island to go to the UK in the 1950s and 1960s, as they genuinely thought they were only in Britain temporarily. I just wasn't happy about how it was done.

How it happened was Marcus and I were living in Hobe Sound where we still felt like newly-weds, when Blossom rang me out of the blue to tell me she's sending our mother home to Jamaica. Dementia isn't easy to handle but I just didn't agree that sending Mama home to Jamaica was the right thing to do. Of course she wanted to go home to live out her life on her island – what Jamaican wouldn't? – and Bloss was doing the right thing there, but she had not travelled by herself since she first left Jamaica to come to England in 1960 and now she was old and sometimes a little confused. In the end, a friend of Blossom's escorted Mama home to Jamaica, who I didn't know at all, which made me somewhat edgy.

That was another thing I was concerned about: what was going to happen when she got there? I didn't even know if I could fit in living in Jamaica at that time because I'd been in Europe or Florida my whole adult life, and Mama had been living very comfortably for twenty years too. Jamaica would be a complete change of lifestyle, because she was going back to live with her sister, my Aunt Sodahl, in Mavis Bank, up at Mount Charles, where I used to carry all that wood on my head! They had just about got a flush toilet by then, instead of the pit toilets they used to have when I was there. It didn't feel right to me, it was as if Mama was going back to the exact life she'd escaped from twenty-five years before, and now she's senile on top of it all. But it wasn't my place to judge, what might have been difficult for me might not bother her and being back in her beloved homeland may well have made up for any discomfort it might have involved. The bottom line was she got her wish and was on Jamaican soil when she passed, now it was a matter of the practicalities.

Wayne told me he thought the funeral was going to be in two weeks, but that couldn't be because I couldn't get there in that time and I needed to be there to pay for it. Which presented its own set of problems: we had no cash flow because we were on that refinancing merry-go-round; the cheque from the tour hadn't come through from the agent yet; and the funeral and the travel expenses were going to cost two or three thousand dollars. I asked my sister to have the morgue hold Mama's body until I could get there, which they did for about a month and of course that added to the cost. Would you believe I borrowed the money to bury my mother from my gardener? His company, Keith & Sons, was a local Hobe Sound contractor; I'd known him for years as his company did the original landscaping for the house and had looked after it ever since, plus I'd never been late with a payment for him and he knew I had money coming in from the tour. If not for him I don't know what would have happened.

My sister flew in from London and we stayed with my half-brother Winston in Kingston. My aunt told me Mama was very happy being back home and when she died she hadn't been ill or in pain. On the day she died she had eaten a big beautiful Jamaican breakfast, complimented Sodahl on how good the food tasted and asked for some more yellow yam, then she just passed away very peacefully as if she'd just stopped. That was some comfort, although I was distressed when I saw Mama lying in the morgue. Because of her age, she would get white hairs growing out of her chin; when she was living with me I would pluck them for her to make sure she was always looking presentable. This couldn't have been happening for a long time before she died, probably before she even came to Jamaica, because she was lying there with a beard that looked like a man's! I asked the ladies at the funeral parlour to shave it off, which they did and I made sure she was laid out in a good dress and I bought a wig for her because by then her hair was very thin. Blossom wouldn't come in with me to view Mama's body: she waited outside while I went in, so she came all that way from London but was unable to go in to see her.

The funeral took place at this big funerary place in Kingston. I asked Winston to say a few words because although he didn't know her that well he was a very good speaker. People appreciated that, her friends and family came and that was the end of Mama. I'm not being callous when I say that, I am just the sort of person that I always want to move forward, especially when there are things you can't do anything about. After the funeral I was thinking about Mama's life and how she came from Jamaica, got her wish for a better life, but because I knew she was always disappointed about Daddy I wondered how happy had she been? In the end she went back to Jamaica and could be buried there, so she got her wish there as well. I was thinking about whether her life was in vain, and my conclusion was that it hadn't been, I hoped I'd done my part to help with that, but I was sure I had made good the promise I'd made to myself in Jamaica all those years ago, that I was going to take care of her.

I think it was hard for Wayne when Mama died. He had always seemed like a happy and contented child, and together with Samantha he was growing up to be a fine young adult. He was always close to my mother and while I couldn't be there all the time being brought up by his grandmother was the next best thing – it was always going to be something of a trade-off, but my being in Boney M. and all it entailed allowed us a comfortable lifestyle. I was determined we weren't going to go back to what it had been like in my childhood, where I was shunted around and we never seemed to have quite enough; he had every material thing he wanted, we all went on some fantastic holidays, and we'd spend the school's long summer breaks in Florida. He did well at school, stayed on and just missed out on going to university. On the whole, life in my immediate family had been good.

When Marcus came into my life it didn't make any difference; in fact, Wayne really loved Marcus. The two of them would hang out together, watching TV, talking about music, Marcus used to take Wayne to gigs . . . they were like brothers. I was so pleased, because Wayne's father Wesley was never part of his life and I thought it such a good thing that my son had a strong male role model in his life. Sometimes at that house in Croydon the three of us would sit talking and laughing until two in the morning! I was back off the road, so I was OK, but I'd have to say to Wayne, 'Haven't you got to be somewhere in the morning?' The three of us weren't monks and a nun either, we'd enjoy a drink and there was often a bottle of champagne on the go. It was a good relationship.

Marcus and I felt confident enough in Wayne to move to Florida and leave him and Mama to look after each other, but when she had her stroke and moved in with my sister, he was left alone in the house. Again, we thought this wouldn't be a problem as he was a young man now, twenty-three years old, had a good job and was ready to make his way in the world. I had bought the house for cash so he had no worries about a mortgage or rent, I was still paying all the bills on it too, and Marcus's brother Sam had made sure everything was decorated and fixed up. Mama was just around the corner at Blossom's, also Marcus's brothers were in London if he had any serious problems. I'm sure he didn't feel resentful or as if we were abandoning him when we went, all of us understood he was in charge of the house now, at least until we came back. We thought it was an ideal opportunity for him to make the jump to adult responsibility without too many pressures, so we left him to enjoy the place.

A few months later I called the house and somebody whose voice I'd never heard before answered the phone! I said to this person: 'Who are you? This is Marcia Barrett, Wayne's mother, and I would like to speak to my son, Wayne Demercado.' Very casually, the chap replied, 'Oh Wayne's gone into town to do some shopping. He'll be a while.' I was boiling by this point, because that would be a worst-case scenario for me – a stranger in my house . . . answering the phone because he's there by himself! All I could say was, 'Oh *really*? Gone out? And *you're* in my house?' I hung the phone up and immediately called Gladys, one of the neighbours there. I asked her what was going on and she said there had been a big party that seemed to have gone on for ages. As Gladys is telling me this, my heart is in my throat. I know Wayne seems to be all right because the guy that answered the phone was so relaxed about him going shopping, but I really can't cope with the idea of strangers on my property. I had always told Wayne and Samantha to keep the doors locked to strangers, and now I'm thinking of strangers going through the private things I have left there. I was worried that they're making a mess of the lovely furnishings and linens that I had bought in Harrods, being careless with the antiques as they don't know what they are . . .

Next I called my sister Blossom, told her what Gladys had told me and asked her to go round and take a look at what is going on – she had a key to the house. The next day she called me back and told me the place was a mess! I wanted to book the next flight from Miami, because I felt the distance was making everything worse. I think Bloss heard how upset I was in my voice, as she convinced me it wouldn't be a good idea for me to come over and see the damage.

It sounded worse than I had been imagining as I waited for Blossom to call back. My heart started pounding so badly I thought I was really having a heart attack. Marcus had to take me down to the bench on the waterfront where he sat me down and I had to breathe in and out, slowly and deeply, about twelve times. When I calmed down – a bit – I knew it made no sense for me to go over, so I asked my sister to salvage what she could, get the place cleaned up and put it on the market. I needed to make a clean break with it.

Wayne moved in with Blossom; she had a big house and he stayed in her box room. I had no sympathy, though. I couldn't bring myself to talk to Wayne because I was so disappointed. From that point of view, Marcus and I racked our brains trying to think what had gone wrong? Was he in with a bad crowd that we didn't know about? We couldn't figure it out, but I was still too mad at him to make any sort of effort to reach out to him.

Looking back, this was such a shame because it really damaged our relationship to the extent that when I was staying at Blossom's to have cancer treatment he only came to see me a couple of times and the tone was very neutral. I can see now that it was a bad time for both of us. At the time I really needed support during my illness; and I felt very sad when he got married in Croydon while we were staying there but he didn't invite Marcus and me or Blossom. The only two people who were invited to the wedding were Samantha and Wesley. I had never met his girlfriend – in fact, neither Bloss nor I even knew he had one. Now, because of this break in our relationship, I have a grandson I've seen once and only have very limited email contact with, and for years the only acknowledgement I've had from Wayne is a couple of words on an email or an emoji on Facebook.

There is hope we can mend things, though, which has come about through me writing this book. When I was going through some boxes of old papers and letters to research some events and check some dates, I came across a letter from Wayne where he sincerely and unqualifiedly apologises for what had happened. It must have taken courage and honesty for him to write that letter.

For years I have wanted some sort of explanation and acknowledgement from him, and when I thought that wasn't forthcoming I thought he didn't care. I realise now that I was so upset that I overlooked this letter so he must have thought I had ignored his apology so I could stay mad at him. Like I said, it really is a great shame – I can't turn back the clock but now maybe we have got a position to come back from.

*Chapter Twenty-five*

# 'Cancer is following me from country to country'

After the troubles with the house in Stuart, it didn't take us long to decide we should move to Germany on a permanent basis. I felt I'd been getting problems from the family, problems with the house, problems from the music business in the US, problems with payments from my Boney M. days; the only place that was showing me any love was Germany.

We stayed in Göttingen at first because that was where the studio was, but settled on Berlin as being the best place to base ourselves because it was pretty easy to get to the studio, and had great transport links with the rest of Germany and abroad. Also, I was getting quite a lot of live work by then, so being in the city would be much better to meet with agents and promoters and raise my profile in the industry in general. Once we'd made that decision, we moved to the city to make apartment hunting easier and checked into a suite in the Mercury Hotel overlooking what used to be Checkpoint Charlie when the Berlin Wall was standing. We engaged a shipping company to bring our furniture from storage in Florida, which turned out to be very funny because we were so looking forward to living amongst our own things again we were constantly online tracking the containers! We were feeling a bit rootless, and we knew having our own furniture would be such an important part of setting up a proper home, and making us feel settled and secure once again. However, I think we took it to extremes as it was like we were waiting for children to return, saying things like, 'Oh my God, our babies are coming! . . . Today they'll be in Hamburg!' We were watching every move!

It wasn't an actual hotel suite we were staying in, as the Mercury had two sides with one entrance for the regular hotel users and another for the suites that long-term guests booked into. It had a nice living room, a little kitchen and a bedroom upstairs; it even had a balcony and we kept it like a little home. We made ourselves very comfortable there, which was just as well because we were there for two years while various realtors showed us a succession of crappy, expensive apartments! Maybe I was being overly fussy, because I hadn't lived in a flat since the early 1970s in Peckham and we'd come from two beautiful spacious houses, but I couldn't see how we were even going to get our furniture into most of the places we viewed, let alone live in them!

We finally found an apartment to suit us, or maybe I should say *apartments* because what we ended up with were the two apartments knocked together to create one big one. It's in a building that's over a hundred years old, with big rooms and high ceilings, and a rear entrance where the servants who lived at the back of the building used to come and go while the bigwigs lived in the front. When we first saw it we loved the proportions, but wanted more rooms, so the landlords suggested putting two flats together. Perfect! They let us design it how we wanted and it was transformed into one lovely apartment, right in the centre of Berlin. We could finally get our furniture out of storage, move it in and start making a proper home for ourselves.

We'd been there for two or three weeks and absolutely loved it, we were getting things into the right places, getting used to the kitchen and starting to feel real cosy. This was exactly the new beginning we had wanted to happen in Germany with all the troubles of the past in the past. Then I started having difficulty swallowing my food.

It wasn't a sore throat, it wasn't tonsillitis and it wasn't getting any better, so we went to our regular doctor who sent me for tests, then I had to see a Professor Bühr who wanted to admit me to a hospital for examination. Marcus and I literally didn't know what to think: on the one hand we knew enough to know when something serious has been found; but on the other we thought there was no way this could be cancer. *Again!* I said to Marcus, 'OK, let's take Norman Vincent Peale's book and my *Survival* magazine and put our trust in our faith.' *Survival* was a magazine I had written in Hobe Sound during my healing intervals while hoping for a book deal!

The professor came in with his team to give me the results and told us there was a tumour on my oesophagus. '*What!*' I heard Marcus say. I too couldn't accept what I was hearing and my first reaction was, 'Professor, just in case it's not cancer . . .' He replied, 'Yes, it is, it's cancer.' By now I was really in denial. 'Nah, Doctor, No, no . . . We can't take any more.' It was as if we didn't believe him or we were just in a state of shock. We'd just got everything back to how it should be and now this setback! I couldn't believe cancer was following me from one country to another.

I was feeling low and Marcus looked dazed, the medical team in their white coats were standing over me, talking quietly and writing notes, while I'm thinking, 'What do I have to do to get free of this?' The professor caught sight of the *Survival* magazine, saw it had my picture on the cover and asked, '*Was ist das?*' When I told him he started reading it and passed it around to the others, then he looked at my body and was showing them my scars: the scar from my first ovarian cancer, I had to turn over to show off the scar along my spine, then this breast and that breast under my lymph node. It was a graphic illustration of what I had been through, and he told the others, 'This woman will beat this; just look at these scars and see how many times she has done it before.'

That was amazing. It was like an injection of confidence and belief just when we needed it most, I looked at Professor Bühr and there was a new vibe in the room. The whole team suddenly seemed galvanised like they were on a mission they couldn't fail: they looked like soldiers who had already won the battle. I knew cancer stood no chance against my faith in God and Professor Bühr's team. Even now, writing it down, I get goose pimples. I knew I was going to be all right – I felt as if a halo had come over my head! I said to him, 'I don't understand the medical terms you are telling me, especially in German, but that's OK. I want you and your team to carry out this operation. Where do I sign? Where does Marcus sign?'

It was after that I discovered how fortunate I was that the cancer had revealed itself at a fairly early stage, as cancer of the oesophagus often has no symptoms at all and goes unnoticed until it is too late. Because I'd had the problems swallowing I got it checked out, so as lucky as you can be with cancer I guess I was. All of this gave me hope.

When reality set in, I got very worried about the surgeons cutting into my throat because my voice is how I make my living and although I wanted the cancer gone, I would be devastated if my vocal cords took a nick. I was asking where, exactly, my oesophagus was and how far away from my voice box is that. They just smiled and told me, 'Oh, not too far!' They assured me that my vocal cords wouldn't be interfered with and I had no choice but to trust them, and rightly so – thanks to the skills of the surgeons I wasn't even hoarse when they finished the operation. Sometimes I see my whole life as something of a miracle.

The next day one of the nurses told me the operation took ten hours, and for a large part of that time Professor Bühr had sent the other doctors away and continued by himself. He was a really remarkable man. To get rid of all the tumour he had to cut out my oesophagus and bring part of my stomach up to where the oesophagus used to be. The only difference it has made to me is that I now have the appetite of a child – I can't eat big portions of food! So at least I never have to worry about putting on any weight now and I can still get into dresses that fitted me years ago!

Right after the operation I remember coming round, seeing Marcus standing there and saying, 'Praise the Lord. Oh hello, Marcus.' I was so relieved my voice was still working normally I went straight back to sleep! They kept me in for nearly a week and during that time it was our twenty-fifth wedding anniversary. Marcus brought a big bunch of red roses and Professor Bühr said it would have been all right for me to have had a glass or two of champagne. I thought, 'Now he's speaking my language!' And the next day Marcus brought one of the two bottles of Moet we had in the fridge and two crystal glasses. That was so funny, popping a champagne cork in a hospital bed, and I couldn't wait to taste it but I took one sip and my head started spinning! *Holy Moses!* I hadn't felt that light-headed from champagne for years! I told Marcus to take it back home where it could wait for me – I wasn't going to waste it!

As I recovered from surgery I was asking about starting the chemotherapy, but Professor Bühr said they were going to ease off that because they didn't think it was really necessary for me to go through it again. He suggested I make an appointment with one of his colleagues, an oncologist named Professor Keilhaus, who is now the oncologist I go and see for my annual check-ups, and they would discuss together if I needed chemo and radiation. Professor Keilhaus was adamant I wouldn't be having any: '*Nein*. We've got to leave you, you don't need chemo, as after all the chemo you have had during your life we have to be very careful. If you get too much of one thing it can give you cancer as well!' That made Marcus and me laugh because it reminded me of a saying we have in Jamaica: Too much of one thing is good for nothing! They made the right decision, too, because every time they saw me after that, they were astonished at how well I was doing, which was a really good feeling and, I hope, the end of me and cancer. For good.

When I was first discharged I had to take it easy and get back into my usually hectic life and my singing very gradually and had to go back to the hospital once a week, where I was becoming something of a celebrity – for medical reasons! Professor Bühr went straight through to a class of students and told them,

'If any of you want to see power, go and take a look at Marcia Barrett-James. Take some power from her, because that is real power!' Professor Keilhaus asked me to give a speech about what had happened to me at a seminar he was organising and I was happy to do so. Another time when I was having my blood tested Professor Bühr asked me how I had handled all these cancers and having them removed like it was nothing more than having a tooth extracted? I told him that all I did was *believe*, believe in myself and believe in the people that were around me doing the surgeries and working on the recovery wards. I told him that it was their skill that gave me the faith I would be OK, that they were the real stars of how I had come through five attacks of cancer. I believed then and I still do now that it is the doctors and nurses who deserve the credit and the admiration and even the wonder at how they do it day in and day out.

Although my voice was unaffected, it was about four months before I could go out on the road and start performing again. I was getting real cabin fever, telling myself, 'I'm getting out of here . . . I'm going to do it . . . I'm going back on stage!' I didn't feel weak, although I looked weak because I had lost a bit of weight and had been moving more carefully.

The worst thing that happened to me during that time was I was sued for two gigs I had to cancel because I was recuperating. The agent I had dealt with was a crook who had taken the money for the shows and had disappeared, leaving me to pick up the pieces, and although the contract had a clause in it about illness, he had not told anybody because he had vanished. There were more people than us looking for him, but because the

313

venue owner couldn't find him and hadn't been notified in time to get another act it looked like I just didn't turn up. Although I knew nothing about it I had become liable for the fee and his expenses, and when the cases went to court I lost on each occasion. We couldn't even pay all the money at once, because I hadn't worked for several months, so we made an arrangement to do it in instalments, which still wasn't right but was better than nothing.

During the hearing, our German lawyer barely spoke up for us, and when I tried to speak to the judge directly all he could say to me was, 'Well you do know you've lost the case!' This is why I've never trusted the German legal system and won't take legal action for a better share of the Boney M. revenue – I had a very good English lawyer for a while, but he's just retired so I'll have to find another one. These are the sort of obstacles it seemed we were constantly coming up against, and although they could be draining in the short term the big picture was I had my health and strength and I was going back on the road.

The first show we had booked was in Mizoram, which is actually in India but is so remote in the north of the country we needed special permits to travel there – back then, even Indians needed visas to visit. When we applied for permits, the Embassy warned us it was a very dangerous place, but it's an amazing place, very beautiful, surrounded by mountains and almost completely cut off; the people look more Chinese than they do Indian and they are mostly Christians. We flew to Calcutta, then it was another five hours on a small plane into Mizoram, then a long drive on mountain roads that didn't have any asphalt and, I'm sure, in cars that didn't have any suspension! There are no hotels so we stayed in guesthouses; the people are very poor but were so warm and welcoming. I visited a local hospital and the whole thing was a real experience.

They loved Boney M. – we were always on television up there – and I think because of 'Mary's Boy Child'/'Oh My Lord' they thought all our songs were Christmas carols. It was an open-air gig for a sold-out crowd of 35,000 and was a bit stop-go because the power failed more than once but we had patience, we got through it and the crowd loved us. Most importantly I had no problems with my voice. Of course that was a relief but I was never in any doubt – I had no symptoms: I wasn't even hoarse; I didn't seem flat; I still had the power and control . . . In fact, once I got on stage I didn't even think about it, because when you're up there in front of an audience it's too late to worry about your voice, you just have to give it one hundred per cent. If I'd had that sort of fear prior to getting out there I wouldn't be free enough to go on to do what I do.

This was a fantastic feeling, knowing things were starting up again and this wasn't such a long detour, but even after the show our adventure wasn't over. The promoter wanted to pay us in local currency, but we insisted on euros as per the agreement, so I requested they sent somebody to fly with us on the little plane to Calcutta to sort it out. While the crew waited in the airport, Marcus and I went out with this agent's representative into the crowded street to a car park where we were to get the rest of the money. We ended up hiding in a car, with me counting the cash and handing it to Marcus who is checking it then putting it in a paper bag – *a paper bag!* All the time we're ducking down in case people see us and think we're doing a drug deal or somebody tries to rob us! It was like we were in a film! We got the full amount and when we walked back into the airport, I put my thumbs up to the crew – mission accomplished – and they started applauding!

By the time we were settled back in our Business Class seats on the flight to Germany, Marcus and I looked at each other and I thought if I could cope with all that I could cope with anything. I knew I was back.

*Part Four*

# SATISFACTION

## Chapter Twenty-six

# 'I refuse to act my age!'

Florida was fantastic and there are many aspects of it I miss, but coming back to Germany was an absolutely brilliant feeling for me – it was the country where I started my career before Boney M., the country that made me famous, where I speak the language . . . It was like a homecoming. Among the shrubbery on our patio, I have three flags: the Jamaican flag, the Union flag and the German flag. They are for my three countries: Jamaica is where I was born so I'll always be a Jamaican; England is where I grew up so it's my second country and I'll always feel part of there too; then comes Germany, which is where I live and have so many good memories from. All the time I was away I kept sentiments for this country, so when we got here to the hotel at Checkpoint Charlie we were ready to go – so ready to go we looked on the last few years as a detour rather than a setback. It was as if I'd been away for a fifteen-year holiday! That particular idea always made Marcus and me laugh because the Hobe Sound house was originally intended as a holiday home.

One of the interesting things about being back in Germany after all those years away was getting recognised all the time as Marcia Barrett of Boney M., because when we were in Florida and anybody came up to us it was usually mistaken identity!

People were always asking Marcus if he was Barry White, or we'd get stopped in restaurants or airports because they thought we were Ashford and Simpson, and once there was this couple who drove all the way from Hobe Sound to Miami – about eighty miles – behind us because they thought we were Peaches & Herb! When we finally stopped they pulled up behind us, jumped out and ran over – we were a bit apprehensive by that point because of the reputation Miami had for carjacking, but they were smiling and said, 'Hey, you guys, can we have autographs?' We must've looked puzzled because then the guy said, 'You're Peaches and Herb, right?' 'Er, no-o-o-o!' Marcus always thinks these incidents are hilarious, but I worry about how these people we are being mistaken for are behaving – we don't want to get into any sort of trouble for something Peaches & Herb did!

Over here in Germany people knew me straight away even before I started getting back on television, because Boney M. are still on all the time and I haven't changed much at all! It's true. Often when I get introduced to younger people as Marcia Barrett of Boney M., the name sinks in and they react with, 'Oh my God! You are an original? Then they start to scrutinise me and I see them thinking, 'How can you be original and look like that?' I have a little laugh to myself and think, 'Thank you, Jesus!'

It's not all by good fortune and good genes, though! I've never stopped keeping fit, although I have to have gym machines at home now because here in Berlin I can't go to the gym without causing a commotion. The same with the sauna, I've always loved my saunas and it was one of the first things we had put in this apartment. Then there's the matter of my posture: while it's well known that 'black don't crack', and I've never smoked so my skin is good, there are plenty of black women of my age with good skin – as I write this I'm two years off seventy – but how do they carry themselves? Sometimes I look at them and their body language looks like they have given up, like they are telling themselves, 'I'm old . . . I'm grey . . . it must all be over for me.' No! Not for me! I'll carry myself upright, with confidence, like I always have done – like I've got things to do. I *refuse* to act my age!

When we moved into our apartment in Berlin in 2009 I said I was going to subtract fifteen years from my age because that was the time taken from me by illness. To us, that move felt like we were at the same point we were in Hobe Sound when the first cancer attacked me, so if I was going to catch up with my solo career I was simply going to take those years back! I think it has worked, too, because mentally I feel fifteen years younger than I am physically.

That is how positive we were thinking when we first got back here: as if fifteen years, four bouts of cancer and losing our home had never happened. In fact, I believe this is why the fifth cancer hit us so badly from an emotional point of view: not simply because it was the *fifth* but because of the timing of it. We figured we had gone back to starting from scratch, just getting financially stable again, the gigs were coming in, then *bang*, I'm out of action again. Even though there was no chemo and I recovered relatively quickly, at times it felt as if we were finished and it took real strength from both of us to gradually pick ourselves back up. If I wasn't saying it out loud there was a voice beeping in my head all day: 'Come on, stay strong, you can't give up now . . . this is what you wanted . . . go back down inside yourself.'

The German audiences might have seemed a bit straight-laced at times – I can remember back in the Boney M. days the effort we had to put in to make them clap along, let alone get up and dance – but that doesn't make them love you any less. If an artist puts themselves into a song, those audiences really appreciate that and will get right into it with them. The same goes for how they think of one of *their* artists off the stage as well: they will be concerned, they will have sympathy and they won't just forget about them if they're out of the spotlight for a while. With German audiences there's a real feeling of 'We're all in this together', so it was a matter of course that I was going to pick up easily from the oesophagus cancer.

Berlin is our home now, even Marcus has settled here in spite of his not learning the language! He misses Florida – mostly the fishing, and he will tell anybody as much – but he knew we had to be realistic and that food needs to be on the table whether he caught it or not. He is a natural man, he loves the world – sometimes I think of him as a surfer who will go with whatever it takes and usually stay upright! He loves that we've been settled for nearly ten years and that I have been free of illness for as long. I'm sure he is as relieved as I am that we are at last moving forward and making music. Never forget, this is a man who gave up touring with Eddy Grant and a good career as a bass player to look after me.

In spite of how it suits us to be here at the time of writing we don't know how Brexit is going to affect us, and the other thing is we don't want to be old and cold, so eventually we'd like to move somewhere warm. We're thinking perhaps Spain, as I can still reach my audience there – there are a *lot* of Germans in Spain!

We're not keen to go back to Florida, even if I stopped working and wasn't looking for an audience. Purely and simply we are not happy with the way the police are treating black people over there; it seems as if the police can shoot who they like and get away with it. We know that anybody can fall victim to that sort of thing because we had our problems in that respect back when we lived there. In fact, one particular incident saw Marcus spend the night in jail for nothing more than asking a chap if he was about to vacate a parking space.

It was in September 1985, we were not long married and still living like love's young dream. We invited my hairdresser Sylvia over from London for a holiday with us. She had become a very close friend – she was a guest at our wedding – and we had a fantastic time showing her around Palm Beach, and the shops and restaurants on Worth Avenue. One night, we had been out to dinner and were enjoying ourselves so much we didn't want the night to end and decided to head to a club in Jupiter, called Banana Max. Marcus and I had been there before and knew it was an upmarket place, like the clubs used to be in London's West End, and we were all dressed to the nines and I was driving our vintage 1941 Chevy, so we knew we'd fit right in. The street outside the club was jumping, so we cruised slowly looking for a parking space when we spotted a guy getting into his car practically right outside. Before he could shut his door, Marcus got out of the car to ask him if he was leaving as we'd take the space. The chap didn't say yes or no, he just looked at

Marcus and said, 'Why don't you go and find somewhere else to park your car?'

Naturally Marcus was taken aback, but before he could even reply, a uniformed policeman has rushed across the road, wrestled him to the ground, cuffed his two hands behind his back and is reaching towards the pistol on his belt! By now Sylvia and I are out of our car and when I see what looks like he's going for his gun I let out the loudest scream I could: '*Oh my God! What are you doing to my husband?*' He looked at me and told me, 'If you don't shut up you'll be going with him!' Then he practically dragged Marcus into the back of the police car. He didn't put up any resistance, because that would have made it worse – he might even have gotten shot – and they drove him away to the jail in Jupiter. We'd lived in that area for ages and we didn't even know there was a jail in Jupiter, that's how law abiding we are! It was terrible, us in our best clothes all ready to have some fun, Marcus thrown to the ground, then bundled in the back of the police car, people standing and staring, Sylvie and I distraught because we'd heard the stories about brutality to black people in American jails . . .

We went home and I had to wake up some lawyers we knew, and they told me, '*Marcus?* We could understand if it was you got taken to jail, but not Marcus!', which made me laugh and helped calm me down. They told us to get all the cash we could together – even Sylvie pitched in – and go down to the jail, which was awful. They'd taken his belt and his shoes and he still didn't really know what was going on, then we were told we'd have to go up to Stuart, about twenty miles away, to pay the bail bond to get him out that night. He still had to go to court, because they'd charged him with disorderly conduct. *Disorderly conduct!* All he did was say to a man, 'Excuse me, but are you going now?'

It turned out the cop was the brother of the man in the car and he'd reacted like that when he saw Marcus approach the car – probably assumed that because Marcus is black he's somehow dangerous, which is how so many police in America think. When we got to the jail and they found out we're law-abiding citizens, not even American, there was a bit of embarrassment, but they had gone so far with it they had to see it through. The policeman and his brother stitched it up so the judge took no notice of Marcus, he was found guilty and had to pay a fine.

It left a bad taste in my mouth about America that never really went away – it might even have been that stress made me ill! That's why I couldn't go back, and especially not with the way things are now with so many black men getting shot by police, Marcus might have died that night just for politely asking about a parking space.

When I came back here to Germany it took me no time to become settled and start moving forward with real confidence, but that doesn't mean I can relax too much. I always have to be ready for a fight, although these days I find it much easier to pick my battles. For a long time I never saw a penny from the sales of the *Come Into My Life* album although I knew plenty of people had bought it – I used to say to Marcus that producer must have a garage full of them selling them under the radar. Then out of the blue I got a cheque for ten euros! We didn't know whether to laugh or cry, but we know it's not worth taking him to court, especially in Germany.

It's like with the money, I'm sure I am owed a better share of the Boney M. royalties. If I had nothing to do or was desperate for cash then I might pursue it. As it stands, I don't think I would ever get to the bottom of it and I am getting on with my life, but I take some comfort from the notion that while I am getting on with my latest adventure Frank has to think about me every day while he remixes my voice and Liz's to try to sell Boney M. yet again.

These days we always make sure everything Marcus and I write or record is correctly copyrighted so there can be no dispute about who contributed what to what, then I have to save my energies for fighting with the booking agents and promoters. It seems so many of them are either trying to get away with ridiculous prices or trying to chip away from what you agreed *after* you have done the show. These days my motto is: 'Treat me with some respect or just leave me alone!' It's as simple as that. God will provide, and I know that He has provided all my life.

Doing all this ourselves can be a pain at times, but I'd rather that than have a manager who just presents me with some cash after a gig and I don't know what has been spent where, or even how much was involved in the first place – don't forget I'm a policeman's daughter. I would advise any artist who's not really big to take charge of their own affairs, since we've been doing that we've found it much more satisfying and if we did ever get another manager we'd understand exactly what it is they were supposed to be doing.

The one thing I don't have in Berlin is Jamaican food, and oh how I miss my Jamaican treats – can you imagine not getting any patties for three years now, since we were last in England? In Florida there were big Jamaican communities near us in West Palm Beach and Port St Lucie, so while Jamaican food wasn't as plentiful as in Brixton or Croydon it was still easy enough to get hold of. In Berlin it's very different. We did find a Nigerian guy here who could bake really good hard-dough bread, which is great, but otherwise we had an experience when we first got here that pretty much put us off.

We found somewhere to buy saltfish and tinned ackee, so I took some back to our suite in the Mercury Hotel and put it on to cook. It seemed to be bubbling more than usual and frothing over the top of the pot but I didn't think too much about that, I turned it down and went to get on with some paperwork. Marcus helped himself but by the time he'd finished eating his body was breaking out in bumps, he was starting to itch all over and his face was swelling up – he looked like a 200-year-old man! He ran to the bathroom to look in the mirror and collapsed. It was like something out of a horror film! It passed the next day – maybe that particular batch wasn't cured properly – but I've stopped shopping for anything like that in Berlin. My hair-dresser often sends us things or if anybody is coming to visit us from the UK we ask them to bring some little delicacies with them. However, since then Marcus won't eat saltfish anywhere other than Jamaica and even then he's nervous about it! It's so funny that I have a couple of tins of ackee and some salt cod in the kitchen, and when I tell him I'm going to cook it he gives me a look and says, 'What? You trying to get rid of me?'

I am still immensely proud of being one of the two voices of Boney M.; and I always will be. Personally, the Boney M.

legacy is very good for me, I'm always very happy to mix the group's hits in with our own material in my shows and I still get a thrill when I hear our original stuff on the radio. But I do wish that in general it had been treated with a bit more respect – the proliferation of Boney Ms touring the world is, quite frankly, becoming a bit of an embarrassment.

Not so long ago I got an autograph request sent to me from America, by a 'fan' to sign the Boney M. photo they'd enclosed, when I looked at the picture I had no clue who any of the people were! I could just about make out which one was supposed to be me and which one might be Liz, meaning the other must be meant to be Maizie, but really none of them looked like any of us! I didn't tear it up or throw it away, I simply put a thick black 'X' on all of their faces and wrote on it 'False line-up, check your facts' and sent it back. I even included two dollars to cover their stamps! So if that's coming all the way from America, where we were never that big, who knows how many other Boney Ms are out there – this sort of thing could never happen to Abba!

It's like the musical *Daddy Cool*, if that had been about Boney M. I'm sure that could have been as successful as Abba's *Mamma Mia* – our record sales were only just behind theirs in Europe – but instead it was all about Frank and his other acts had to be included, which I think confused people. Marcus and I were flown over from Florida to be at the premiere in London, Liz was there, Maizie didn't want to go which was a shame, and Bobby was still alive but I don't know if he was invited because he wasn't there. At the end of the performance Frank got up on stage and announced, 'Ladies and gentlemen Marcia Barrett and Liz Mitchell are here tonight . . .' When we walked up and took a bow and the place went *crazy*! The two of us got a much bigger applause than the musical itself – imagine what it would have been like if all four of us had been there? As it was, the two of us got a reception that, I believe, showed it was Boney M. who were the real stars of that story. I don't think *Daddy Cool* was an actual flop, and Frank's still putting it on in various places, but it should have done a lot better, which was a shame.

Right now I'm very happy. Berlin is our home, the flat is lovely, and we are working as much as we want, with gigs taking me seriously enough to support the party of seven travelling with me in the sort of comfort I feel I've earned. We are still recording and although we have plans to release music we're not putting ourselves under pressure. I give talks and make motivational speeches about war or the environment or pertaining to my illnesses, and I am an Ambassador for the Institute of Cultural Diplomacy here in Berlin, an international organisation set up to promote greater trust and understanding between cultures. I really enjoy all of that; being able to use my position as Marcia Barrett of Boney M. to directly help or inspire people is a privilege I'll always work to live up to.

I genuinely believe my life has been blessed and if I'm looking for proof of that I think back to my early childhood in Jamaica, up there in Mount Charles, when my cousins were all going to organ lessons and I couldn't because my auntie said my mother hadn't sent any money for them. I was so sad, and when I heard the beautiful organ playing up there I would stand in the gulley crying. Sixty years later, music has given me all sorts of unbelievable adventures and is still providing for me.

However, I also believe my life is far from over – I *really* do have plans. Marcus and I have reached a point we're both satisfied with but I want to go further. I want to do a little acting, because portraying a song properly is acting, as you have to get into it and tell the story by going through the range of emotions. Another desire of mine is to be offered to sing the title track of a James Bond film. I want to give proper lectures based on my experiences. But most of all I look forward to working with a live band again with no more half playbacks. After all those years with Black Beauty Circus I feel very confined; now I want an eleven-piece band with my husband on the bass and as musical director, and when I hit the stage it's *bam*!

One thing that isn't going to happen is a Boney M. reunion. Not because we've had any big falling-out, we've just all got our own lives and have moved on too far to go back to that situation. The last time we were altogether was at Bobby's funeral and although it was a very sad occasion it was actually a lovely get-together. Of course all the press there wanted to know if anything more permanent was going to happen, although we all very cordial in front of the reporters and didn't actually deny it, we all knew it wasn't to be. I'm sure of this because I had this magnum of Boney M. champagne that was given to me in Moldova after my presentation of Boney M.'s music – it had a gold Boney M. label and seal on it, and was in a beautiful silk-lined box. I had issued an open invitation to the others saying I didn't want to open it until we were all gathered together to drink it. I know Liz and Maizie have been in Berlin since then but I haven't see them and that bottle sat around for years before Marcus's daughter Nikki and her family visited us in Berlin when we decided to pop the cork and *enjoy*!

The most beautiful thing about now is that I'm alive and kicking, I've got my dignity and nobody can take away what I can do and what I have done – that's in the history books for anybody to see. After the amount of times I've been back down to nil then each time got back up, and Marcus has had the patience and the strength to see me through, I know the sky's the limit.

Forward!

# Boney M.: The Golden Years

## Albums

*Take The Heat Off Me* (1976)

*Love For Sale* (1977)

*Nightflight To Venus* (1978)

*Oceans Of Fantasy* (1979)

*The Magic Of Boney M. – 20 Golden Hits* (1980 – Compilation)

*Boonoonoonoos* (1981)

*The Christmas Album* (1981)

*Ten Thousand Lightyears* (1984)

*Kalimba De Luna – 16 Happy Songs* (1984 – Compilation)

*Eye Dance* (1985)

*The Best Of 10 Years – 32 Superhits* (1986 – Compilation)

*The 20 Greatest Christmas Songs* (1986 – Compilation)

## Singles

'Baby Do You Wanna Bump (Part 1)'/'Baby Do You Wanna Bump (Part 2)' (1975)

'Daddy Cool'/'No Women No Cry' (1976)

'Sunny'/'New York City' (1976)

'Ma Baker'/'Still I'm Sad' (1977)

'Belfast/'Plantation Boy' (1977)

'Rivers Of Babylon'/'Brown Girl In The Ring' (1978)

'Rasputin'/'Painter Man' (1978)

'Mary's Boy Child – Oh My Lord'/'Dancing In The Streets'
(1978)

'Hooray! Hooray! It's A Holi- Holiday'/'Ribbons Of Blue'
(1979)

'El Lute'/'Gotta Go Home' (1979)

'I'm Born Again'/'Bahama Mama' (1979)

'I See A Boat On The River'/'My Friend Jack' (1980)

'Children Of Paradise'/'Gadda-Da-Vida' (1980)

'Felicidad (Margherita)'/'Strange' (1980)

'Malaika'/'Consuela Biaz' (1981)

'We Kill The World (Don't Kill The
World)'/'Boonoonoonoos' (1981)

'Little Drummer Boy'/'6 Years Of Boney M. Hits (Boney M.
On 45)' (1981)

'The Carnival Is Over'/'Going Back West' (1982)

'Zion's Daughter'/'White Christmas' (1982)

'Jambo (Hakuna Matata)'/'African Moon' (1983)

'Somewhere In The World'/'Exodus (Noah's Ark 2001)'
(1984)

'Kalimba De Luna'/'Ten Thousand Lightyears' (1984)

'Happy Song'/'School's Out' (1984)

'My Chérie Amour'/'Sample City' (1985)

'Young, Free And Single'/'Blue Beach' (1985)

'Daddy Cool – Anniversary Recording '86'/'B.M.A.G.O'
(1986)

'Bang Bang Lulu'/'Chica Da Silva' (1986)

**6,859,000** singles sold in the UK, making Boney M. the fourteenth best-selling UK singles act of all time

Over **130,000,000** records (singles and albums) sold worldwide

**Eight Number One** singles in Germany; **five Top 10** singles; and **five Top 20** singles

**Ten Top 10** singles in the UK

Boney M. are in the **Guinness Book of Records twice** for topping the biggest selling singles ever charts, with 'Rivers of Babylon' and 'Mary's Boy Child'

Boney M. were **the first Western pop group to perform in the former Soviet Union**, at the invitation of President Leonid Brezhnev

Boney M. **performed before Her Majesty the Queen** at the Royal Variety Show in 1979

## Acknowedgments

It was Pauline, Eddy Grant's daughter, who suggested I wrote a book during a conversation we had at her home together with her father and Marcus in 2013, after over three decades of not seeing each other.

The conversation then led into the search of the perfect ghost writer, someone who would actually get my story and come on board with their experience in the field. Pauline suggested Lloyd Bradley, who turned out to be the perfect choice. Thank you, Pauline for your awarding instinct!

Lloyd – although we hadn't met in person until last August in Berlin, you listened to my story via Skype on sessions that would sometimes last three hours! Both Marcus and I felt very comfortable chatting away with you for hours at a time. The technical mishaps we sometimes had didn't hinder us from bouncing back and picking up the pieces in our next recordings. Thank you for allowing the readers to imagine that I'm standing before them in a room just telling my story. The people who know me personally will no doubt say, 'That's Marcia'. Thank you, thank you, Lloyd for a brilliant job!

Now, I couldn't have done this book by myself. For all the historical information I needed to talk about, I had to lean on to my teammates who had more Boney M. clippings, photos, etc. than I had time to collect over these decades.

To Daniel Diezi, who always took care of my graphics; Danni Lange, who has constructed my websites; and Shaun O'Shea, who wrote articles together with Daniel in the years I was unable to: thank you, dears, for standing by my side ever since you were teenagers. Teamwork is magic!

Marcus – I would like to thank you with all my love, as your wife and closest friend, for being so beautifully patient in having had less family hours with me during the making of this book. May God bless and keep you always!